When Harlem Was Jewish
1870–1930

When Harlem Was Jewish
1870–1930

Jeffrey S. Gurock

New York   Columbia University Press   1979

Library of Congress Cataloging in Publication Data

Gurock, Jeffrey S   1949–
When Harlem was Jewish, 1870–1930.

Bibliography: p.
Includes index.
1. Jews in New York (City)—History.
2. Harlem, New York (City)—History.   I. Title.
F128.9.J5G87   974.7'1'004924   79-14768
ISBN 0-231-04666-9

Columbia University Press
New York   Guildford, Surrey

To My Wife, Pamela

Contents

Illustrations

Acknowledgments

It is my grateful and pleasureable duty to acknowledge the many individuals who assisted me—intellectually, socially and emotionally—in the writing of this book.

The idea of writing a history of Jewish Harlem evolved out of discussions with Dr. Zvi Ankori, my teacher and mentor during my early years at Columbia University, over my early impulse to study the nature of black–Jewish relations in the urban setting during the first decades of this century. It was he who so thoughtfully suggested that to understand properly the origins and development of interracial attitudes and stereotypes and the roots of urban neighborhood conflict, about which others have written so extensively and with such varying degrees of objectivity, one must first be well schooled in the fundamental social realities—the day-to-day lives of these two groups—which influenced perceptions and pronouncements. My subsequent search for such a social setting led me quickly to Harlem, the site of one of the first major twentieth century black–Jewish residential encounters.

The multitude of issues and events comprehending a history of Jewish Harlem, which clearly transcends the story of interracial relations, was crystallized for me, however, only after careful prodding from my teacher Dr. Ismar Schorsch, whose early questioning of the projected scope of my work helped me see many of my localized concerns in their broader historical perspective. To both of these able and concerned scholars go my thanks for their aid in launching this project.

The greatest proportion of research on my New York City neighborhood was completed, interestingly enough, in Cincinnati, Ohio, where as a Visiting Fellow in American Jewish History at the Hebrew Union College–Jewish Institute of Religion, I was able to study the Yiddish press along with the bits of extant communal documentation at that school's magnificent American Jewish Archives and American Jewish Periodical Center. My sincerest thanks to Dr. Samuel Sandmel and Dr. Michael A. Meyer for inviting me to study at their institution, and to Mrs. Fanny Zelcer (AJA) and Mrs. Moira Steiner (AJPC) for their invaluable day-to-day assistance in their respective institutions. Grateful acknowledgment is extended to Mr. James Marshall for granting me permission to examine the papers of his father, Louis Marshall, on file at the American Jewish Archives. Thanks are also due to the Memorial Foundation for Jewish Culture for their generous fellowship grants during the academic years 1974–1975 and 1975–1976.

On my return to New York, I was able to complete my research at the Jewish Division of the New York Public Library, the New York City Municipal Reference Center and Municipal Archives and at the Office of the County Clerk for New York County. My thanks to the staffs of each of these institutions for expediting my search for materials.

The writing of my dissertation, which formed the basis for this book, was completed under the close guidance of Dr. Naomi W. Cohen of Hunter College of the City University of New York and Dr. David J. Rothman of Columbia University. Dr. Cohen, who, while visiting at Columbia University in 1972–1973, assisted me in both the writing of my M.A. thesis and in the preparation of my first published article, graciously and selflessly agreed to serve as my second reader after her return to Hunter. My thanks both to her and to Dr. Rothman, my sponsor, whose probing questioning and strict adherence to clear and concise expression forced me almost against my will to seek the limits of my intellectual potential. I am also grateful to Dr. Kenneth T. Jackson of Columbia University, an expert in urban history and quantitative method, who aided me in the development of the methodology used in my study of state and federal census materials. Dr. Jackson gave willingly of his time and skills both during the academic year and beyond. I was also privileged to have him chair my doctoral defense. Drs. Herbert J. Gans and Marvin Herzog of Columbia University and Arthur Goren of Hebrew University also read my manuscript and I have benefited from their learned comments. These scholars and the many others who answered my queries have my most profound gratitude.

Despite this greatly appreciated intellectual assistance from the academic community, I am convinced that my project would not have been completed if not for the great emotional support of several friends and relatives. Dr. Norman and Susan Cohen and their children welcomed my wife and me into their home in Cincinnati, beginning a friendship which continues now in New York. My colleague and friend Benjamin R. Gampel and his wife Miriam Schacter also stood by me throughout the work. My brother, Noah David Gurock, helped with many of the technical aspects of my presentation. He and his family share in the joy of my completed endeavor.

My wife, Pamela, to whom this book is dedicated, shared with me the insecurities and frustrations that are part of any creative effort. She more than anyone else helped keep alive for me the vision of a completed project.

My final and greatest thanks are reserved, however, for my parents, Jack and Leah Gurock, who sacrificed much to enable their children to study Torah, which led to the critical study of Jewish history and ultimately to the writing of this book. They possessed the wisdom and steadfastness of character to permit their children to decide upon their own careers, confident in the knowledge that if you provide them with the proper tools, their choice will be the appropriate one.

Bronx, New York   J. S. G.
Fall 1978

When Harlem Was Jewish
1870–1930

introduction

Uncovering a Forgotten Community's History

The geographical place-name Harlem evokes in most contemporary Americans the imagery of a deteriorated inner-city neighborhood: the metropolitan area's first and most famous black ghetto. Few people are aware that between the close of the Civil War and the end of World War I—the decades that immediately preceded the black shift uptown—Harlem was home to a large variety of other ethnic and religious enclaves, including, for example, a Jewish community of well over 100,000 people in the 1910s. Indeed, between 1870 and 1920 Harlem's Jews, Italians, Germans and Irish outnumbered uptown's black population. And it was within this period that Harlem was transformed from a sparsely populated suburban, almost rural, settlement to a fully developed new center-city neighborhood, and finally to the blighted urban area it is today. Those who have chronicled the saga of the development and ultimate decay of this well-known section of the metropolis have generally neglected the histories of uptown's pre-black ethnic communities.

This historical oversight is particularly apparent with regard to Harlem's Jews. Three generations of Jews lived uptown and constituted in their heyday not only Harlem's single largest ethnic group but also America's second largest new immigrant Jewish community. Harlem was surpassed only by the Lower East Side as a center attracting those originally from Eastern Europe. But popular writers and American and Jewish historians have not shown much interest in describing and

studying this large and variegated community. When Jewish Harlem
has been described, the focus has invariably been on it as the temporary home of the upwardly mobile East European immigrant or as the
first Jewish community to decline under the impact of black migration. Too many other and even more significant aspects of Harlem's
Jewish history have been sadly neglected.

Historians of nineteenth-century German-Jewish life in America,
for example, have not examined and analyzed the experiences of
Harlem's early German-Jewish settlers who, due to the then narrow
physical limits of city life and the absence of strong communication
links between downtown and what was then suburbia, were separated from the major locus of Jewish life. These historians, who have
often described and extolled the pioneering community-building efforts of the Jewish merchant-peddler living in the towns and cities far
removed from the major East coast Jewish population centers, have
overlooked those uptown merchant–pioneers who faced the same
types of problems and displayed a similar commitment to developing
Jewish institutional life as did their known counterparts on the Western frontiers. This important early aspect of both local Harlem and
general German-American Jewish history has been universally overlooked.

Those concerned with the history of this particular neighborhood
and city and those interested in analyzing and determining a general
pattern to intracity migration and areas of immigrant settlement have
failed to examine in any great detail the complex set of forces directing East European migration up to Harlem at the turn of the century.
They have contented themselves with, as previously indicated, the
perception of this community as solely the home of upwardly mobile
Jews who moved uptown as a reflection of their newly acquired affluence and newly achieved acculturation. They have not detailed the
migration story of Harlem's other Jews; poor and less-Americanized
individuals who settled for a variety of other social and economic
reasons.

Students studying the geographical limits of ghetto civilization have
similarly ignored the truly significant transplantation of the immigrant
way of life from the Lower East Side to Harlem. The close communication links established and maintained between downtown society and segments of the uptown community and the contributions
of Harlem labor and socialist groups to their respective citywide

movements, which clearly evidence the pervasiveness of the Lower East Side lifestyle outside the ghetto, have apparently been deemed unworthy of serious consideration.

Others who have traced the ideological and practical roots of contemporary Jewish attempts to combat assimilation have also ignored the Harlem experience. Scholars have always associated the beginnings of this intracity battle with the suburban neighborhoods of the 1920s and 1930s. Pioneering uptown-based efforts—as early as the turn of the century—to fashion a new type of Judaism totally consistent with Jewish tradition and American ideals and attractive to those alienated from older religious forms have been overlooked. The principles championed in Harlem and the institutions created there to reach the newly acculturated Jew, that foreshadowed later Jewish communal efforts, have not been considered.

Finally, the history of Jewish Harlem's rapid decline during the first decade following World War I has not been given sufficient attention. Although historians of the uptown neighborhood have clearly delineated the course of one major "push" factor in Jewish outmigration, the so-called "black invasion," other push factors—such as the great physical deterioration of the neighborhood prior to the black takeover—and such "pull" factors as the rise of new, better-built neighborhoods attractive to now affluent immigrants and their children, have yet to be studied.

This present work accordingly opens with a description of Harlem Jewish life in the 1870s when uptown was a remote outpost of German immigrant life, separated by inadequate transportation from downtown population centers. It then proceeds to trade the emergence of Harlem in the 1880s and 1890s as a vibrant growing Jewish neighborhood, as rapid transit lines reached uptown and the first wave of new immigrants pushed thousands of Germans out of the ghetto. It goes on to chronicle and analyze the impact of the moving of tens of thousands of East European Jews uptown after the turn of the century, noting the variety of push and pull factors contributing to the development uptown of two economically and socially distinct immigrant communities. It points out the similarities in lifestyle between Harlem's second ghetto residents and their brethren still on the Lower East Side. And it points up Harlem's important contribution to the formulation of Jewish anti-assimilation strategy. This history of Harlem Jewry closes with a detailed evaluation of the concert of forces directing Jewish out-migration after World War I. These and other subthemes constitute the first major effort to accord a measure of historical recognition to an until-now forgotten community's history.*

* This study shows only minor concern with analyzing the response of Harlem Jewry to issues and events affecting the general American and world Jewish communities. For although in many ways a separate community from the Lower East Side, Harlem, and the other major Jewish neighborhoods of the metropolitan area of that time, were also parts of a Greater New York community and responded as one community to problems facing Jews elsewhere. There was no specifically "Harlem" regional or sectional approach to Jewish concerns, such as Zionism or anti-Semitism, setting it off from her sister settlements elsewhere in the city.

chapter 1

The Early
Years, 1870–1900

At the close of the Civil War, New York's residential neighborhoods were severely overcrowded. Nearly a million people—workers in the city's growing industrial plants, merchants, jobbers, storekeepers in its many diverse commercial emporia, businessmen and financiers of every rank and description and immigrants from a variety of Western and Central European states—were concentrated into the lower sections of Manhattan Island. The poorer and immigrant elements in New York society competed for the limited space in the overcrowded downtown tenements and boarding houses south of 14th Street, while those with greater economic resources lived in the better-built but heavily populated northern midtown sections between 14th and 42d streets.[1]

New York did possess vast resources of unimproved territory suitable for residential expansion north of 42d Street. But real estate operators were reluctant to expand uptown into areas isolated from the central city by the absence of efficient rapid transit lines. Manhattan's twenty-nine omnibus lines provided crosstown service and uptown transport as far north as Yorkville and the city's five horse- and mule-drawn city car lines ran north to the tip of Manhattan, but service in each carrier was slow and unreliable. So while builders awaited the construction of speedier transportation as a prerequisite for further expansion, uptown New York remained, according to one contemporary real estate man, "this dreary region of rocky eminences and marshy depressions, stray houses interspersed among a legion of scattered shanties." Urban dwellers were left to struggle with the problems of overcrowding, while civic leaders pressed municipal officials for necessary improvements.[2]

New York's Jewish residents—40,000 strong and predominantly of German birth or ancestry—lived both in the dangerously over-populated downtown quarter and in the less critically overcrowded midtown sections of the city. The poorer and unacculturated elements were housed in the old Jewish quarter bounded by Canal, Elm, Mott, and Bayard Streets, a now run-down section which only decades earlier had been home for the most affluent and Americanized segment of German-Jewish society. This section remained a predominantly Jewish quarter for succeeding generations forming as it did part of the western boundary of the later Russian-Polish immigrant ghetto.* The richer, native-born or Americanized elements in 1860s Jewish society sought accommodations in the ethnically mixed midtown neighborhoods above Grand Street on the East Side. Prior to 1865, few Jews ventured north of 42d Street.[3]

During this period, Harlem—that part of New York's Twelfth Ward lying north of 96th Street to the Harlem River on the East Side and north of Central Park at 110th Street to 145th Street and east of Morningside Park and St. Nicholas Park on the West Side—was still physically and socially separate from the central city.† It retained much of the rural character of the "little village on the outskirts of the city" which it had been during the eighteenth and nineteenth centuries.

---

*The term "ghetto", as used here and elsewhere in the new immigrant Jewish and Italian contexts, refers not to an officially designated area from which certain groups could not move, but to a section of a city to which many of the same ethnic group flocked, for the most part voluntarily, due to their common economic position and social orientation. These ghettos should not be confused with the legally enacted ghettos of Europe nor with the American urban ghettos into which blacks were often trapped by economics, covenant and convention.

† There exists no legally defined modern community of Harlem. The "colonial" Harlem village ran approximately from 74th to 129th streets from the East to Hudson rivers. The term "Harlem" was also used extensively during the eighteenth and nineteenth centuries to designate all of upper Manhattan Island. Accordingly, the geographical boundaries of Harlem used here were based on the following less-than-legally official criteria:

a) *Government Studies of Harlem Conditions and Private Jewish Surveys of the Uptown Community.* Harlem was studied several times during the late 1920s and 1930s by government and Jewish officials. Each time the area was defined a little differently. The boundaries used here are in basic agreement with what appear to be the most generally accepted geographical limits, as determined by these contemporary observers.

b) *How Harlem dwellers and other New York Jews defined this community.* In study-

Large sections of territory between Fifth and Lexington avenues were totally unimproved or were pockmarked by one-story wood shanties. Much of the lower portion of Harlem east of Lexington Avenue was still covered by streams from the Harlem River. Its only noteworthy landmarks were the National Stockyards that ran from 97th to 102d streets between Second and Third avenues and a small bridge that crossed Third Avenue at 106th Street. The one substantially developed section of Harlem lay above 110th Street, east of Third Avenue, where most residents both lived and worked. One- to four-story combination store–dwellings predominated, covering most available land on both sides of Third Avenue, north to 125th Street. Third Avenue, described by one contemporary as Harlem's "Broadway where we all went to do our shopping," was the main street of this suburban settlement. Today's congested 125th Street, destined to become Harlem's major crosstown commercial center, was then still "a lane, in fact all the thoroughfares were lanes."[4]

Harlem's major transportation link with downtown population and cultural centers was the Third Avenue horse-car lines. Extended to Harlem in 1853, this primitive form of mass transit brought the village within one and a half hours' travel time of City Hall. Not long after the arrival of the horse cars, a steamboat service linked 125th Street with Peck Slip downtown. But this marine transportation line ran only during the summer, and infrequently even then. Neither form of transportation contributed much toward bringing Harlemites into close communication with their fellow New Yorkers. The isolated uptown settlement remained, according to one contemporary, "a rural retreat of the aristocratic New Yorker and its chief charm [was] its well bred seclusion."[5]

Not long after the end of the Civil War, a small group of German-Jewish merchants ventured north from the Lower East Side to set up shops and to establish homes within Harlem's Third Avenue commercial district. Perhaps the earliest known Harlem Jews decided to relocate to avoid downtown overcrowding or perhaps to take advantage of expanding commercial opportunities uptown. In all events, these

ing the locations of institutions calling themselves "Harlem-based", it was determined that few, if any, were situated outside the boundaries established for this study. For a complete discussion of the social, cultural and demographic determinants of the geographical term Harlem, see my "The History of the Jewish Community of Harlem, 1870–1930" (Ph.D. diss., Columbia University, 1977), pp. 8–9.

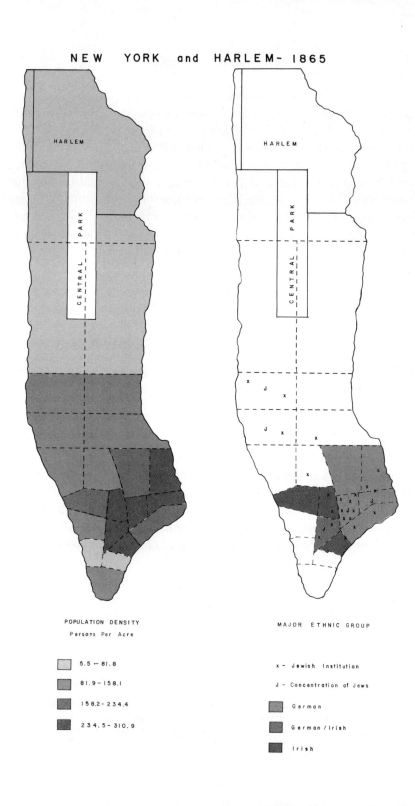

NEW YORK and HARLEM- 1865

HARLEM

CENTRAL PARK

HARLEM

CENTRAL PARK

POPULATION DENSITY

Persons Per Acre

5.5 – 81.8

81.9 – 158.1

158.2 – 234.4

234.5 – 310.9

MAJOR ETHNIC GROUP

x – Jewish Institution

J – Concentration of Jews

German

German/Irish

Irish

pioneers settled within close geographical proximity of each other, and began almost immediately to establish uptown the essential basic institutions normally associated with a nineteenth-century German-American Jewish community.[6]

The primary impetus for creating their own Harlem synagogue, Hebrew school, and social organizations, and even for acquiring their own separate burial grounds, was their physical and social isolation from the downtown centers of Jewish life. Perhaps this sense of remoteness from fellow Jews was felt most acutely by those Orthodox Jews who wished to pray on Sabbaths and Holidays in their former "city-synagogues" and who were frustrated by the logistical impossibility of walking over five miles to the nearest downtown services. Even less observant Jews may have felt a similar longing for the opportunity to meet, pray and socialize with old friends and coreligionists. They would have gladly traveled by omnibus to services. But they too were stymied; in their case by Harlem's primitive transportation system which made intracity commutation so difficult. Harlem's first merchant-pioneers undoubtedly quickly realized that they could not rely upon downtown institutions for their own spiritual inspiration and religious leadership. And what of the next generation growing up in a remote outlying area bereft of contact with Jewish educational and social organizations? What chance did Judaism have to become— or remain—an important force in the lives of those unschooled in its ways and unaffiliated with its institutions?[7]

Responding to this difficult challenge of perpetuating group cohesion and a sense of Jewish identification in their new neighborhood, a group of newly arrived Harlem Jewish businessmen began meeting late in 1869 to inaugurate plans for regular Sabbath and Holiday services at the Harlem Savings Bank at 124th Street and Third Avenue. These early leaders included Marcus Marx, a hatter and clothier who moved his family from East Broadway to Third Avenue at 110th Street; Israel Stone, a former downtown clothier who set up shop next door to Marx on Third Avenue; brothers Samuel and Gershom Boehm,

Map 1. New York and Harlem in 1865
Source: United States Industrial Commission Report of the Immigration Committee on Immigration, vol. 15, 1901; Hyman B. Grinstein, *The Rise of the Jewish Community of New York 1654–1860,* 1945; *The 1866 Guide to New York City,* 1866. Map by L. Salit.

liquor dealers, late of Beaver Street, then of 125th Street; and jeweler
Isaac Peiser, formerly of Elm Street and now also a resident of 125th
Street. Their early efforts on behalf of the time-honored Jewish tradition of community-building led to the official incorporation of Congregation Hand-in-Hand in 1873 with twelve charter members. Harlem's first synagogue remained for over a decade the focus of uptown
communal life.[8]

Congregational growth within this small community remained slow
for its first several years because of several bitter disputes among
members over the synagogue's ritual practices. Congregation Hand-
in-Hand, although nominally Orthodox, did from the very start permit
one noteworthy departure from traditional religious procedures.
Mixed seating was allowed during services because, according to one
early congregational chronicler, "there was no gallery available" for
women in the rented quarters. A more deliberate reform was initiated
in 1877 with the introduction of an organ into the synagogue. This
more radical break with Orthodoxy caused several members to attempt to create their own Congregation Tents of Israel in a nearby
hall. One year later, a second group left the synagogue over new
proposed reforms, leaving Congregation Hand-in-Hand with a membership of only seventy. Having so limited a Jewish constituency to
draw from to begin with, the congregation could ill afford to lose any
dues-paying members. And although neither of the competing
splinter synagogoes survived for any appreciable length of time, Congregation Hand-in-Hand remained weak from the splits and was unable to raise sufficient funds either to build its own sanctuary or even
to retain a full-time cantor or rabbi. The laity of Harlem's first congregation continued to hold services in rented halls until the beginning of the 1880s.[9]

The congregation did, however, succeed during these early years in
meeting a more pressing communal problem by helping to establish
the Shangarai Limud Talmud Torah of Harlem, a free Jewish religious
school founded in 1876 under the leadership of the Carvalho family.
Solomon Nunes Carvalho, formerly of Liberty Street, an artist by profession and a member of one of America's most distinguished Sephardic families, arrived uptown in time to be a charter member of the
congregation. A man soon to involve himself in a variety of Jewish
and general communal social and educational organizations, Carvalho
joined with his wife in alerting the community to its obligation to edu-

cate the next generation of Jews. Rather than wait for the congregation to inaugurate religious instruction for children and recognizing
the paucity of funds available to Hand-in-Hand, they decided to establish a small school in their own home which served some forty-five
children by 1874. The Carvalho school became the Shangarai Limud
school in 1876, when the congregation's newly formed ladies' auxiliary took exclusive control of educational activities. The school's constitution specifically provided that only women could be active
members of the educational society. It did, however, grant the all-
male congregational school committee advisory status, and more importantly, financial control over the society, making the chairman of
the school committee an ex-officio member of the women's board of
managers. The women, led by Sarah Carvalho who served as school
superintendent, were to provide a staff of unpaid volunteer instruc-
tors, while their husbands controlled the purse strings. This school—
the forerunner of Temple Israel's Hebrew Free School of Harlem—
succeeded by 1880 in attracting some two hundred students to its educational program. With the establishment of a school in their own
neighborhood, religiously committed Harlem parents no longer had
to face the dilemma common to most Jewish families—to this day—in
settlements or towns remote from the major centers of Jewish learning: Whether to send their children, especially their sons, away to
school and risk a break in family cohesion or to keep them at home
and hope they acquired a love for Judaism through observation of
and participation in family-oriented religious ritual.[10]

Harlem's early communal leaders were concerned with all phases
of their members' lives and thus moved, in 1879, to purchase a ceme-
tery plot in Bayside, New York. Again the remoteness of Harlem Jewry
from their downtown coreligionists necessitated a separate uptown
communal effort. The small burial area, purchased by Marcus Marx,
served membership needs until 1895, when new larger territories
were acquired in lower Westchester. The latter purchase made it no
longer necessary for mourners to travel by ferry directly across the
North (Harlem) River to bury their dead in the countryside.[11]

Marcus Marx, Solomon Carvalho, and several other founders and
early members of Congregation Hand-in-Hand were also important
charter members of uptown's earliest Jewish social organizations; the
Harlem YMHA and the Harlem Lodge of the B'nai B'rith established in
1879 and 1882 respectively. In fact, the Y and B'nai B'rith membership

lists overlapped with those of the Congregation and Talmud Torah. Generally those families that affiliated with the congregation and its school also participated in Harlem Jewish social club life. Carvalho, for example, was the first secretary of the Harlem Y and may well have been instrumental in influencing the organization to hold a social benefit ball in 1880 to support the Talmud Torah. Marx and Israel Stone were charter members of Lodge #254 of B'nai B'rith and in 1882 represented their branch in negotiations with Yorkville brethren over a possible merger of small neighborhood branches. Concerned as they were with maintaining Judaism as a fundamental part of their lives, these religious communal leaders undoubtedly saw in the Y and the B'nai B'rith another means of strengthening Jewish family and neighborly ties within the small settlement. These Jewish social organizations, as one historian has pointed out, were designed to provide leisure-time programs and activities under Jewish auspices attractive to "Jews of all convictions and orientations." With the incorporation of these institutions, it became possible from that date forward for uptowners to live a full Jewish existence outside the center of New York Jewish life.[12]

However, to the dismay of the congregational leaders, many Y and Lodge members failed to share their dedication to synagogue life and chose not to join or attend the settlement's religious institutions. Supporters of Hand-in-Hand were greatly troubled by "sparse attendance" at services and severely chastised their neighbors for "thinking that all Judaism requires is to join the YMHA and attend its entertainments." The YMHA itself was once criticized by a local Jewish newspaper for demonstrating an unconscionable lack of concern for Jewish religious traditions by scheduling a boat ride on the Jewish fast day of Tisha B'ab. The Y was directed "to consult a Jewish calendar" before arranging for an entertainment on a day of Jewish national mourning.[13] Harlem's early religious communal leaders struggled with a problem that would later confront all subsequent Jewish leaders working in more contemporary suburban settlements: How to reach that large segment of the community that desires only minimal affiliation with local Jewish life while assimilating into general society.

The Harlem YMHA was also dedicated to serving the cultural needs of the greater uptown community. Harlem Jews of this early period—a small minority within a predominantly gentile neighborhood—closely identified with and sought to contribute to the social, political, and cultural life of their local community. And the Jewish Y, through an ongoing series of public lectures given by prominent uptown citizens during the early 1880s, expressed the community's dedication to aiding in the cultural enrichment of all Harlemites. These lectures may have also contributed directly or indirectly to greater understanding and acceptance of the Jews by their gentile neighbors. At least one lecturer, in speaking from the Y podium on the recent history of Harlem, admired the contributions Jewish merchants were making to Harlem's commercial growth and clearly indicated that, in his opinion, uptown Jews had earned the respect of their fellow citizens. The lecturer, Colonel Alonzo Caldwell, a popular contemporary chronicler of Harlem life, identified by name several Jewish storekeepers who "try to please their customers by competing with downtown merchants" and directed his audience to patronize local businessmen, stating "it is better for the purchasers to leave his dollars in Harlem . . . you can trade now in nearly all things as cheap in Harlem as elsewhere." Caldwell also emphasized the importance of tolerance and cooperation between Christians and Jews, calling upon all uptowners to continue "cultivating the friendliness as of yore in 'ye ancient village' and leave animosities and contentions to other localities."[14]

Many Harlemites apparently seconded Caldwell's philo-Semitic sentiments as evidenced by the prominent role accorded Jews in Harlem patriotic and political activities. David Carvalho and David Rutsky—both members of Hand-in-Hand—served, for example, on the Committee of Management of the 1886 Independence Day Celebration Association of Harlem. Participation in this community-wide patriotic event, organized under the auspices of the local post of the Grand Army of the Republic, was, according to its leader, the joyful obligation of "all Harlemites, white or black, Democrat or Republican, naturalized or native-born."[15]

A further indication of the Jews' acceptance in the general Harlem society was their active participation in both of Harlem's major political parties. Six uptown Jews, including Rutsky and Benjamin F. Peixotto, were among the first members of the Harlem Republican Party founded in 1888. Peixotto, former United States Consul to Bucharest, lived out the last years of his life in Harlem, affiliating as a member of the Harlem synagogue and the Republican Party. The Democratic Party could boast of thirteen Jews among its original members including the Carvalhos, young Jacob Cantor—who was destined to become both an uptown state senator and president of the Borough of Manhattan—and Cyrus Sulzberger and Daniel P. Hays, founders of the important Anglo-Jewish periodical *The American Hebrew*.[16]

Jews also participated in a variety of uptown German immigrant cultural organizations, forming as they did an important part of that group's intracity migration of the late 1880s. Jews were active in organizations like Amitica, a literary group formed in 1887, with "its object the study and cultivation of the German language among its members."[17]

Another way in which Harlem Jews demonstrated their desire to be part of uptown society was by contributing time and money to Harlem's charitable organizational activities. Several prominent synagogue members affiliated with the Harlem Relief Society of the City of New York, founded in 1892. And some years earlier the Harlem Jewish Y had held a charity ball for the benefit of the Irish Relief Fund. Jews' interest in this charity reflected compassion for a suffering people or, more likely, their desire to be part of a district-wide campaign run by local neighborhood Irish-American charitable groups.[18]

The only recorded instance of social prejudice—so common a problem for socially mobile German Jews in many localities during the late nineteenth century—marring Harlem's seemingly harmonious intergroup relations was the temporary exclusion in 1899 of Jacob Cantor from membership in the Harlem Club. Cantor, by then a well-known attorney and recently elected State Senator from Harlem's 10th District, was proposed for membership in this prestigious local men's club by two of his gentile friends. The election of this universally respected professional and public servant should have been no more than a formality. It became a bit of a public scandal when several members attempted to blackball his election "solely on the ground of his being Jewish." Cantor was soon elected, however, because, according to one Jewish observer, "the electors were too refined and had too much of an American sense to judge a man on his religion alone."[19]

During the 1880s Harlem's era as a remote sparsely populated semirural settlement ended. The uptown area was drawn into the orbit of city life by the extension of the Second and Third Avenue railroads to the northern tip of Manhattan in 1879 and 1880 respectively. These long-awaited rapid transit improvements cut travel time between Harlem and City Hall nearly in half, facilitating greater uptown participation in a variety of city activities. More importantly, it at long last brought the borough's large expanses of undeveloped lands within reasonable commutation time of Lower Manhattan's business, office and industrial districts, convincing local real estate operators that Harlem and other uptown districts were now suitable residential neighborhoods. And although realtors may have feared that the forty-five minute ride from Harlem to downtown might still pose a logistical problem for some inner city dwellers looking to relocate—especially those of the lowest economic strata who had to be at work downtown very early in the morning—they nevertheless reasoned that many more long-suffering New Yorkers would perceive commuter problems as a minor annoyance when compared with the more oppressive problems of overcrowding.* Accordingly, in 1880 New York real estate operators embarked on a then-unparalleled wave of residential construction that transformed Harlem almost overnight. By 1885, when the focus of real estate development shifted to the West Side and Morningside Heights sections of Manhattan, nearly half the East Harlem lands south of 125th Street were covered with tenements, brownstone flats, and private homes.[20]

During the first era of large-scale residential construction Harlem builders focused their attention primarily upon those properties near or adjoining the elevated lines. During 1881—the year of the most pronounced building activity—more than two-thirds of the buildings completed in Harlem were constructed within the streets and avenues east of Third Avenue and north of 100th Street. In fact, nearly one-fifth of all uptown buildings constructed during that year were situated on the streets between Second and Third Avenue. The then newly designed dumbbell tenements and older railroad flats predominated east of Third Avenue "covering all the vacant space" and providing shelter for "the great working population" that began establishing roots in East Harlem during the era. Even when first

---

* The trip from Harlem to the Lower East Side on the Second and Third Avenue "Els" took over forty-five minutes. That meant that approximately one and a half hours were lost daily by commuters from uptown. The rate from the Battery to Harlem was set in 1875 as not to exceed 15 cents and to the Bronx, no more than 17 cents. Special "rush hour" or "commission hour" rates were established for uptown and the Bronx. Travelers from Harlem paid only 7 cents a ride if they rode between the hours of 5:30–7:00 A.M. and 5–7 P.M.

introduced in 1879, the dumbbell tenements failed to provide decent accommodations. But for workers previously trapped in the front, rear and makeshift tenements that pockmarked their overcrowded downtown neighborhoods, residence even in a dumbbell tenement in the still relatively uncrowded uptown district meant a significant improvement in the physical conditions of their lives.[21]

Contemporary critics of the dumbbell tenements scorned this new type of uptown construction, believing it made Harlem "one of the most depressing quarters in New York." Criticism of the old railroad flats was even more pronounced as many sensed that they represented the first step in creating what would later become the slum neighborhood of Harlem. As one observer put it: "It is curious and discouraging to see how little influence the advance in planning and architecture, especially of apartment houses have had upon the common reign of these edifices."[22]

The erection of smaller numbers of three-story brownstone dwellings along Second and Third Avenues received far more approval. These buildings provided better accommodations for "the army of clerks and bookkeepers and others, who now that rapid transit is a reality chose to settle uptown rather than look for residential relief in New Jersey or Brooklyn." Brownstone residences were also popular on the less-populated sections of Lexington and Madison Avenues and in the slightly improved and lightly populated Madison and Fifth Avenue district, the home of "the finest houses" of Harlem's most affluent residents. Real estate operators pointed with pride to the grand uptown houses complete with "the parlors and various chambers being gotten up in a manner which would do credit to houses of greater pretensions."[23]

The construction of the elevated railroads and the resulting New York building boom of the 1880s occurred at a most crucial juncture in the history of New York City. In 1881—almost immediately after the uptown lines were finished—the already severely overcrowded metropolis became the destination of thousands of Jewish immigrants from Eastern Europe who fled to these shores to escape the atrocities of pogroms and the deprivations of greatly restricted occupational opportunities. Arriving in the Port of New York virtually penniless, they had almost no option but to settle in the poorer, densely populated, section of the Lower East Side, the home of the less-affluent segment of the earlier Irish and German immigrations. Joining the

Jews in settling downtown were also thousands of Italian immigrants who had begun arriving en masse several years earlier. Were it not for the new residential areas in Harlem and elsewhere created in the early 1880s, which siphoned off the many Irish- and German-American tenement dwellers capable of fleeing this new Southern and Eastern European invasion, New York may well have been unable to absorb the new immigrants.[24]

Harlem, Yorkville, and to a lesser extent the new West Side neighborhoods, did serve as major safety valves for the thousands of Irish and Germans—among them many German Jews—who had acquired by the 1880s enough economic resources to escape the downtown ghetto for new uptown neighborhoods. New Irish and German residential areas sprung up in the wake of the downtown dislocation in each of the several newly developed regions north of 42d Street, east and west of Central Park. The German emerged as the predominant group in Yorkville, while the Irish gained control of the West Side's Twenty-second Ward, settling along the route of the Eighth and Ninth Avenue "Els." Both groups settled in large and almost equal numbers in Harlem, constituting by 1890 nearly one-half of the district's residents and overwhelming those of native American ancestry who now represented less than one-third of an expanding uptown population.[25]

The evacuation of downtown by these "old immigrant" groups was so remarkably quick and complete that by 1890 the Tenth Ward, bordered by Grand, Norfolk, Division Streets and the Bowery, once the home of a predominantly German population, had become 70 percent Russian-Jewish.* By that date similarly large immigrant popula-

---

* It is impossible to determine from United States and New York Census of Population manuscripts exactly what proportion of the Russian and Polish immigration was Jewish. Historians have assumed, however, that the overwhelming majority of Russians and Poles living in New York's immigrant Jewish neighborhoods during the era of mass East European migration to the United States were of Jewish ancestry. This widely held assumption is predicated primarily upon the work of the demographer of Jewish immigration, Samuel Joseph. He argued in 1914 that the majority of East European immigrants to the United States before World War I were Jewish and the majority of these Jewish immigrants chose to settle in the northeastern urban centers. See Samuel Joseph, Jewish Immigration to the United States, 1881–1910 (New York: Columbia University Press, 1914), pp. 102, 107, 195.) Thus it is most likely that the statistics for Russians and Poles closely approximate those for Russian and Polish Jews. This assumption is furthered by my own study of those federal and state census manuscripts available. I found few instances where Russians and Poles enumerated in Harlem's Jewish districts had other than "Jewish-sounding names." Those few names were, of course, eliminated from the manuscript sample, for the purposes of my study.

tions also concentrated in the neighboring Seventh and Thirteenth wards, encompassing such well-known "Jewish streets" as Rivington, Monroe and Catherine. The 1880s also saw the Italians gain control of the formerly Irish tenement territories west of the Russian-Jewish settlement. Thompson, Sullivan, Grand, Broome, and Houston streets all became part of an emerging Italian ghetto that also included large parts of the formerly German-Irish Sixth and Fourteenth wards.[26]

The burgeoning Harlem community not only attracted low-income immigrant workers from the Lower East Side to its tenements and their moderately affluent fellow downtown brethren to its better-quality brownstones. It also became home for a considerable number of very affluent midtown residents who bought or leased the limited number of luxury homes and apartments built in the still lightly populated northern regions of Harlem's Fifth Avenue. And although the West Side and Morningside Heights sections also offered abundant residential opportunities to the city's rich, Harlem attracted more than its share of New York's "older and wealthier" citizens. One contemporary student of Harlem life has argued that by the late 1890s "few neighborhoods in the entire city had so disproportionate a number of wealthy native-born American and 'old immigrants' as did this north-western section of Harlem." The Sulzbergers, Hays, Peixottos, and other prominent old Jewish families joined with other "people of taste and wealth" in settling this "residential haven" from a deteriorating midtown.[27]

Late in the 1880s Harlem also became home for a relatively small number of Italian immigrants who followed the Irish and Germans out of the overcrowded Lower East Side to Harlem in search of work in the uptown construction industry. These recent immigrants, with the most minimal of economic resources, settled with the poorer element of uptown society in the east-of-Third Avenue tenement district. And although the older immigrant groups would remain numerically predominant in the area bounded roughly by 105th and 120th streets, Third Avenue and the Harlem River, until the turn of the century, the arrival of these first uptown Italian settlers signaled the beginning of a new era of urban ethnic dislocation that would eventually lead to the establishment of a twentieth-century "Little Italy" neighborhood in this part of Harlem.[28]

The opening of Harlem to large-scale residential construction and intracity migration dramatically altered the fortunes of early Harlem

Jewish institutions. For Harlem's oldest synagogue, it meant a new era of growth and development; it attracted to its membership rolls many of the newly settled affluent German Jews. Buoyed by this new financial security, in less than a decade Congregation Hand-in-Hand grew from a small chevrah—so poor that in 1880 it was unable to contribute even ten dollars to the United Hebrew Charities' Free Burial Society—to one of New York's leading Reform religious institutions ensconced in an architecturally magnificent Temple Israel—at 125th Street and Fifth Avenue, the crossroads of Harlem's wealthiest district.[29]

The congregation began showing signs of growing economic strength when it purchased in 1882 the Grace Episcopal Church, which it had been leasing for several years, as its first permanent home. Not long thereafter, the congregation took another step by hiring Dr. Maurice Harris as its first full-time Rabbi. The English-born Harris began his association with the Harlem group in 1881. As a student at the Emanu-el Theological Seminary, he served the congregation as a "volunteer nominally paid" part-time preacher. Upon attaining his rabbinic diploma from the New York-based institution, Harris received a call for full-time service at Hand-in-Hand.[30]

A self-described advocate of moderate Reform practices, Harris quickly inspired some significant modifications in the previously Orthodox ritual of the congregation. He immediately introduced more English-language prayers into the service and soon convinced his laity to abandon the Orthodox siddur completely in favor of the English language Minhag Jastrow so popular with the left wing of the nineteenth-century Conservative or Historical School of Judaism. Later, in 1894, when the new Central Conference of American Rabbis, of which Harris was an early member, adopted the Union Prayer Book for use by Reform congregations, Congregation Hand-in-Hand adopted that standardized prayer book for its services. But Rabbi Harris was moderate, advocating the continued observance of the traditional religious "second holy day" of Festivals and defending the right of traditionally oriented members to continue to wear a skullcap or hat during services.[31]

Not all congregational traditionalists accepted Harris's religious approach. Those who preferred the old ritual ways were particularly incensed by the congregational majority decision to follow the Rabbi in adopting the Jastrow prayer book. The dissent caused such ill will within membership ranks that a "peace conference" had to be called to reconcile synagogue factions. Both Myer S. Isaacs, son of Samuel

M. Isaacs, a leading Historial School spokesman, and Dr. Kaufmann Kohler of the Reform Temple Beth-El addressed the reconciliation meeting. They succeeded in convincing both sides that "the necessity of peace in synagogue life transcended all other ritual and personal considerations." Both leaders called upon worshipers to somehow settle their differences harmoniously "and to support their present executive and minister."[32]

Congregation Hand-in-Hand demonstrated its new standing as one of the city's most important Reform groups in 1888 when it built a suitable synagogue building and reorganized itself as Temple Israel of Harlem. The choice of the 125th Street at Fifth Avenue site for the Temple was dictated, according to Rabbi Harris, by "the movement of the [affluent] Jewish community to the West Side of Harlem." The Third Avenue at 110th Street edifice was deemed "too small and too far east" for the congregation's growing membership. By then, of course, Temple Israel could boast of a most impressive membership which included representatives of several of the city's most important Jewish families. Daniel P. Hays, Vice-President of the Temple in 1888 and its President beginning in 1890, was a scion of an American Jewish family that traced it genealogy to before the Revolutionary War. Cyrus L. Sulzburger, of that famous German-Jewish family, was a trustee of the congregation and served as chairman of its Religious School Union. Benjamin Peixotto, the noted diplomat and statesman, himself of Sephardic ancestry, added even more prestige to the Temple by his participation on the congregation's Board of Trustees. These famous Jews combined with the many professionals and successful businessmen to finance Harlem's first landmark Jewish institution. Temple Israel remained at its Fifth Avenue location until 1903 when it followed it most affluent members further west to the newly constructed Central Harlem neighborhood and relocated in even more grand surroundings at 120th Street and Lenox Avenue.[33]

The presence of many former midtown New Yorkers on its membership rolls and the improved direct communication lines between Harlem and the city also inspired greater Temple Israel participation in a variety of Greater New York Reform communal activities. The most noteworthy new link was the Harlem Temple's Sisterhood of Personal Service founded at Rabbi Harris' request in 1891. This uptown charitable organization was modeled after the Temple Emanu-el Sisterhood which had come into existence several years earlier to assist in the care of the city's immigrant poor. The midtown organization and the several other congregational relief committees it inspired may well have reflected local denominational recognition of and affinity for the "social gospel" plank adopted by Reform Jews under their Pittsburgh Platform. Reform leaders meeting in 1885 had declared it "the duty of Jews in full accordance with the spirit of Mosaic legislation" to participate in solving the great social problems of modern times. Rabbi Harris pointed to the good work done by Emanu-el's women when he proposed the creation of the Harlem Sisterhood. "A congregation," he declared, "can and must be the center for a large amount of good. A society has been formed in this city—that I would like you to make your ideal—whose only dues are 'personal service'." [34]

The women of Temple Israel responded to the Rabbi's appeal and organized a society that sponsored a sewing circle for the poor of East Harlem, a Perserverance Club for uptown working girls, and a free kindergarten for needy tenement children. In 1894, the Sisterhood established official ties with downtown Reform charitable and relief organizations, becoming the uptown affiliate of the United Hebrew Charities. Later in that decade, as poor East European Jews started settling in large numbers among Harlem's poor German Jews in the Third Avenue tenement district, Temple Israel surrendered part of its district-wide charitable responsibilities to two smaller German Jewish women's organizations, the Amelia Relief Society and the Deborah Relief Society which operated in the Yorkville–Lower Harlem areas. These cooperating organizations were destined to expand their benevolent activities when poor immigrant Jews migrated to Harlem after the turn of the century. [35]

While the new transportation links proved to be a great boom to the internal development of Temple Israel and to the expansion of congregational contacts with city-based institutions, these same rapid transit improvements, ironically, hastened the decline of the early Harlem Y and the Harlem Lodge of the B'nai B'rith as important social organizations. Both groups had been founded originally in remote Harlem by their respective national leaderships who were concerned with providing membership benefits to individuals incapable of attending meetings and functions in the central city. By 1885, however, with Harlem emerging as just another residential neighborhood in close contact with an expanding metropolis, organizational leaders realized that uptown-bound members could still retain their active affiliation with their present midtown and downtown branches and older Harlem residents could now readily participate in all city-wide activities. Local Harlem branches were now, in their opinion, simply duplicating the work of their neighboring city organizations. The YMHA of midtown New York was believed to be well within reach of Harlem residents. And the B'nai B'rith maintained several branches in the immediate Yorkville area within even closer proximity to the Harlem brethren. It is not surprising, therefore, that in 1885, the fifty-one members of the Harlem Y liquidated their assets and pooled their funds with the larger New York group. A year later, the Harlem Lodge consolidated with the nearby Lebanon Lodge #9. More than two decades would elapse before each of these organizations would re-emerge—under totally different contemporary circumstances—as important parts of the Harlem Jewish social scene.[36]

The large German-Jewish migration to Harlem in the late nineteenth century not only changed the developing courses of existing Jewish institutional life but also led to the relocation of several downtown institutions within the uptown community. The arrival of these congregations uptown underscored the obvious transformation of Harlem from an outpost of Jewish life, housing a small community of merchant-pioneers, to a growing neighborhood attractive to many different segments of German-Jewish society. Chevrah Anshe Chesed, a small German Conservative-Orthodox congregation founded in 1876 at Beekman Place near 50th Street, became part of the Harlem religious scene in 1893. This was the final stop on a long congregational odyssey which saw a small group of families who wished to live and worship together migrate from midtown in 1879, to Yorkville in 1883, and finally to Harlem. There they reorganized themselves as an open congregation granting membership to all German Jews who wished to affiliate, and joined with Temple Mount Zion to serve the Lower Harlem Community. Temple Mount Zion had been established in a small neighborhood public hall several years earlier by a small contingent of German and Hungarian Jews who had broken from Yorkville's Congregation Har Sinai. Not long after its incorporation in 1888, Congregation Mount Zion changed its denomination from Orthodox to moderate Reform, raising the possibilty that the earlier dispute may have been over the ritual practices of the Yorkville congregation.* These two synagogues grew rapidly in membership and prestige and were soon destined to play important roles in Harlem social work, serving both their German and the East European constituency.[37]

Congregations Beth Tephilah and Ateres Zvi were both established in 1890 to serve those migrants who had served contacts with downtown or midtown congregations and who desired to affiliate neither with the old, affluent Temple Israel nor with the other small transplanted Conservative or Reform congregations. Congregation Beth Tephilah typified the "private" synagogues that proliferated in all Jewish immigrant neighborhoods. It was owned and operated by a Reverend Samuel Distillator, a Russian Jew who operated this Orthodox German† congregation out of several small rented halls during the 1890s. Distillator also served the uptown community in the triple capacity as a local *Mesader Kedushin* (performer of marriage ceremonies), *Mohel,* and ritual slaughterer, and advertised his varied talents in both the Yiddish and Anglo-Jewish press. He also gained a measure of notorious publicity in 1892, when he was arrested by Health De-

* It is often very difficult to determine accurately the denominations of nineteenth-century congregations. Relatively few Reform congregations affiliated with the early Union of American Hebrew Congregations (founded in 1873), and the so-called Conservative-Orthodox or Orthodox congregations had no such national body until the founding of the Union of Orthodox Jewish Congregations of America in 1898. In addition many nominally Orthodox congregations such as the early Hand-in-Hand and Anshe Chesed, permitted mixed seating; other Conservative congregations utilized mixed choirs in their services in clear variance from contemporary understandings of Orthodox ritual practice. Finally, one cannot base synagogue denomination even on the background of the pulpit rabbi. For at least in Harlem, several rabbis served at a number of congregations with apparently totally different denominational orientations.

The designations, Orthodox, Conservative-Orthodox, Moderate Reform, and Radical Reform, as used in this chapter, are, therefore, based upon my own study of the ritual practices of local congregations and are predicated upon the following criteria:

a) *Orthodox*—strict segregation of the sexes during prayer, use of the traditional prayer book.
b) *Conservative-Orthodox*—mixed seating permitted, use of Jastrow or other English-language prayer book, but no organs or mixed choirs used during the services.
c) *Moderate Reform*—mixed seating and use of organ and mixed choir permitted but men still wore hats and prayer shawls during the services. Affiliation with the U.A.H.C. obviously denotes Reform.
d) *Radical Reform*—mixed seating, use of organ, and mixed choir permitted; affiliation with the Union and no hats or prayer shawls.

† Synagogues were designated "German Congregations" on the basis of the following criteria: a) The languages of prayer and discourse were German and English, and b) the founders of the congregation or the majority of the members were of German ancestry (when that could be determined.)

HARLEM IN 1890

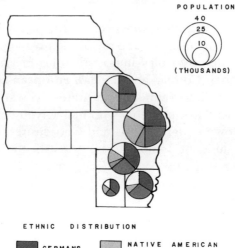

POPULATION

40
25
10

(THOUSANDS)

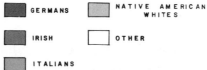

ETHNIC   DISTRIBUTION

GERMANS   NATIVE   AMERICAN
                            WHITES

IRISH   OTHER

ITALIANS

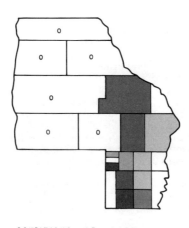

CONDITIONS   OF   LIFE

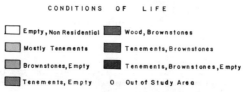

Empty, Non Residential   Wood, Brownstones

Mostly Tenements   Tenements, Brownstones

Brownstones, Empty   Tenements, Brownstones, Empty

Tenements, Empty   0   Out of Study Area

Map 2. Harlem in 1890

Source: United States Department of Interior Census, Census Office, *Vital Statistics of New York City and Brooklyn Covering a Period of Six Years Ending May 31, 1890,* 1894. Map by L. Salit.

partment officials for operating a butcher shop without an approved city code permit.[38]

Congregation Ateres Zvi replaced Congregation Hand-in-Hand as the major religious institution for Jews living near 125th Street and Third Avenue. This congregation, like Ansche Chesed, was run according to Conservative-Orthodox strictures and is most noteworthy for its being the first Harlem German congregation to openly solicit East European members through advertisment in the religiously oriented *Yiddishes Tageblatt*.[39]

Probably the most widely noted German-Jewish institutional migration was the removal to Harlem in 1899 of members of Congregation Shaarei Zedek, one of New York's oldest and best-known congregations. There they founded, after much quarreling, an uptown branch of their Henry Street Synagogue. The question of a possible congregational relocation first attracted public attention when in 1897 a group of synagogue leaders, headed by real estate operators Bernard Galewski and Aaron Levy, attempted surreptitiously to sell their downtown synagogue in Harlem. Other trustees, upon hearing of the move, quickly went to court and received an injunction blocking final real estate negotiations until board members could have the opportunity to vote on the projected sale and relocation. When the Board of Trustees finally considered the Galewski-Levy plan, a majority voted to maintain the congregation where it was on the Lower East Side.

Galewski, Levy, and their minority of dissenters continued to press their fellow congregational leaders for assistance in establishing a Shaarei Zedek presence in Harlem. Finally in May 1899, uptown and downtown factions agreed to an appropriation of $6,000 for the construction of a synagogue for Harlem-bound members in return for their official resignation from the downtown congregation and their forfeiture of all chevrah (mutual benefit) privileges, including the important right of burial in the cemetery plot held by the downtown congregation. The uptown branch was to become a completely separate entity with no official ties whatsoever with the Henry Street synagogue. The dissidents willingly accepted their exile and used the "severance payment" to build a synagogue on 118th Street east of Lenox Avenue, in a newly built section of Central Harlem. They also hired Rabbi Leopold Zinsler away from the downtown congregation in the hope of adding greater prestige to the Harlem synagogue and the community it served.

Although officially divorced, Harlem Shaarei Zedek people maintained close contact with downtown members because residents of the Lower East Side were constantly abandoning the ghetto for Harlem during the first decade of this century. Finally in 1910, the last remaining leaders of the downtown faction agreed to the disposal of the Henry Street property and officially moved the congregation to Harlem. Still, they steadfastly refused to negotiate amalgamation with the uptown group immediately, preferring to hold separate services in a local public hall. Finally, in 1914, peace came to Congregation Shaarei Zedek when all factions were reunited as a single larger representative congregation in the 118th Street synagogue.[40]

The time of German numerical predominance and institutional hegemony in Harlem Jewish life proved to be of only limited duration. Not long after the German Jews completed the major phase of their evacuation of the Lower East Side, small groups of East European Jews began establishing their own colony in Harlem. As early as 1890 approximately thirteen hundred Russian Polish pioneers had already settled in Harlem, residing in almost equal numbers in the better Irish-German neighborhood, west of Third Avenue, and in the mixed ethnic tenement district east of Third Avenue. These first Russian settlers founded their first congregation, Nachlath Zvi, in 1891, and their first religious school, the Uptown Talmud Torah, a year later.[41]

These early Russian immigrant settlers were, however, only the first pathfinders for future waves of East European intracity migrants who would begin arriving uptown in earnest after 1895.* By the early 1900s, Russian Jews would constitute the overwhelming majority of Harlem's Jewish residents and a whole new set of communal institutions would have appeared on the uptown scene, all designed to serve the many needs of a large, ever-expanding immigrant population.

---

* Like the Germans before them, the early East European settlers constituted in the very beginning a remote outpost of Jewish life far removed from the hub of immigrant settlement. The remoteness of the early colony is graphically illustrated through an examination of the *Yiddishes Tageblatt,* an important Yiddish daily of the period. Between 1888 and 1891, only two articles dealing with Russian Jews in Harlem appeared in the periodical. Harlem's immigrant synagogue was not included in the lists of hundreds of permanent and temporary synagogues which appeared in the Tageblatt before the Jewish New Year. Any quantitative analysis of the economic activities of these Russian settlers has been made impossible by the lack of extant federal census manuscripts for 1890 and state manuscripts for New York County for 1892.

chapter 2

The Arrival of the East European Jew Uptown, 1895–1910

The migration at the turn of the century of large numbers of East European Jews from the downtown ghetto of the Lower East Side to a new Jewish immigrant quarter in Harlem generally has been viewed as part of the group's economic and social advancement. Contemporary observers often depicted Harlem as the home of the upwardly mobile Jewish immigrant. One writer spoke of "a great Jewish bourgeoisie" living in an uptown neighborhood "made up entirely of East Siders who have outgrown their station." Another remarked that "Harlem is the goal" of the newly successful business entrepeneur and noted that "the further uptown he moves the larger, one may be sure is his bank account." So too, in his recent study of Harlem's history, Gilbert Osofsky argued that the participation of Jews in the uptown building boom of the late 1890s "reflected their economic mobility. To live in Harlem became a symbol of good times for many East European Families."[1]

These popular and scholarly perceptions fit only one segment of the uptown community, which settled in Harlem after 1903 along the wide thoroughfares of Lenox Avenue and in the spacious six- and seven-story elevator apartments of Madison and Fifth Avenues. But they were neither the first nor the largest group of East European Jews to leave the ghetto for Harlem.

Many more migrated in the hope of making economic progress than as a result of having achieved financial success. Fundamental to their decision making was the perception that resettlement in Harlem did not even require a basic change in their work routine. They could continue, as they had done downtown, to live in close geographical proximity to their work, while seeking economic advancement and avoiding severe ghetto overcrowding. A closely related combination of factors, including the proximity of home to office but more importantly the possibility—at least during the temporary glut in new uptown building construction after 1900—of living in uptown housing superior to and cheaper than the better grade of ghetto accommodations for only slightly more rent than then charged for downtown tenement housing, influenced others. Still other uptown-bound migrants had the decision to relocate made for them by physical changes in the ghetto. Urban renewal and municipal improvement occurring during the peak years of immigration forced many with no prior intention of moving uptown to seek accommodations outside the ghetto. Included in this group were thousands of newly arrived immigrants who were never given the opportunity to settle downtown and who looked immediately to Harlem. The decision-making process leading to the settlement by 1910 of 100,000 Jews in several distinct Harlem neighborhoods was far more complex than has been previously suggested.

Although Harlem did house a small group of East Europeans as early as 1890, the era of mass uptown migration did not commence until after 1895. Until that time most immigrants, wishing to escape the physical problems of an overcrowded, deteriorating Lower East Side, or to explore new economic opportunities outside the downtown ghetto, looked to the new Jewish settlement in the then outlying Brownsville district. For many immigrant Jews, the decision to relocate in Brownsville was facilitated by their ability to follow occupations similar to those performed on the Lower East Side. Many needle trades workers, for example, migrated to Brownsville when their employers moved their sweatshops across the river. More limited numbers of Jewish building trades workers and other skilled and semiskilled workers found employment in a variety of locally based shops and industries. Very few Brownsville Jews had to travel back to the Lower East Side to earn a livelihood.[2]

Harlem of the early 1890s offered far fewer occupational opportunities to the prospective East European Jewish settler. No Harlem Jew rivaled Brownsville's Elias Kaplan who moved his large factory and workers to Brooklyn. The cigar-making industry, which gave employment to thousands of Russian immigrants, had only begun to shift its large factories from the Lower East Side to Yorkville and southeast Harlem. It was, of course, possible for immigrant factory workers to live in Harlem and to commute to their downtown industries on the Second and Third Avenue "Els." It is questionable, however, how many low-salaried sweatshop workers actually considered uptown relocation worthwhile when they contemplated rising almost an hour earlier in the morning and paying fifteen cents a day carfare in order to reach the Lower East Side to begin their long working day.* Jewish building trades workers, who were destined to play so large a role in later uptown construction activities, also found it difficult to secure employment in the Harlem of the early 1890s. Building activity, which had peaked in the mid-1880s, had been in decline for several years. Jews had to compete with members of other ethnic groups for the few jobs that did remain.[3]

Thus, Harlem's limited immigrant employment opportunities undoubtedly restricted uptown settlement to those relatively few Russian-Jewish settlers who could be classified within one of the following occupational categories: Successful skilled workers who could afford to leave the downtown factory district to settle in Harlem and set up their own small shops, or who were talented or valuable enough to arrive at work later than the normal worker; those few Jewish building trades workers who were able to find work in Harlem's construction industries; small shopkeepers and peddlers who were willing and able to live and work in Harlem away from their steady Russian-Jewish clientele; and professionals, large manufac-

---

* It is noteworthy that Harlem, unlike its sister settlements in Brownsville and Williamsburg, was never home for a large needle trades industry. In 1900, for example, only 1,245 women's garment workers were employed in some ninety-three plants located north of 42d Street. Twenty-two years later, 11,832 worked in that area, constituting only 7.9 percent of the needle trades work force. The men's clothing and textile industries also produced low figures for the uptown district. These statistics did not include the small independently owned tailor shops which may have existed in the uptown districts. See *The Clothing and Textile Industries in New York and Environs* (New York: 1925), pp. 67–68.

As far as the early Harlem tobacco industry is concerned, of some 724 cigar manufacturers located in the New York area in 1892, only 139, or 19 percent, were located north of 59th Street, and only 43, or 5 percent, were situated within Harlem. See Trow's *Business Directory of Greater New York, 1892* (New York, 1893), pp. 227–37. The directory does not indicate how large each of the establishments was.

turers and businessmen who had risen out of the working class and who were no longer tied to an externally established time schedule. But most Russian immigrants did not fall into these categories. Migration to Harlem remained the province of only the truly exceptional immigrant.

The attractiveness of Harlem, even for the most extraordinary immigrant settler, was greatly reduced by the paucity of decent available housing. The old, now densely populated tenement district east of Third Avenue offered only the prospect of rapidly deteriorating dumbbell tenements and railroad flats, similar to those that predominated on the Lower East Side. And although the uptown district continued to remain far less congested than downtown, these tenements were not very much of an inducement to migrate. The smaller number of superior types of brownstone flats and apartments that stood west of Third Avenue were, as always, in very short supply. Even the most upwardly mobile Russian-Jewish families were slow to consider a move uptown.[4]

The primary factor that induced most Jews to move uptown after 1895 was a change in the Harlem real estate market. For the first time new types of housing, superior to that available on the Lower East Side, and at rents comparable to or lower than those downtown, were widely available. Indeed, this construction provided the very necessary opportunities for work. The center of this new construction was the previously underdeveloped segment of East and Central Harlem. The impetus for renewed speculation in Harlem lands was the expectation of improved rapid transit facilities that would make that part of Harlem more accessible to downtown.

Real estate developers had sufficient cause for optimism. The first steps in improving mass transit had already taken place. In 1895, the Metropolitan Street Railway Company, which had built overhead trolley lines from Battery Park to Central Park West in the early 1890s, extended its lines eastward across 116th Street through Central Harlem. This new system, which finally made it possible for Central Harlemites to reach downtown for only one five-cent fare, was still seen as too slow for those having to travel downtown daily. Still, real estate operators anticipated that the time was finally ripe for the long-awaited construction of a subway system linking downtown with Harlem and the Bronx.[5]

Central Harlem's residents had been agitating for a subway system for many years. One Harlem neighborhood weekly began as early as 1890 to criticize city officials for not recognizing that "New York and especially Harlem is losing population and growth constantly because of the lack of facilities for quick and comfortable transit between the north and south ends of Manhattan Island." They argued that "it is made apparent every day that something must be done towards providing rapid transit or the results will be serious."[6]

The municipal government responded half-heartedly, creating in 1891 a permanent commission that was empowered to lay out a route for the subway and to negotiate with landowners for possession of parcels located on the projected route. The commission was not empowered, however, to build or operate the system. Those rights were to be offered for sale to the highest public bidder.

After over a year of protracted negotiations with some reluctant Knickerbocker landowners who wished to preserve the suburban character of their neighborhood, the commission reported, late in 1892, on a proposed subway line that would run from the Battery up the West Side along Broadway to Kingsbridge Road in the West Bronx, and up the East Side along Madison Avenue across the Harlem River into the East Bronx. The rights to build this rapid transit system were subsequently offered at public sale, but when no responsible bidder appeared, the "permanent" commission was temporarily dissolved and rapid transit plans were tabled.[7]

Harlem's real estate and business people continued to push for rapid transit. The *Harlem Local Reporter,* which played a major role in rallying uptown forces, spearheaded the struggle, coining the oft-repeated slogan "Fifteen Minutes to Harlem." "A rapid transit system which will bring 125th Street within fifteen minutes of the City Hall will be the greatest boom New York City can ever have."[8]

Municipal leaders finally responded affirmatively to uptown needs in 1894 by passing a new rapid transit act that provided for public construction of a subway system, conditional on public approval of a referendum on mass transit to be held in the upcoming municipal election. And when the referendum was overwhelmingly approved in November of that year, Harlem's long struggle for rapid transit appeared to have ended in victory.[9]

Anticipating the construction of the newly approved rapid transit system, Harlem realtors and builders began to invest heavily in Central Harlem lands. A local trade journal estimated that enough "cheap semi-urban homes" were built between 1895 and 1900 on previously unoccupied sections of Madison, Fifth, and Lenox avenues to accommodate approximately 30,000 new settlers. The blocks located along 110th to 120th streets between Madison and Fifth avenues showed the most pronounced growth during this period. Of the ten square blocks situated in this area, six had a building concentration of between 90 and 100 percent of available land utilized. The other four square blocks were between 50 and 90 percent built-up.[10]

The construction boom in the late 1890s was also stimulated by the desire of real estate developers to complete construction before new building regulations went into effect in 1900. The New York City Building Code, which failed to satisfy even the most minimal hopes of tenement house reformers, was, nevertheless, seen by builders and speculators as a source of increased construction costs and lower profits. Poorly constructed buildings, rushed to completion by builders fearful of new regulations, augmented the ready supply of apartments available to prospective tenants.[11]

But the expected great demand for Harlem housing did not immediately materialize. Numerous unforeseen legal and financial problems delayed construction of the long-anticipated approved rapid transit system. The newly developed sections of Harlem remained inaccessible to downtown and attracted relatively few new settlers. Soon—even before the end of this pre-1900 building boom—some thoughtful realtors realized that they had overspeculated in Harlem lands. And as early as 1898, complaints were heard from builders about a "tenant dominated" real estate market.[12]

Fearful of suffering substantial losses on their investments, realtors began to grant long terms of free rents to attract prospective tenants. Harlem landlords also started to list available apartments in the Yiddish press. A typical advertisement read:

> The Voice of Joy, the Voice of Gladness, The Voice of the Bridegroom, the Voice of the Bride. Young couples and growing families can receive a practical, decorated three-room apartment for $8.50-$9.50 in the great new Steinway Apartment House. Do you want an elegant place for cheap rent?[13]

The competition among realtors to fill up their partially rented buildings was so keen that by 1900 a "rent war" was underway in Harlem and the Bronx. The problem reached such critical proportions that in April 1900, forty-seven property owners in the Twelfth, Twenty-third and Twenty-fourth Wards met to form a Protective Association of Harlem Property Owners for the expressed purpose of creating "an extensive union of uptown real estate operators to do away with some of the evils which have made Harlem real estate unprofitable." The new association hoped to crack down on those realtors who promised to maintain minimal base rents and then quietly offered tenants several months free rent.[14]

During this period of renewed large-scale construction and relatively low rents, thousands of Russian-Jewish families moved uptown. The pages of the Jewish and real estate press were filled with discussions of the migration of the "prosperous and Americanized" Russian Jew who was ready to escape the ghetto and able to take advantage of this temporary glut in the real estate market. They spoke of a bourgeoise Russian-Jewish immigrant who was willing to pay middle-income rents of twenty to thirty dollars a month for accommodations superior to and cheaper than the better grade of apartment on the Lower East Side. Contemporaries also noted that the prospect of living in houses with "greater privacy, larger quarters" and the possibility for some of "becoming a landlord" were important additional factors influencing the decision to move uptown.[15]

Joining these residential "bargain hunters" were several thousand Jewish building trades workers who sought Harlem's "frontiers" in search of employment. Offering their services to "lumpers" (building subsubcontractors) at rates considerably less than those of other workers, Jewish painters, paperhangers, carpenters and decorators soon gained a firm foothold in their industries. Their efforts also earned them the well-articulated enmity of the Irish-dominated construction trade unions. In 1896, for example, John F. Chalmers, secretary of the Amalgamated Society and Joiners No. 5, complained to the New York State Bureau of Labor Statistics that his men had been "knocked out of the work of fitting up flats in the Harlem district" by, among others, "Polish Jewish scabs" who were willing to work "for $1.50–$2.50 a day," leaving union men to find employment in other construction fields.[16]

Chalmers's colleague, David Callahan, president of the Amalgamated Painters and Decorators of New York, also charged that "Polish Jews, Hebrew Workmen" had taken "all the work done east of Third Avenue, from the Battery to the Harlem River." These workers, he reported, "work for wages that no respecting mechanic would think of accepting for his labor—some as low as 80¢ a day," making it "impossible for us to compete with them." Callahan also argued that American landlords, in their overwhelming desire to hire workers at the lowest possible wages, had overlooked the crucial fact that the Jewish scab's labor "is inferior and they perform much less daily than a first-rate mechanic." Despite this consistent unionist opposition to immigrant lumping, and to their later entrance into the ethnically exclusive construction workers' Brotherhood, Jewish building trades workers continued to migrate to Harlem.[17]

Less publicized but equally important was the removal to Harlem of thousands of other former downtown tenement-dwelling Russian Jews who were crowded out of the Lower East Side when their homes were torn down to make way for large factories and small public parks. Ironically, much of the overcrowding that resulted from the building of these public and private "improvements" was caused indirectly by the efforts of urban progressive reformers to improve the lot of the immigrant.

The problem of tenement house work was a central theme in the literature of reform. Progressive agitators struggled throughout the 1890s for passage of effective antisweatshop laws both in Congress and in numerous state legislatures. But their efforts met with only limited success. Only three highly industrialized, heavily populated states—New York, Massachusetts, and Illinois—passed any sort of health protection legislation. And laws in each of these states were easily circumvented both by enterprising bosses and by wage-hungry employees. The Congress contented itself with an 1894 investigation of the evils of the "sweating system," but passed no legislation. The problem of tenement sweatshop work still awaited effective solution when the new century began.[18]

Reform pressure was, however, strong enough to convince some large manufacturers to remove their sweatshops from tenements. Accordingly, new warehouses and factories were built all over the East Side to accommodate the "mercantile movement" out of the tenement. And the Lower East Side experienced an unanticipated loss of badly needed residential space as many tenement houses were torn down to make room for factories. Their displaced tenants were forced to find new homes within the already overcrowded ghetto or to seek new accommodations elsewhere in the city. Confronted by this unexpected consequence of well-meaning reform efforts, many immigrant tenement dwellers decided to move to Harlem.[19]

Reform pressure for the construction of public parks for the poor had a similar effect on residential space. The agitation for "public parks and recreation piers for the people" dated from the 1880s. In 1887, Mayor Abram Hewitt secured passage of a Small Parks Act that authorized the Board of Street Opening and Improvement to select and build small parks in New York's tenement districts and to spend up to one million dollars a year on the project.

The Board failed to fulfill its mayoral mandate and spent only one-half million dollars in the eight years between 1887 and 1895. Reformers, led by Danish-born muckraker Jacob Riis, charged that Tammany Hall, under the pretense of public economy, neglected to spend the appropriated funds properly. They cited the case of the Mulberrry Bend Park as a prime example of the Board's foot-dragging on construction. Plans for the park were filed in 1888. Six years later, the city had still not taken possession of the site.

The New York State Assembly Tenement House Committee reexamined the question of public recreation in 1894. Committee members reported that although over one-thirteenth of New York City's land was used for parks, only one-fortieth of that park land was located south of 14th Street where one-third of the population resided. They called upon the legislature to respond to the needs of the urban population, and establish a permanent State Commission on Public Parks. As a result of the Committee's agitation, an 1895 law provided for the compulsory expenditures of at least three million dollars for construction of small parks. Under it, construction of Mulberry Bend Park was finally begun in 1895.[20]

In that same year, Mayor William Strong requested the Federation of East Side Workers to appoint an advisory committee to suggest sites for additional East Side parks. The resulting Advisory Committee on Small Parks of 1897 was headed by former Mayor Hewitt. Jacob Riis served as the Committee's secretary. They counseled that the city acquire parts of some eleven blocks in the ghetto's Tenth Ward for use as public play areas. This committee's recommendations, and continued pressure from other reform circles, led to the creation by 1902 of some seven new parks on the Lower East Side.[21]

Still, these public improvements contributed to the overtaxing of already scarce residential space. The building of the Division Street

Park, for example, required the condemnation of tenements housing some 4,000 people. Once again, many Lower East Side dwellers were faced with the choice between crowding in with friends and neighbors downtown or looking elsehwere. Many chose to join the movement to Harlem.[22]

By 1900 Harlem was home for an economically diverse Russian-Jewish community of approximately 17,000.* Although numbers of immigrant Jewish families could be found scattered throughout Harlem, their major concentrations were in the predominantly Irish-German East Harlem neighborhoods south of 110th Street. Most of the more affluent Russian Jews joined their Irish and German counterparts in settling in the moderately populated, mixed tenement, brownstone flat and apartment house section west of Lexington Avenue. Their poorer brethren crowded into the densely populated working-class tenement district east of Lexington. Few Jews settled in East Harlem's growing "Little Italy," that heavily populated tenement section bordered roughly by the East River and Third Avenue between 105th and 120th streets.[23]

The economic diversity of residents in these East Harlem "Russian-Jewish" districts is revealed clearly by the 1900 Federal Census of Population manuscripts. In the West of Lexington Avenue district, almost six of ten heads of households were engaged in either high or low white-collar occupations. Approximately 15 percent of them were employed as professionals, manufacturers, or as businessmen; high white-collar callings. An additional 45 percent were working as clerks, salespeople, peddlers or as semiprofessionals; low white-collar fields. (See table A.1)

Russian Jews in the Western District showed an even greater concentration in white-collar occupations than did the general population.[24] Some two-thirds of all Jewish heads of households could be classified within the highest two occupational categories; three out of every four of these high white-collar workers were either major pro-

---

* In 1902, the newly formed New York City Tenement House Department published a study of the tenement house population of Manhattan based on the 1900 Federal Census of Population manuscripts. A study of these statistics indicates that 3,404 Russian-Jewish families lived in Harlem in 1900. My own study of 275 Russian-Jewish families enumerated in the same manuscripts reveals that the average Russian-Jewish family consisted of 4.9 people. Projecting that figure for a Jewish family population of 3,404 results in a total population of approximately 17,000. See New York City Tenement House Department, *First Report, 1902–03,* vol. 2. (New York: 1902–03).

HARLEM POPULATION CHARACTERISTICS—1900

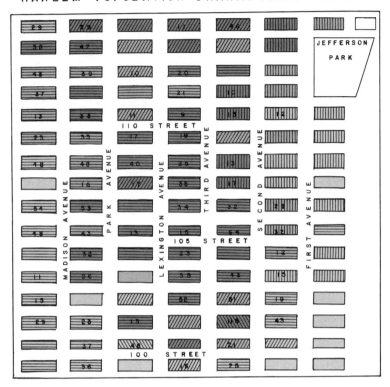

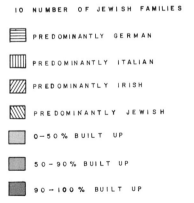

10   NUMBER OF JEWISH FAMILIES

▤	PREDOMINANTLY GERMAN
▥	PREDOMINANTLY ITALIAN
▨	PREDOMINANTLY IRISH
▧	PREDOMINANTLY JEWISH
▢	0–50% BUILT UP
▩	50–90% BUILT UP
■	90–100% BUILT UP

Map 3. Harlem Population Characteristics, 1900
Source: New York City Tenement House Dept., *First Report, 1902–3,*
vol. 2. *Atlas of the City Of New York, 1898.* Map by L. Salit.

prietors, managers or officials. Within this category were the real estate operators and large clothing manufacturers most generally associated with the Harlem migration.[25] (See table A.2.)

Another broad indicator of the high level of socioeconomic advancement enjoyed by these Jews is the types of occupations followed by low white-collar workers. Some 68 percent were engaged in clerical and sales work. Another 13 percent were employed in semiprofessional fields. To be employed as a clerk, bookkeeper or stenographer, one had to have acquired a better-than-average command of English verbal skills and at least some exposure to the American educational system. Similarly, the successful salespersons or semiprofessionals—particularly the agents, auctioneers, insurance salesmen and adjustors and buyers dominating our sample—ambitious of attracting customers and clients outside his or her own ethnic group, had to gain a facility in English and a general understanding of American attitudes and preferences. These individuals constituted a higher-status occupational subgroup above the other segment of the low white-collar class; peddlers, small shopkeepers and dealers of all sorts who dealt primarily or exclusively with members of their own ethnic group. (See table A.2.)

The occupational profile of heads of households residing in the East of Lexington Avenue district was fundamentally different. The overwhelming majority of these workers was engaged in skilled and unskilled occupations. Close to one-half of all workers in this district were employed as skilled laborers, while more than one-quarter were working at semiskilled, menial service or unskilled jobs. Only one of four individuals was employed in either high or low white-collar fields and only three in every one hundred could be classified in the high white-collar category. This "Eastern District" was fundamentally working class. (See table A.3.)

Russian Jews residing east of Lexington Avenue were also predominantly proletarians. Here, approximately six out of every ten Russian-Jewish heads of households were employed as skilled laborers. These individuals were divided occupationally almost equally among those employed in the needle trades (36 percent), in construction (34 percent), and in other skilled occupations (30 percent). Another 8 percent were working at less-than-skilled jobs.

The relatively lower level of Eastern District Jewish socioeconomic achievement is highlighted further by the predominant number of peddlers and small shopkeepers in the low white-collar category. Some 84 percent was engaged in small proprietary, managerial and official occupations that required a relatively lower degree of interaction with general American society. Russian Jews were, however, significantly more occupationally advanced than other working-class groups in their area. Close to 90 percent of Jewish blue-collar workers were employed at skilled jobs.* Only 60 percent of the general blue-collar population could be classified within that category.[26] (See table A.4.)

These occupational statistics also reveal that Jewish migrants of every economic class pursued occupations not exclusively tied to the Lower East Side. As was the case in Brownsville in the early 1890s, it is apparent that in confronting the problems of ghetto overcrowding, the immigrant's desire and ability to either work near his home or at least to avoid having to commute on a regular basis or at a set time daily was a prime factor in determining whether he would remain downtown or seek accommodations elsewhere. Most Jewish white-collar workers faced no logistical barriers to migration. Ghetto manufacturers, businessmen, managers and professionals, for example, who were free to set their own schedules, could and did reside in Harlem and conducted their business either at home, downtown, or in other parts of the city. Real estate operators and speculators also found residence in Harlem most convenient. They were able to transact their business in parcels and securities on Harlem's "Real Estate Curb" at 116th Street and Fifth Avenue and were thus not obliged to travel on a regular basis to the downtown central business district. Clerks, salespeople and semiprofessionals who found work in stores and offices in midtown, Yorkville or Harlem were similarly able to live

*These figures correspond to Jewish-other immigrant statistics for New York at large. Moses Rischin points out that "an estimated 66 percent of the gainfully employed Jewish immigrants between 1899–1914 possessed industrial skills—a far greater number than that of any other immigrant group." Thomas Kessner has shown that the Jews arrived with far greater industrial skills than did the Italians. Comparing the occupational distribution of the two groups in 1880, Kessner observed "fifty-six percent of the Jewish working population did manual work. Here, however, one finds a sharp distinction from the Italian. While 53 percent of the Italian workers were unskilled only .6 percent of the Jews were unskilled. Twenty-five years later, the percentage of unskilled Jewish workers had risen to only 1.7 percent, while the percentage of unskilled Italian workers had dropped only 12 percent. A difference of 40.2 percent still separated the two groups". See Rischin, The Promised City: New York's Jews, 1870–1914 (Cambridge, Mass.: Harvard University Press, 1962), p. 59 and Thomas Kessner, The Golden Door: Italian and Jewish Immigrant Mobility in New York City, 1880–1915 (New York: 1977), pp. 61, 69.

and work either in their own neighborhoods or at least close to home. And small shopkeepers, peddlers and dealers of all sorts, who may have operated out of uptown's so-called "Jewish Market" of 98th to 102d streets between Second and Third avenues, were able to live in Harlem and serve the needs of the expanding Jewish settlement.[27]

Harlem's blue-collar job market also permitted downtown's skilled and unskilled workers to migrate and settle uptown. The construction industry offered great opportunities for those Jewish painters, carpenters, paperhangers and decorators who were willing to work for less than union scale wages. (One-third of all Jewish skilled workers in the east of Lexington area were employed in the construction industry.) The relocation uptown of many tobacco factories in the late 1890s provided neighborhood employment for many other Jewish workers. By 1900, some thirty-one factories employing more than fifty workers, constituting 40 percent of Manhattan's total tobacco factories, were relocated between East 59th and 110th streets, east of Third Avenue. Close to 20 percent of Eastern District Jewish skilled workers were employed in this industry and most probably found work in neighborhood factories either in Yorkville or Harlem.[28]

The only major group of ghetto workers who could not easily live and work uptown were those employed in the needle trades. In their case, the absence of both local industry and efficient rapid transit linking workers with downtown factories may have been the determining factor limiting their numbers in the uptown settlement. In any event, needle trades workers constituted at most only one-third of the skilled labor force and 22 percent of all Jewish workers.

The some 17,000 Russian Jews who had migrated to Harlem by 1900 were only the first phalanx in a massive "Jewish invasion" of uptown. In the next decade, some 80,000 more Russian Jews would move to Harlem, transforming the section's ethnic makeup. They supplanted the Irish and the Germans as the dominant ethnic group south of 125th Street and west of Third Avenue. Their poorer element would continue to carve its own separate Jewish niche, east of Third Avenue directly south of an expanding Little Italy. Their most affluent group would move west of Fifth Avenue and would become a major component in a new fashionable middle-class settlement constructed north of 110th Street, east of Morningside Avenue. By 1910, Harlem was the home of the second largest concentration of immigrant East European Jews in the United States.[29]

This second, post-1900, stage of the East European uptown migration, which saw Harlem emerge as a major center for immigrant Jews, was precipitated by a set of forces similar to those which had first sparked movement out of the downtown ghetto. Continued slum clearance, municipal improvements, new building code regulations and the further incursion of business establishments into residential areas combined to tax, and finally destroy, the absorptive capacity of the downtown ghetto.

Once again, the efforts of city planners and social reformers to improve conditions in ghetto areas contributed to the depletion of residential space downtown. In April 1901, after a generation of continuous prodding from such progressive reformers as Robert De Forest and Lawrence Veiler, the New York State Legislature finally approved an effective tenement house reform bill. The legislation prohibited the further construction of the dumbell and rear tenements that predominated on the Lower East Side. According to the new law, every residential building completed after January 1, 1902 had to allow for direct natural lighting of every room and to conform to such minimal health and safety standards as separate toilet facilities for each apartment and safely constructed fire escapes. The law also created the New York City Tenement House Department which was empowered to oversee future building construction and to monitor the improvement of existing tenements. The era of cheap, unsupervised, low-rent construction on the Lower East Side had, at least officially, closed.[30]

Although downtown realtors had been especially active in opposing tenement reform legislation, they were soon to realize the economic profitability of the new building code. They recognized the emergence within ghetto society of a new Russian-Jewish business elite, composed of successful manufacturers, dealers and shopkeepers who desired and were able to pay for the modern, more expensive type of apartment that was to be built under the new regulations. Eager to remain downtown, near their factory or business, these newly affluent immigrants wanted to live in houses that reflected their economic station. "New Law construction," one contemporary predicted, might well transform the East Side ghetto into "the kindergarten for the small merchant whose name is afterward seen on Broadway."[31]

The creation of a middle- to high-rent district within the immigrant ghetto reduced further the number of buildings available for the poor and raised rents in the remaining old-law tenements. One representative of the real estate industry noted that "poor tenants were being forced into the miserable rookeries, the front and rear tenements" and were being made to "pay twenty dollars for four rooms, fifteen and sixteen for three miserable tenements and ten dollars for three rooms in the rear tenements."[32]

The number of dwellings available for the poor of the Lower East Side was reduced again by the condemnation of hundreds of buildings to make room for the Williamsburg and Manhattan bridges. In 1900, parts of fourteen blocks lying along Broome, Delancey, and Norfolk Streets and the East River were torn down to make space for the Williamsburg Bridge. This important municipal improvement, which would eventually facilitate the migration of thousands of Jews to Williamsburg and Brownsville, caused 17,000 people—the overwhelming majority of them immigrant Jews—to lose their homes. Many thousands more were evicted soon thereafter from the vicinity of Pike Street to make room for the Manhattan Bridge.[33]

The disturbance of population resulting from the building of these bridges was so pronounced that the New York City Parks Department, fearful of an imminent critical ghetto housing shortage, suspended further construction of small parks downtown after 1902. Noting the city's new, more careful, approach to municipal improvements, one contemporary observer advised that "until there is some indubitable indication that the tenement house population has a tendency to distribute itself more than at present, it would be well not to dispossess any more people."[34]

This second major contraction of residential space in less than a decade could not have occurred at a more inopportune juncture in the city's history. The ghetto "face-lift" was completed at the very moment when the tide of Jewish immigration to the United States was reaching its peak. During the first decade of the twentieth century some 976,000 Jews fled to these shores, primarily to escape the widespread violence that attended the Kishinev and Gomel pogroms of 1903 and the aborted Russian revolution of 1905. The overwhelming majority of these new migrants—like the tens of thousands before and after them—chose the Port of New York as their final destination and sought jobs and homes within the crowded sections of the city already populated by immigrants from their old home town or country. The overcrowded Lower East Side, soon to be home for more than one-quarter of the city's total population, staggered under the weight of this new wave of immigrants. And those concerned with the future of the city and/or the welfare of the immigrants began calling for new efficient means of "breaking up the ghetto."*

German relief organizations, for example, which had been striving for close to a generation to develop workable large-scale immigrant dispersal programs, increased their efforts. In 1901 the Industrial Removal Office, a branch of the Baron de Hirsch Jewish Agricultural Society, was created and charged with coordinating a continent-wide effort to find jobs for immigrant Jews outside the major eastern centers. Perhaps the Office's offer of certain employment in a more salubrious setting would induce many immigrants to leave the urban ghettos.[35]

This ambitious relocation plan, like all other paternalistic immigrant dispersal schemes, failed. New York remained the home for the majority of immigrants; the desire of the East European Jew to live among his own kind continued to outweigh most economic inducements. Immigrants feared traveling to strange new cities away from the Jewish atmosphere that permeated the immigrant ghetto. It was difficult enough for them to adjust to their removal from the traditional Jewish society of Eastern Europe. The unacculturated Jews were socially and psychologically unprepared for life outside their ethnic community.

A far more popular immigrant dispersal plan was the one undertaken by thousands of individual Jewish families in removing from the Lower East Side to Brownsville, Williamsburg, and Harlem. While hundreds of thousands of new immigrants were crowding into the downtown ghetto, tens of thousands of others were flocking to the newly established Russian-Jewish settlements. For at least one immigrant editorialist, the intensification of intracity migration after the

* Samuel Joseph has estimated that New York was the destination for some 696,000 Jews in the first decade of the twentieth century. That figure constitutes 64.2 percent of all Jewish immigrants in those years. Samuel Joseph, *Jewish Immigration to the United States 1881–1910* (New York: Columbia University Press, 1914), p. 195.

Another indication of the higher intensity of the post-1900 migration is the fact that in 1886, during the first decade of mass East European migration, an average of fifty-four Jewish immigrants were admitted to America each day. Twenty years later, 417 were arriving daily. See Rischin, *Promised City*, p. 270.

turn of the century was proof of the immigrants' ability to redistribute themselves. "The problem presented by the congestion in the ghetto," he asserted, "will solve itself. As a matter of fact it is solving itself already. A strong tendency to move to less congested districts, where the environments are more pleasing and the housing accommodations more ideal manifests itself in Harlem and the Bronx Borough. Both contain a large Jewish population which is constantly being increased by those who are withdrawing from the ghetto."[36]

Harlem immediately attracted the greatest number of new settlers. Its closer proximity to the Lower East Side, its ready supply of relatively cheap apartments, its existing Jewish community, and its soon-to-be completed underground rapid transit system made it a logical choice for Jewish settlement. The Williamsburg Bridge, which would facilitate future migration to Williamsburg and Brownsville, would not be completed until the end of 1903. The Manhattan Bridge would not be finished until 1909. By the time these facilities opened, some 80,000 more Jews had relocated in Harlem.[37]

As the northward migration intensified after 1900, the available supply of vacant apartments quickly started to shrink. Harlem realtors, who only a few years earlier had bemoaned the oversupply of accommodations—the so-called "tenant-dominated" market—were slow to respond to this new wave of migration. They were fearful of once again overspeculating in underdeveloped Harlem lands. Even the signing of a new rapid transit contract assuring cheap, quick travel between downtown and Harlem failed to stir investment. Real estate operators, according to one observer, had been conditioned by "a generation of delay and disappointment to expect new disappointments." The passage of the new Tenement House Law also contributed to the doubts and fears of the operators. They were not sure of the profitability of the more expensive new-law tenements in previously underpopulated and moderately populated areas.[38]

The conservatism of Harlem real estate operators coupled with the ever-increasing volume of uptown migration created a temporary housing shortage in Harlem by 1903. Stephen McCormack, a Harlem real estate operator, reported in April 1903 that whereas "there used to be a waiting list of apartments now there is a waiting list of tenants. As a result, rents are going up."[39]

The uptown housing shortage continued only until the fall of 1903, when a period of widespread real estate speculation and building construction came into full swing. Recognizing the true dimensions of the demand for accommodations in Harlem, real estate operators abandoned their earlier reluctance to invest. The value of all existing uptown buildings soared when landlords circumvented the strictures of the new law by remodeling old-style tenements for a cost of only a few thousand dollars. The great demand for uptown housing, according to one real estate operator, "galvanized into life a class of building which had been dead for years."[40]

The tearing down of thousands of small three-story private residences in East Harlem and their replacement with six-story new-law tenements was also economically profitable. Most of these homes were located in the previously lightly populated areas of Madison and Fifth Avenues, immediately north of 100th Street and away from most rapid transit facilities. Still, the pressure to provide housing for all of Harlem's new residents made even these relatively remote East Harlem properties economically profitable.[41]

The real estate boom also affected large sections of Central Harlem. These properties, due to their inaccessibility to most rapid transit facilities, had remained relatively undeveloped during the building booms that hit East Harlem in the early 1880s, and the Morningside Heights area of Manhattan later in that decade. Even when widespread construction was resumed in Harlem late in the 1890s only those parts of Central Harlem bordering on Fifth Avenue were significantly improved. Private dwellings and apartment houses of a quality superior to those constructed anywhere in East Harlem were scattered all along the wide-open thoroughfares of Fifth and Lenox Avenues. The anticipated completion of the long-awaited subway in 1904 set off the first full-scale building activities on Central Harlem lands. New-law tenements and apartment buildings were erected all over Central Harlem as far north as the Harlem River and as far west as Morningside Park. An elegant new community was constructed along the newly laid subway lines. And by 1906, practically all the vacant land in the uptown district had been built over. Speculators would subsequently have to look to Washington Heights, The Bronx and Brooklyn for real estate investment.[42]

Thousands of Russian immigrants entered into the real estate market as heavy investors in Harlem properties during this post-1903 phase of uptown development. For these Jews, Harlem was not—or was not only—a new residential haven within city limits. It was a huge parcel of undeveloped land; virgin territory offering great pecuniary rewards to the skilled or lucky investor. Real estate speculation was seen by upwardly mobile Jewish merchants and businessmen as a safe investment that would increase their holdings and at the same time accord them with the social prestige worthy of the established landowner. "Real estate," one journalist commented, "was the only form of investment popular downtown. Stocks and bonds were practically unsaleable on the Lower East Side."[43]

Abraham Cahan, editor of the *Forward,* in his classic saga of immigrant life *The Rise of David Levinsky,* described the intoxicating effect the real estate boom had upon certain elements in downtown society.

> Small tradesmen of the slums, and even working men were investing their savings in houses and lots. Jewish carpenters, house painters, bricklayers or installment peddlers became builders of tenements or frame dwellings— real estate speculators. Deals were being closed and poor men were making thousands of dollars in less time that it took them to drink the glass of tea or sorrel soup over which the transaction took place. Women too were ardently dabbling in real estate.[44]

Thousands of investors, according to Cahan, dreamed of becoming like "Max who but two years ago was a poor operator, lean, bent and worn out with work, who stepped aside for every man and wore a ragged old coat." "Now," Cahan continued, "his face is beaming, a large diamond sparkles on his shirt front and his face wears that peculiar expression, which tells you without words that Max has a large bank book in his pocket."[45]

Jewish investment in Harlem properties took several different forms. Those speculators who possessed considerable capital negotiated with the well-known Knickerbocker families of Harlem for purchase of the underdeveloped lands lying along the proposed subway route. These large tracts were then parceled out to smaller investors who contracted them to builders, many of them Russian Jews themselves, who erected new-law tenements and apartments in Central Harlem. Several of these larger investors directed a considerable portion of their profits back into the uptown community and helped sponsor a variety of Harlem social and cultural organizations. They were respected by many Jewish Harlemites as individuals who in making economic progress in America had not forgotten their roots or their less-fortunate brethren.[46]

David A. Cohen was typical of this type of socially responsible Harlem investor. Born in Suwalk, Russo-Poland, in 1854, Cohen migrated to the United States in 1880. His successful career in business and real estate parallels in many respects that of Cahan's fictional character, David Levinsky. Beginning at the bottom of the economic ladder as a housewares peddler, Cohen in a very short time emerged as a leading downtown entrepreneur. By the 1890s, he owned both a tinware business and a clothing factory. Later in the decade, he entered the real estate industry and became president of Gold and Cohen Realtors. Cohen was also a major stockholder in the Universal Construction Company, a firm founded by members of Congregation Kehal Adath Jeshurun of Eldridge Street, which Cohen himself attended.[47]

After 1900, Cohen removed to Harlem and acquired several tracts of uptown land. One was situated along Seventh Avenue at 114th Street. Another was located at 136th Street and Lenox Avenue. Probably his most dramatic Harlem business transaction was his selling of a parcel lying on 114th Street at the Corner of Seventh Avenue to the now-affluent German-Jewish Congregation Ansche Chesed for $108,000.[48]

Cohen and his son, Elias, also became well-known in Harlem Jewish communal circles. The senior Cohen was elected president of the Uptown Talmud Torah, a position he held until his death in 1911. Elias A. Cohen was a member of the board of directors of both the Uptown Talmud Torah and Temple Ansche Chesed and was secretary of the Harlem Federation Association.[49]

Those investors with far less capital speculated primarily in "remodeled" old-style tenements in East Harlem. Groups of small-time investors pooled their limited funds to purchase (or in some cases only lease) these cheap tenements. They made the few necessary alterations and quickly raised rents to cover their expenses and to afford them a fast return on their investment. Turnover in the ownership of these properties was very brisk. Investors moved from one tenement to the next in search of quick profits and rents were hiked every time a parcel changed hands.[50]

Relations between these "get-rich quick" investors and their local community were never good. They were often condemned as "the greatest schnorrers [beggars] of the ghetto, men who save every penny, live in dirt, neglect their families the whole year to raise sufficient capital to invest and become a landlord."[51]

And they were—even more importantly—accused of carrying their insensitivity to community needs as well. Critics castigated them for failing to recognize how their selfish activities threatened the security of all newly settled Jews in this ethnically mixed section of town. "Christians in general," one critic pointed out, "do not move as quickly as Jews. For many years Christians live in the same house without a raise in rents. Then the Jewish landlords come and raise the prices on these houses. It has gone so far that Christians are already showing their might and are once again looking to get even with the 'Sheenies.' "[52]

The conflict between those who viewed Harlem as home and those who looked upon the community primarily as an area for investment first peaked in March 1904, when small neighborhood protective associations were formed to resist the obnoxious rent-gouging practices of some uptown landlords. Most East Harlem protest committees were formed on an ad hoc basis by residents of single buildings threatened with rent hikes. Committee members solicited contributions from their fellow tenants and lawyers were engaged to represent their interests. When landlords were successful in obtaining court orders directing tenants to pay their rents, strikers often responded by organizing the complete evacuation of the effected building. Picket lines were thrown up in an attempt to prevent landlords from acquiring new tenants. In one incident such a maneuver led to violence between Harlemites and police had to clear protestors from a strike-bound property.[53]

Harlem protestors were inspired in their struggle by the example of downtown tenement dwellers who a few weeks earlier had initiated their own rent strike. Residents of the Lower East Side were moved to action by the attempts of downtown real estate operators to increase rents on the quickly diminishing supply of formerly cheap old-style tenements. The movement to resist high rents quickly spread to Brownsville and from there to Harlem and even to some sections of the South Bronx.[54]

Uptown protestors were also influenced by the active support emanating from all local socialist and some labor groups. For groups like the Harlem Workmen's Circle, the struggle against specific insensitive Jewish landlords was only symptomatic of the ever-present general problem of landowner oppression of generally helpless workers. Viewing the strike as such a struggle, uptown radicals sought to lead and expand the scope of the still limited fight. They organized a mass rally at the Harlem Terrace in April, 1904 and set plans for the creation of a district-wide rent strike headquarters. A coalition of radical groups called upon all Harlem residents desirous of organizing against their landlords to appeal to their good offices for assistance.[55]

When the rent strike finally ended several weeks later, socialists all over the city proclaimed it a success. The problem of rent gouging did not end, however, with this first protest movement. Some four years later a new more extensive wave of tenant protests would hit New York's immigrant neighborhoods, protests dedicated to solving many of the same problems apparently solved in 1904.[56]

The Russian Jewish mass movement to Harlem after 1900, which saw Jews gain control of certain sections of neighborhood real estate both as residents and as investors, was only the most pronounced element in a multiethnic invasion of uptown that caused the complete transformation of the district's ethnic balance. Harlem's residents had been previously predominantly white and either native-born or of West European ancestry. Irish and German hegemony ended during the first decade of the twentieth century as Italians joined the Russian Jews in expanding their earlier acquired footholds in the community, and Blacks made their first major incursions into Harlem. Between 1900 and 1910, the combined uptown Irish-and-German population dropped from approximately one-half to less than one-fifth of the total, as Harlem came to house three new major ethnic-racial neighborhoods; one Russian-Jewish, one Italian, and one Black.[57]

Most Russian Jews and Italians arriving after the turn of the century settled in those sections of Harlem already occupied by their coreligionists or fellow ethnics. The East Harlem neighborhoods lying immediately south of 110th Street and east of Fifth Avenue which had attracted most of Harlem's first Russian-Jewish settlers continued to attract the majority of Jewish migrants. By 1910, it held close to one-half of Harlem's 100,000 Russian Jews. This constituted more than one-half of that neighborhood's total population. Of the 50,000 Russian Jews residing elsewhere in Harlem more than 29,500 (59 percent) settled within the seven Central and East Harlem census tract districts clustered immediately north and west of 110th Street and Fifth Avenue. The remaining quarter of Harlem's Russian-Jewish population was scattered among those regions of uptown extending north of 120th Street.[58]

Italians demonstrated an even greater proclivity for self-segregation in one particular section of Harlem as their enclave east of Third Avenue expanded to accommodate their own more limited post-1900 uptown migration. By 1910, some 59,200 Italians had relocated in an uptown ghetto which had grown to embrace all of East Harlem lying east of Third Avenue and south of 125th Street except for one area, 99th to 104th Streets between First and Third Avenues, where Jews clearly predominated. Relatively few Italians chose to settle outside the pale of this "Little Italy." The approximately 13,000 Italians who lived elsewhere in Harlem amounted to no more than 15 percent of the population in all other census tract districts.[59]

The first decade of the twentieth century also witnessed the first major Black incursion into uptown. Although limited numbers of Black families were to be found throughout Harlem as early as the 1880s, there was no identifiable Black section of Harlem comparable to "Little Italy" or the emerging Jewish section west and south of the Italian enclave until well into the first decade of this century. Black families could be found on blocks located as far south as 96th Street and Second Avenue and as far north as 146th Street and Eighth Avenue. In fact, as late as 1902, the New York City Tenement House Department reported 1,127 Black families living among thirty-one square blocks scattered throughout the uptown area.[60]

Harlem's first predominantly Black neighborhood was established in the northern parts of Central and East Harlem after 1905. By the end of the decade, more than two-thirds of Harlem's 22,000 Black residents had settled in a neighborhood bordered roughly by 133d and 140th Streets, Park and Lenox Avenues. Blacks constituted the largest single group in this newly built section of Harlem, constituting as much as 50 percent of the total population in one specific area lying between 133d and 140th Streets, and Fifth and Lenox Avenues. Blacks remained concentrated within this limited northwest territory until after World War One, when they made their major incursion into the predominantly Jewish sections of Lower Central and East Harlem.[61]

The early years of the twentieth century also witnessed a significant shift in the economic distribution in the East Harlem areas under Jewish control. The patterns of uptown residential life changed rapidly during this era of pronounced residential expansion and massive immigrant resettlement. Once ideal or acceptable residential areas were almost overnight beset with problems common to all heavily populated areas, and lost much of their glamor. And new neighborhoods

Harlem landscape, 116th Street and Fifth Avenue, c.1880
Museum of the City of New York

Temple Israel of Harlem, 205 Lenox Avenue, as it is today
Oscar Israelowitz

Temple Israel of Harlem, c.1920

Oscar Israelowitz

Temple Ansche Chesed, 114th Street and Seventh Avenue

Oscar Israelowitz

Congregation Shaarei Zedek, 23 Wes 118th Street

Oscar Israelowi

Congregation Ohab Zedek, 18 West 116th Street, c.1910

Congregation Ohab Zedek

Street scene—schoolchildren crossing Lenox Avenue, c.1910

Museum of the City of New York

Cantor Joseph Rosenblatt of Congregation Ohab Zedek,
Harlem's most famous cantor

Congregation Ohab Zedek

CONFERENCE HELD IN VESTRY ROOMS FIRST HUNGARIAN CONGREGATION OHAB ZEDEK · 18 W. 116 TH ST. N.Y.CITY.

Meeting of the Board of Trustees, Congregation Ohab Zedek, c.1915

Congregation Ohab Zedek

HARLEM POPULATION CHARACTERISTICS—1910

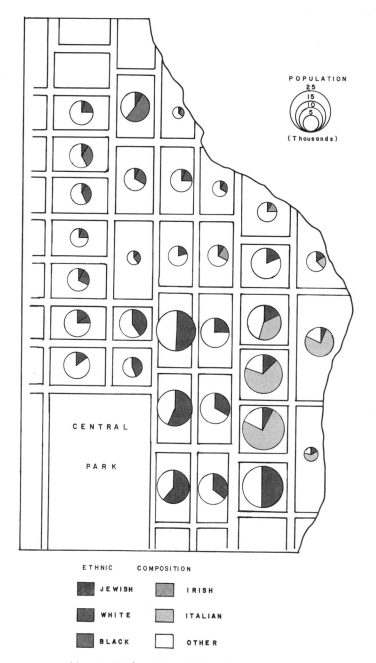

Map 4. Harlem Population Characteristics, 1910
Source: Walter Laidlaw, *Statistical Sources for Demographic Studies of New York*, vol. 1, 1910. Map by L. Salit.

were built, absorbing those seeking to reside in the best section of uptown. Such was the case with the old "West of Lexington Avenue" district of East Harlem, which had attracted most of Harlem's early more affluent Russian-Jewish settlers. It was inundated by thousands of poorer Jewish settlers; they settled in the new tenements built on previously vacant lands or which replaced the small private dwellings that had dotted Fifth and Madison Avenue's landscape. By 1910, this once moderately populated section of uptown contained population densities in excess of 480 and 560 persons per acre. As this neighborhood began to be weighed down by overcrowding, East Harlem's white-collar class began leaving for new, better accommodations either elsewhere in Central Harlem or outside the uptown area. And their old neighborhood was quickly proletarianized.[62]

The basic shift both in general neighborhood composition and in the Russian-Jewish economic profile was well under way as early as 1905. By that year, the percentage of all heads of households engaged in all types of white-collar occupations had dropped some 12 percent, from 60 to 48 percent of the total work force. The decline was felt equally within the high and low white-collar categories. (See Table A.5.)

The changes in the Russian-Jewish occupational hierarchy are far more striking, indicating that many of the most recently settled East Harlemites were the first to leave the neighborhood. The proportion of Jewish heads of households engaged in white-collar callings, for example, dropped from two-thirds to only one-half of the work force between 1900 and 1905. And Jewish high white-collar workers, numbering between one-quarter to one-third of the Jewish work force at the turn of the century, dropped to 20 percent of the total five years later. The percentage of "clerical and sales" workers in the Jewish low white-collar category also dropped precipitously; from 68 percent of the total in 1900 to 34 percent five years later. This latter shift is particularly significant because these workers—as has been previously noted—by virtue of their having better-than-average command of English verbal skills and some exposure to American education, constituted a high socioeconomic subcategory above the general low white-collar class of peddlers and small shopkeepers. It is apparent that many of these clerks, bookkeepers and secretaries joined the Jewish and non-Jewish professionals and large-scale entrepreneurs in abandoning early-twentieth-century East Harlem. They were all quickly replaced by proletarians; primarily skilled Jewish laborers whose proportion in the now predominantly Jewish work force rose from 26.5 percent to 43 percent in this half-decade of rapid change.[63] (See Table A.6.)

This ongoing shift in uptown residential patterns was clearly noted by the Yiddish press of the day. One contemporary witness to the economic decline of the East Harlem neighborhood reflected on the combination of economic and social pressures that motivated many Jews to desert this once-elegant uptown territory. "The Best of the Jews," he observed, had in 1900 made "the entire area in and around Fifth Avenue the aristocratic settlement of Jews. When one asked these people where they lived, they proudly stated 'on Fifth Avenue', as if they were close friends of 'Brother Carnegie'. But it was not long before that area became crowded and poor people who could not pay high rents on the East Side began to move in. It is now becoming crowded on the Avenue and in the Park and the 'world' is now considering moving again."[64]

The object of their considerations was, in many cases, the new-law tenement and apartment house district constructed along the route of the new subway lines in Central Harlem. This neighborhood, which boasted of a type of accommodation far superior to anything available elsewhere uptown, emerged during the first decade of this century as a home for a large segment of New York Jewry's most economically advanced and socially acculturated element. "The better class of Jews," desirous of avoiding ghetto surroundings and able to pay above-average rents, flocked to this new residential area. When contemporary writers spoke of the new Jewish quarter uptown populated by former denizens of the Lower East Side who had broken the economic and social bonds of the ghetto, they were in actuality referring to that section of Harlem lying west of Fifth and north of 110th Street. Many of East Harlem's more affluent settlers, crowded out of their homes by thousands of their poorer brethren, moved due west and participated in creating the elite Russian-Jewish neighborhood west of Fifth Avenue.[65]

Most of Central Harlem's settlers were employed in high-status occupations when the district was starting to absorb large numbers of Russian Jews. By 1905, an overwhelming proportion of the section's residents were engaged in white-collar occupations. More than two out of every three heads of Central Harlem households followed either high or low white-collar pursuits. Close to one-quarter of the district's work force could be classified as holding high white-collar jobs. Of the one-third of the work force engaged in blue-collar pursuits, some 20 percent were employed as skilled laborers. (See table A.7.) [66]

Russian Jews in Central Harlem showed an even greater concentration in the high and low white-collar occupational categories than did the general population. Three out of every four Russian-Jewish heads of households in that district were employed in the two white-collar occupational categories. A full one-quarter of the Russian-Jewish work force labored in the high white-collar field. And the overwhelming majority of Russian-Jewish low white-collar workers were engaged in the higher-status "clerical or sales" work subcategory for that group of employees. (See table A.8.) [67]

Far removed, both geographically and economically, from Central Harlem's affluent Russian-Jewish neighborhood was that Jewish district located east of Third Avenue, immediately north of 96th Street. This former Irish-German working class neighborhood, which as early as 1900 had been troubled by the problem of overcrowding, emerged during the first decade of this century as the home for "a class of Jews who want to live uptown but cannot pay uptown rents." Its residents were described by at least one observer as people "who had moved uptown without checking to see what kind of area it really was." [68]

Although the area east of Third Avenue never approached the Lower East Side in terms of overcrowding, its density of population exceeded that of almost every other uptown area. In 1905, three of the ten blocks in the census tract district from 99th to 104th Streets between First and Third Avenues, had population densities in excess of 500 persons per acre. The block on 101st to 102d between Second and Third Avenues had a density above 600, a figure which would have been considered very high on the congested Lower East Side. Four of the remaining seven blocks in the district contained more than 400 persons per acre. The only area of East Harlem more densely populated was "Little Italy," situated immediately north of 105th Street, east of Third Avenue. Several blocks within that district showed population densities in excess of 700 to 800 persons per acre. [69]

Large-scale immigrant resettlement during this era of neighborhood-wide change merely strengthened this district's already well-established occupational hierarchy. Close to one-half of the total labor force remained concentrated within the skilled worker category. Three of every four workers could be classified as laborers, either skilled, semiskilled or unskilled. And the percentage of workers in the highest occupational category remained well below 5 percent of the total work force in an era where Russian Jews replaced the Irish and the Germans as the predominant ethnic group in the area. (See table A.9.)

The expanded Russian-Jewish element in the population duplicated the general blue-collar economic profile. More than one-half of the Jewish working force could be classified as "skilled" and six out of every ten workers could be described as "blue-collar." Jewish high white-collar workers continued to avoid this area, constituting less than 5 percent of the population. (See table A.10.)

Besides attracting many of the downtown ghetto's less affluent residents, the district east of Third Avenue also drew to its midst many newly arrived immigrants who came directly from Europe to East Harlem. In 1905, close to one-fourth of the Jewish heads of households in that territory had been in the United States five years or less at the time of enumeration. Their economic distribution showed a slightly greater concentration in the blue-collar occupations than did the general Jewish population. Close to two-thirds of the Jewish heads of households were engaged as skilled laborers. Seven out of ten were employed in all types of blue-collar jobs. Those not engaged in blue-collar pursuits were working almost exclusively in the petty proprietary area—as peddlers and small shopkeepers who were able to serve the needs of a Jewish neighborhood located outside the Lower East Side without first becoming Americanized.

The knowledge that Harlem attracted not one but many different groups or classes of Jews that migrated to several distinct uptown neighborhoods for a variety of different social and economic reasons not only furthers our understanding of New York's Jewish history but more importantly points out weaknesses in certain generalized assumptions about the basic nature of intracity migration and immigrant settlement life. Until recently scholars, projecting from several pioneer sociological studies of Chicago's immigrant communities, have theorized that all American cities housed clearly designated areas of immigrant settlement, each displaying certain well-defined and fundamentally different economic and social characteristics. Areas of first settlement—the so-called ghetto areas—situated "close to the central business district in an interstitial area in the throes of change from residence to business and industry" are, according to the regnant theory, "the point of entry from which enterprising [immigrants] are seeking to escape." These congested slum areas are permeated by transplanted European culture and are populated by the masses not yet possessed of the economic resources and social skills to seek residence elsewhere in the city. Areas of second settlement, better residential neighborhoods located "at that distance beyond the factory belt" on the borders of the major urban centers, are supposedly populated by immigrants "recruited" from areas of first settlement. It is in these new neighborhoods that "the character of the ghetto is remodeled under the influence of wider contacts and a larger world." And it is here that immigrants begin to "throw overboard most of the cultural baggage" of European and ghetto life. Thus, according to the theory, the migration from one area of settlement to the next is a most crucial event for the immigrant both as an indication of his heightened economic power and his abandonment of ghetto culture.[70]

The story of East-European Jewish uptown migration and settlement that has been outlined here clearly demonstrates the inapplicability of this all-too-simple Chicago-based paradigm to America's largest immigrant center. The Harlem historical experience indicates, for example, that newly arrived immigrants can be found both within the so-called ghetto and without, and demonstrates that here terms like "areas of first and second settlement" do not refer to static geographical localities but to differing types of settler behavior. The uptown neighborhood that displayed the basic physical characteristics of an area of second settlement and that attracted most of its settlers from downtown areas was also simultaneously an area of first settlement for others who chose Harlem as their initial home in America. Harlem's complex Jewish economic distribution—which included the affluent "recruited" to new better-built homes, uptown-bound workers seeking employment in expanding Harlem industries, as well as many of the poor forced from downtown tenements to uptown industries— similarly demonstrates that the neat Chicago-based perception of newly affluent immigrants as the first and most numerous intracity migrants also does not apply to the New York experience.

The Chicago phenomenon resists eastward transposition because many of the key elements directing the saga of Jewish migration up to Harlem—particularly the availability of cheap housing and job opportunities outside the ghetto and the contraction of downtown living space due to slum clearance and municipal improvements—simply did not obtain in the midwestern city. One might further suggest that since these forces do not seem—at least at first observation—idiosyncratic either to the group, neighborhood or city understudy here, it might well be that the presumed all-inclusive Chicago-based pattern may fail to typify the growth history of many, if not most, other great American cities. If this indeed be proven the case, then this Harlem case-study, already intrinsically and specifically important for what it indicates about New York and the character of its East European Jewish communities, may gain its greatest significance for helping reorient our general understanding of the basic character of intercity migration and immigrant settlement life.[71]

chapter 3

Harlem in Its Heyday—The Two Communities

I: The Second Ghetto

Harlem's multifaceted communal experience also points up the difficulties of generalizing from one city's experience to that of all others and strongly indicates the need for a broader conceptual understanding of the processes of urban immigrant life. To be sure, the uptown area of second settlement attracted a considerable number of Jews whose migration underscored their desire to break the social bonds of the ghetto. These newly acculturated individuals—as predicted—built a variety of new social and cultural organizations that reflected their overriding concern with becoming one with general culture. But even these settlers broke with the generalized pattern of second-settlement behavior by demonstrating a profound commitment to fashioning uptown a new type of "American Judaism," totally consistent both with Jewish tradition and American principles, in place of their discarded ghetto Jewish identity. And they were only one segment of an even more complex uptown community.[1]

A second, totally distinct, community was built in this "peculiarly mixed settlement of our people"—as one contemporary described it—by those who migrated not primarily out of social choice but out of economic necessity. These Jews, though geographically removed from the ghetto, continued to maintain close contact with downtown and constructed communal institutions fundamentally different from those expected in an area of second settlement. They sought to transplant the all-pervasive spirit of ghetto culture to Harlem and looked

for solutions to their social and economic problems in close cooperation with and much in the same way as did those still downtown.
Harlem's old-world and ghetto religious institutions—landsmanshaft
self-help organizations, chevrah congregations, countless small
cheders and European-style yeshivas—and its Jewish radical organizations transplanted from downtown—Workmen's Circle branches, Socialist Party groups and Jewish labor unions—all testify to the existence of a "second ghetto" community created uptown and
supported by those who showed—each in his or her own way—little
inclination towards "throwing the cultural baggage of the ghetto
overboard."[2]

What was the positive aspect of ghetto life which these Harlem migrants extolled, preserved and transplanted uptown? Certainly its fundamental character was not always apparent to contemporaries. To
unsympathetic outside observers the Jewish ghetto was only an overcrowded, unsanitary tenement district; an eyesore to be avoided by
respectable society. To City Health officials, the narrow, dank Jewish
quarter was noteworthy only as an incubator of the "white plague,"
tuberculosis, which threatened the health of all who resided in or
who came in contact with the immigrant district. And to an over-
zealous, anti-Semitic Police Commissioner, downtown was an incubator of crime and delinquency, and immigrant Jews were among the
most proficient "burglars, firebugs, pickpockets and highway rob-
bers" in the entire city. None of those people chose to look beyond
the many day-to-day problems of adjustment associated with what
one government census statistician described as "the most densely-
populated ward in the city, crowded with Russian-Polish Jews of unsanitary habits."[3]
  There was, however, a positive facet of ghetto life that lay beneath
the squalor of the physical ghetto and was almost unintelligible to all
but the tenement dwellers themselves. It was that certain joy and certain security felt by immigrants living among their own kind and experiencing the "Jewish atmosphere" that permeated the immigrant
settlement. For many immigrants the ghetto was, as one contemporary philosopher has described it, "a fortress as much as it was a
prison."[4] The landsmanshaft synagogues, the socialist and laborite
societies and debating clubs and the innumerable small coffee
shops—where for the price of a cup of coffee, one could listen to

anonymous ghetto philosophers of every political stripe hold forth on every possible contemporary and historical problem—all provided the immigrant with a degree of consolation and a feeling of belonging in adjusting to foreign American surroundings. It was this form of Jewish group identification rooted in transplanted European and downtown ideas and institutions that the founders and supporters of the "second ghetto" community worked to transmit and preserve in Harlem. These notions were certainly apparent both in the day-to-day activities of Harlem's many landsmanshaft synagogues as well as in the outlook of those ultra-Orthodox Jews who, as we will see later, opposed the modernization efforts of the founders of the Harlem Talmud Torah movement. Both groups sought to maintain transplanted European ideals of religion and of community. But the desire to retain ghetto goals, values and ties is best defined and seen most clearly within the idiom and activities of uptown's Jewish socialist and radical movements and organizations. And it is to the life of this radical subcommunity that we now turn our attention.

Uptown-bound Jews began initiating efforts to duplicate ghetto cultural conditions in Harlem as early as 1898 with the founding of Branch #2 of the Workmen's Circle, the socialist fraternal organization. Joseph Anapol, a long-time resident of East Harlem and a founder of uptown's first Workmen's Circle branch, recalled these early community-building efforts. Looking back in 1929 on his movement's over thirty years of service to the East Harlem community, Anapol described how his group had succeeded in creating a downtown cultural center for radical thinking Jews uptown. He detailed how a group of radicals, formerly of the Lower East Side, had recognized the need for a "socialist home away from home." These pioneer-leaders understood that Arbeiter Ring members—who now lived and worked uptown—found travel downtown for late Friday night meetings and debates impractical, especially when they were due back in Harlem early the next morning. And they were aware that physicians hired by the movement to service the health needs of its members were reluctant to visit patients living in Harlem. Recognizing that they and their fellow uptown members were being deprived of the major social and practical benefits of their movement, Harlem Workmen's Circle leaders appealed to their downtown comrades for help in establishing a network of social, educational and fraternal services in their own neighborhood. The branch charter granted to Harlem Branch #2 early in 1898, guaranteeing such assistance, served as a model for similar agreements reached over the next few years between the parent organization downtown and affiliate groups in Williamsburg, Brownsville and the Bronx.[5]

Harlem's Workmen's Circle membership lists were swelled during these early days by an amalgamation with another newly created radical organization, the Harlem Socialist Press Association. This latter group was composed of former members of Local #16, District 32 of the Socialist Labor Party, who had been forced out of the party over their support of the Social Democratic *Forward* in its ongoing struggle with other Socialist dailies. Its leaders, Abraham Baroff and A. Persky, viewed affiliation with the Workmen's Circle group as a viable means of spreading the *Forward*'s brand of radical thought among the numbers of Jewish workers settling uptown. Bolstered by their participation, the Harlem branch was able to rent a public hall for meetings, hire a local doctor to serve as "physician on call" for uptown members and began the job of establishing itself as a center for socialist thought and activity for the Harlem-bound proletariat.[6]

Branch #2 was already a well-known center of uptown Jewish life when H. Lang arrived in the United States and settled in Harlem in 1904. Describing himself later as a "spiritual representative for many young men who migrated to these shores" during the peak years of Jewish immigration, Lang recalled how fearful he and his fellow immigrants were of settling outside of the "secure" immigrant hub. "Harlem," Lang remembered, "seemed to us remote from the Lower East Side, downtown where there were the Jewish folk masses. We knew downtown was filled with lectures and debates. Harlem seemed to us a forgotten spot without the spiritual atmosphere which we desired."

Lang credited the Harlem Workmen's Circle—of which he was an official—with having "simply saved the new immigrants," by "creating the desired radical immigrant atmosphere in Harlem." He recalled that when a center was needed for radical Jewish thinkers, "a central place" was established by Branch #2 not far from the "corner of 101st Street," where Jews who sought day-work in the building trades lined up. Clubrooms were established on that block and "on the walls were hung pictures of Marx, LaSalle and Bakunin," reflecting the multiplicity of socialist and radical ideologies supported by Harlem workers. Branch #2 also created a Robert Owen Club, an organization which maintained a small library and made copies of the socialist *Forward* and *Zukunft* and anarchist *Frei Arbeiter Stimme* available to members. These activities helped smooth the new immigrant's adjustment to foreign surroundings and "soon," according to Lang, "we young immigrants in Harlem were no longer miserable."[7]

At this time, Branch #2 began making its most important contribution to the life of Harlem's Jews—and to the life of its movement in general—the organization of New York's first Socialist Sunday School in Harlem in 1906. The establishment of this institution dramatically symbolized the beginnings of a fundamental shift in the outlook of the Jewish socialist fraternal and educational organization. When the Workmen's Circle was founded in 1892, its primary goal was to provide its members with illness and death benefits. Educational work seemed secondary to fraternal activites. The creation of the Harlem Children's Educational Circle meant that education and the propagation of Jewish socialist ideas would become the dominant goal of the movement. The Workmen's Circle was soon to be known as "an idealist, educational organization which also paid sick and death benefits."[8]

The impetus for this change in organizational outlook may be attributed to the infusion after 1905 of Russian-Jewish Bundist ideology among New York's immigrant masses. The Bund—the General Jewish Labor Alliance of Russia, Poland and Lithuania—was founded in 1897 as the Jewish wing of the Russian Social Democratic Party. In its early days, the Bund viewed itself as a cosmopolitan socialist organization and rejected all forms of Jewish nationalism as "bourgeois." Yiddish—a form of national expression—was used by the Bund but only as a means of spreading socialism among the Jews of the Pale of Settlement. By 1900, however, the Bund recognized that the Jewish workers whom they hoped to lead and serve were innately nationalistic; they were reluctant to abandon their national-cultural heritage for unrealized promises of universal socialism. Accordingly, the Bund adopted a uniquely Jewish socialist posture. Such leaders as Chaim Zhitlowsky and Vladimir Medem argued that Jewish socialism reflected the struggle of a small minority group for political and cultural expression. Expressions of a particularly Jewish national identity within the socialist context through the medium of Yiddish literature and poetry were now to be strongly encouraged. Bundists argued that their ideology was quite different from the bourgeois, imperialistic nationalism of the West, which all good socialists rejected. This divergence with orthodox Marxism caused the Bund to split with the Russian Social Democratic Party in 1903, and to establish its own separate socialist movement among the Jews of Russia.[9]

The nationalistic phase of Russian Bundist history continued until 1914 when the movement became a casualty of the massive dislocation of Russian Jews during World War I. During its relatively short period of independent existence, the Bund did succeed, however, in inspiring, among other things, a cultural renaissance among the Jewish masses of the Pale. Yiddish replaced Russian as the language of the Jewish intellectual in Russia. Yiddish poetry and fiction flourished there as well. Hence, when thousands of Jewish socialist radicals fled Russia after the aborted 1905 Russian Revolution, they brought Bundist notions with them.[10]

The Bundists added a new vitality to existing American socialist life. Their agitation, through the Socialist Sunday School movement, for a heightened sense of socialist ideological commitment among Arbeiter Ring members, was but one of the ways in which these recent immigrants sought to change the face of immigrant life. And it was in Harlem that these new educational programs were first initiated.[11]

Harlem Workmen's Circle members were greatly taken by Bundist propaganda. They were convinced that radical ideas were important not only to the present immigrant generation but to future generations. They therefore felt a great obligation to transmit their enthusiasm for secular Jewish national socialist values to what they hoped would be a rising group of American-born leaders. The curriculum of the Harlem Children's Educational Circle, sponsored by the uptown Arbeiter Ring branch, reflected just such a commitment. In the Socialist Sunday School, children were exposed to courses on socialism, radicalism and trade-unionism and received instruction in Jewish history and literature. American-born public school teachers sympathetic to radical goals were hired, and instruction was conducted in English to serve the needs of a new generation of American Jews.[12]

It was through this school that Harlem radicals illustrated most dramatically that residence outside the ghetto was no cause for the lessening of their attachment to ideals first fostered in Europe and transplanted to the Lower East Side. The Harlem Socialist Sunday School served as a model for ten similarly constituted schools organized over the next half-decade on the Lower East Side and in Brooklyn, and represented uptown's greatest contribution to the perpetuation of socialist ideals within New York's European Jewish community.[13]

These first Socialist Sunday Schools were plagued by a dearth of money and of skilled teachers. The national leadership of the movement, according to its Harlem leaders, was "concerned with a multitude of workers' problems, and the problem of a 'Socialist Sunday School' was considered a luxury." The supporters of socialist education claimed they received little support, "not from the national office and not from the local institutions." Finding qualified teachers willing to work for low wages caused continued problems. School officials constantly complained that there were simply too few teachers to service all the children who desired to study in Workmen's Circle schools.[14]

The combination of these two major problems caused the temporary decline of socialist school activities in 1911. Advocates of the Workmen's Circle school movement continued, however, to fight for national office support for their educational plans. Finally, in 1918, the Eighteenth National Conference of the Workmen's Circle appropriated adequate funds for a new Yiddish-language school system by approving an eight-cent per year tax on its entire national membership. The first new Workmen's Circle school was opened in Williamsburg in November, 1918. Later that month, a second school was established in Harlem. By 1919, ten Yiddish schools were in operation in New York State and in seven other cities outside the state.[15]

The links between the downtown centers of radical thought and the uptown community were strengthened further by the five other city-wide socialist organizations that established branches in Harlem. Although advocating different strains of socialist ideology, they were united in the belief that Harlem was fertile territory for the transmission and propagation of radical ideas.

The Jewish National Workers Alliance of America, an organization of twenty-four branches scattered throughout the Jewish sections of New York, established two branches in Harlem, both at 104th Street and Madison Avenue. They were joined there by a branch of the Ludlow Street-based Jewish National Radical School, when the school began operations uptown in 1912, and by the Poalei Zion, the Socialist Zionist organization, which initiated uptown activities in 1905. The

Jewish Socialist Federation of America established an uptown branch of its movement at an adjacent location on 104th Street and Madison Avenue. These organizations, along with numerous other smaller radical landsmanshaft organizations (some of which ultimately affiliated with the Workmen's Circle), all helped to spread and strengthen socialist ideals, first fostered on the Lower East Side, among those living in the new uptown Jewish quarter.[16]

The emergence around 1910 of strong Jewish building alteration trades and bakers unions within the Harlem working class settlement also testifies to the continued importance of ghetto concerns and issues among Jewish workers residing uptown. In fighting for the right to organize and in finally gaining grudging recognition both from their employers and other opponents, these Harlem Jewish workers showed that uptown residence did not preclude membership in the downtown-based Jewish labor movement. On the contrary, Harlem Jewish builders and bakers showed that uptown unionists could play leading roles in labor agitations that affected not only themselves but all Jewish workers wherever they resided in New York City.

In organizing themselves into a viable union, Harlem's Jewish alteration building trade workers had to overcome both the opposition of powerful uptown building bosses and the animosity of their fellow non-Jewish construction trade unionists. Jewish construction workers were employed almost exclusively in the alterations trades. Employment opportunities in the new building area were controlled by the ethnically exclusive, Irish-dominated construction unions. Few Jews were able to obtain the union card needed to secure work in that more lucrative employment field. Scabbing for "lumpers"—never a profitable practice—became increasingly more difficult after 1900 as the unions grew in strength. The only major concession on membership granted Jewish workers by the established gentile construction unions during this period was the admission of 1,000 Eastern European Jews to the rolls of the Amalgamated Painters' Union in 1901.[17]

Excluded from the new building area, Jewish laborers settled for the lower paying alteration work and after a while began to agitate for higher pay through their own unions. After one false start in 1907, the first Alterations Painters' Union, which included members from a variety of construction trades, was formed in Harlem in 1910. The up-

town-based union quickly gained recognition from the United Hebrew Trades, and soon established four branches in other parts of
New York City and nearby towns. In 1911, the five alteration union
locals, representing in theory 20,000 workers, 75 percent of whom
were Jewish, federated under the name International Painters' and Paperhangers' Union.[18]

This new union's first major effort on behalf of local alteration
workers began in June, 1913, when uptown Local #1 joined with
locals on the Lower East Side and Brooklyn in developing plans for a
city-wide strike of New York builders. The major goals of the proposed strike were to be the unionization of 15,000 "exploited" workers and the establishment of "union conditions" in all local building
projects. Three strike headquarters were established: Delancey Street
on the Lower East Side, Grand Street in Williamsburg and Workmen's
Circle Branch #2 headquarters in East Harlem. Each center was
charged with organizing its members for a projected August general
strike.[19]

The general strike was called during the second week in August and
by August 29, 1910, the sympathetic *Forward* triumphantly announced
that 200 bosses had already settled with the union. Two days later, it
reported that so many employers had come to strike headquarters to
settle with the union, that a schedule of appointments had to be arranged for union leadership to be able to meet with all bosses who
wished to capitulate. Less than two weeks later, it was announced
that the strike had been settled and that "union shop" conditions had
been achieved. According to this report all workers returning to work
had to obtain union permits to retain their jobs.[20]

The only disquieting feature of the strike for union leadership was
the antagonistic attitude displayed by the established A.F. of L.
Brotherhood of Painters. This federation of non-Jewish, new building
construction unions had sent scabs to undermine the struggle of the
alteration workers. The Yiddish press contended that fear of competition and racial hatred had motivated their actions. Relations between
the unions continued to deteriorate for over a year as each group persisted in scabbing against the other. Finally, in November, 1914, after
years of "unofficial" warfare and a short period of intense "official"
conflict, an amalgamation was achieved linking Jewish and non-
Jewish construction workers. The International became a local in the
Brotherhood of Painters.[21]

This alliance did not automatically reverse the course of Jewish-Christian relations in the building trades. The official unity reached by union leaders was not universally accepted by the laboring rank and file. Many Christian painters, according to published reports, still felt "race hatred and economic competition which hurt the effectiveness of the union." In April, 1915, union officials attempted to reduce the points of intergroup conflict by arranging for a meeting between "old" International and Brotherhood factions to "promote understanding and unity among workers."[22]

The Harlem Baker's Union was faced with the even more difficult task of dealing with fellow Jewish scabs in finally establishing itself as the representative of uptown Jewish bakers. This labor organization was formed in June, 1903, by former members of the defunct downtown Local #36 who had migrated uptown in the hope of finding work at decent wages. Jewish bakers on the Lower East Side had experienced great difficulties in attempting to organize; downtown bosses had adroitly blocked most labor agitations by hiring newly arrived immigrants who were willing to endure harsh bakery working conditions for less than union scale wages. Harlem labor organizers hoped that uptown bosses would have a smaller work force to choose from and would have to deal with unionists.[23]

When Harlem bakers began to agitate for the right to organize, uptown bosses responded by declaring a lockout in all uptown shops and importing nonunion bread from other parts of the city. Harlem unionists reacted to this challenge by immediately calling for a strike. Picket lines were thrown up around local bakeries to prevent scab bread from entering the neighborhood. Unionists also appealed to uptown radical organizations to direct their members to buy only bread that carried the union label. This agitation soon reduced the effectiveness of the owner's lockout, and the owners were ultimately forced to readmit the unionist to work.[24]

The uptown bakers' struggle intensified in January, 1904, when six major Harlem Jewish-owned bakeries were struck by unionists who complained that their bosses were forcing them to work longer than the ten hour day established by the New York State Legislature. Uptown bosses were also accused of placing false union labels on bread produced elsewhere. City Board of Health officials were criticized for their alleged collusion with baker bosses in accepting bribes for overlooking obvious health violations.[25]

This second uptown bakers' strike continued sporadically for six months. Unionists again watched carefully to prevent the sale of falsely labeled bread uptown. They went so far as to deliver union bread from Brooklyn and elsewhere to local groceries themselves in order to stop their bosses from substituting scab bread. This uptown disturbance took on further city-wide dimensions when Jewish bakers from all over New York decided, on January 28, 1904, to each donate one dollar from their week's wages to the uptown bakers' cause. This strike and several other minor worker-boss confrontations ultimately led to a grudging acceptance of "union conditions" by uptown bosses.[26]

These early union victories were, however, extremely short-lived. The success of uptown bakers caused many unorganized downtown workers to migrate uptown to reap the benefits of "union conditions." Harlem bakery owners capitalized on this newly created over-supply of labor by reneging on numerous negotiated agreements. Scabs replaced unionists in many uptown shops and unemployment mounted among those committed to union organization. Union membership dropped off sharply and leaders feared that the conditions that had previously blocked organization downtown were being duplicated in Harlem.[27]

Bakers' Union officials responded to this threat by propagandizing among all uptown workers the merits of collective action. More importantly, they lent their active support to new unionization efforts on the Lower East Side. They argued logically that if "union conditions" could be achieved downtown, this would halt or at least reduce the flow of workers uptown, which so threatened their own position. Uptown labor leaders worked closely with downtown comrades in several unsuccessful downtown union actions initiated in 1905, and ultimately in the successful organization effort of 1909. Through these efforts, Harlem bakers reaffirmed the close interdependence of Jewish proletarian groups in all sections of New York.[28]

Uptown groups preaching radical solutions to immigrant social and economic problems and advocating the development of a true downtown socialist atmosphere in Harlem were also important to that segment of local Jewry that may have not been particularly inclined towards radical ideals. Many uptowners supported organizations like the Workmen's Circle from a nonideological standpoint, backing local agitators when these radicals championed the pragmatic day-to-day consumer problems of uptown residents. Temporary allegiance to socialist-oriented organizations, which lasted only for the duration of a particular crusade, was also quite attractive to some of East Harlem's non-Jewish immigrant residents who ordinarily had little organizational contacts with Jewish radical groups.

Uptown residents were, for example, quick to rise in support of the "ladies' auxiliary" of the Workmen's Circle in its 1902 campaign to reduce uptown Kosher meat prices through a boycott of Harlem meat markets. This early attempt at consumer activism began on May 16, 1902, when the Ladies' Anti-Beef Trust Committee, composed of members of the Women's Branch #2 of the Workmen's Circle, called for a neighborhood boycott of uptown butchers "in the vicinity of 98th-100th Streets" in protest over what they declared to be exorbitantly high Kosher meat prices. The committee began the boycott by going from house to house to request that neighbors refrain from buying meat until prices dropped. Picket lines were thrown around local meat markets and women who sought to defy the protest movement were stopped and "convinced" of the merits of the boycott.[29]

One day later, the protest committee held a mass meeting at Central Hall on Third Avenue, where money was collected and plans completed for the expansion of the "meat struggle." Strike leaders also announced that "Bohemian Christian neighbors" had taken heart from the example of Jewish protestors and had themselves begun to protest against the high prices charged in Harlem's non-Kosher meat stores.[30]

This first attempt at consumer activism lasted nearly a month and was marked by several instances of violence. On May 19, 1902, for example, two neighbors, Sarah Blitzstein and Tina Tass, were arrested for disturbing the peace while picketing a nearby butcher shop. According to newspaper accounts, a butcher named Wegderwitz had attempted to "smuggle" a chunk of meat out of his picketed store on Second Avenue in the hope of selling it downtown. His efforts were blocked by a "gang of women" who tried to steal the meat and drove him back into his store. This initial disturbance caused "hundreds of men and women" to congregate outside the butcher shop. Frightened but determined to break the blockade, Wegderwitz sent his daughter to call for the police. The officers successfully drove a wedge between the protestors and led Wegderwitz "as one leads a bridegroom to the marriage canopy" to the safety of the elevated railroad. Blitzstein and Tass were arrested when they laid down on the "El" tracks, blocking Wegderwitz's escape. The two women were joined in custody by Esther Warfel who was arrested for "ripping a chicken from the hands of a woman" who sought to pass through the Committee's picket line.[31]

The meat boycott entered a new stage on June 13, 1902, when it was announced in the *Forward* that Branch #2 had decided to open a cooperative butcher shop in Harlem. It was their idea to deflate artificially the price of Harlem meat by opening an ad hoc wholesale meat market which would compete successfully with the established high-priced butchers. Any profits derived from this cooperative venture would be turned over to women protestors. This plan was quickly put into operation and according to the Branch's highly sympathetic historian "existed over a year and a half and practically stopped the butchers from raising prices."[32]

This first limited attempt at cooperative consumerism inspired the creation in Harlem in 1903 of a branch of the New York Industrial Cooperative Society which had been formed two years earlier by a group of downtown radicals who modeled their organization activities after those of the English Rochdale cooperative system. The Rochdale cooperative pioneers of the late nineteenth century had argued that for a cooperative venture to compete successfully against capitalist enterprises, it must organize a "controlled market," wherein all members of the co-op pledge to buy all the necessities of life exclusively from the cooperative stores. According to this system, once assured of a consistently reliable clientele, the cooperative store could afford to offer its members good products at wholesale prices. Whatever profits were derived from the venture would be turned back to the membership in the form of dividends. Once firmly established, the cooperative movement would also attract nonmembers to its shops by offering quality articles at reasonable prices.

The keys to the success of this or any other cooperative system were the ability of the cooperators, in the first instance, to attract committed investors to its program and secondly, its success in organizing its membership for a controlled market. The New York Industrial Cooperative Society attempted to adapt the Rochdale system to the American ghetto experience by establishing a network of ten retail stores on the Lower East Side designed to serve a variety of downtown consumer needs.[33]

In 1903, in the hope of capitalizing on what was assumed to be an atmosphere for consumerism created by Branch #2's first efforts, the New York Industrial Cooperative Society founded a combined bakery and butcher shop in Harlem. In announcing the opening of the cooperative venture, the society was quick to point out that its soon-to-be implemented Rochdale system marked a significant advancement over previous "spur of the moment" consumerism. Strike-time efforts were characterized as "one-quarter cooperative," offering only "cheap meat under Rabbinical supervision." The new organization pledged itself to an additional goal: to make the "power of the cooperative ideal felt in Harlem."[34]

The uptown cooperative movement's goals of providing high quality, low cost consumer goods for its members quickly led it into conflict with the then newly established Harlem Bakers' Union which was agitating for recognition by uptown bosses. The Harlem Cooperative was attacked by the union for its hypocrisy in allegedly supporting bakery owners' attempts to break the union. These uptown radicals were accused of joining with other "capitalist" retailers in selling scab bread from the Lower East Side and Brooklyn. The Label Agitation Committee of the United Hebrew Trades castigated the Cooperative as "union-busters" and warned that if the co-op did not agree to use only union bread, an action would be initiated by the United Hebrew Trades.[35]

Cooperative leadership responded to this attack by charging that the Harlem Bakery strike and lockout was caused by the "conspiracy" of union leaders to line their own pockets, and not their purported desire to improve the lot of the average worker. The Harlem Co-op announced that it would "gladly" pay the one-cent a loaf increase demanded by the union to support a wage hike, if they could be sure it would "give the poor baker a possibility to work a human work day, but it seems as if the goal of the union is to enrich the profits of some union bosses."[36]

The uptown cooperative movement survived only until April, 1904. Its quick demise was due more to its inability to gain a large base of constantly committed followers than to its opposition to uptown baker union leadership. The Harlem Co-op and, for that matter, all New York Jewish co-ops of that era, failed because few Jewish families on the Lower East Side or in the working-class section of Harlem ever accumulated sufficient assured income to invest in a cooperative venture. And even if they had the money to join the movement, most immigrant householders found it simply more convenient to purchase their necessities of life from private storekeepers who were often known to extend such important personal services as credit to steady customers during periods of individual financial crisis.[37]

Uptown radicals learned the lesson that mass enthusiasm for spur-of-the-moment consumerism was not easily translated into an ongoing grass-roots protest movement. The only consumer activities undertaken uptown after the dissolution of the Harlem Branch of the New York Industrial Cooperative were, ironically, those of the Jewish Bakers' Union Local #305, which established several temporary cooperative bakery and grocery stores during strike periods.[38]

Harlem radical organizations played an important role in a second neighborhood consumer crusade when, in January, 1908, Harlem tenement dwellers decided to join a new wave of rent strikes that "spread like wildfire over all the poor quarters of New York." The 1908 rent strike was far more organized than was the 1904 disturbance. Some ad hoc neighborhood tenant groups still conducted localized protests, such as one conducted by residents of 100th Street and Second Avenue. But most of the major Harlem-based activities were initiated by a coalition of five Jewish radical organizations which combined to form the Anti-High Rent Socialist League of Harlem. Most uptown tenement dwellers committed to forcing landlords to reduce tenement house rentals looked to the League for leadership.[39]

The district-wide umbrella organization was composed of Branch #2 of the Workmen's Circle, the 26th Assembly District Socialist Party, the Lodzer Bundist Unterstutzen Verein (which was destined to become a branch of the Arbeiter Ring in 1909), the Socialist Territorialists, and the Group Charmigal, a socialist literary organization.[40]

The League decided at its organizational meeting of January 5, 1908, to appoint a nine-man committee to coordinate strike activities. Working from its headquarters at Madison Avenue between 104th and 105th Streets, representatives were sent throughout the neighborhood to convince Harlemites of the merits of the agitation. The organization also called for mass meetings to publicize the strike's objectives and collected money to pay whatever legal fees arose out of eviction litigation. The rent strike lasted more than a month and affected more than forty-five different Harlem tenement houses, the majority of them located in the working-class section east of Third Avenue, south of 105th Street.[41]

Jewish agitation in their areas was applauded by neighboring Italian tenement dwellers who appealed to the Harlem League for assistance in conducting their own limited tenant protest. On January 10, 1908, a tenant protest committee representing the radical Italian newspaper *Il Momento* turned to the Harlem League suggesting that the two ethnic groups work for common goals against landlords. The Italian delegation was well received and several Italian tenants who had been evicted from their homes received money from the Harlem League to find new accommodations. Five days later, the *Forward* reported that a "great spurt" of protest activity had hit the Italian quarter and that mass meetings were being held within Little Italy. The activities of the Harlem League also attracted the attention of non-Jewish tenement dwellers in the South Bronx. On January 11, 1908, the uptown socialist group was invited to help form an organization similar to itself in the outlying borough. The Harlem League decided to work with the Bronx German Socialist Party in organizing northern radical forces.[42]

Despite both their dedicated efforts to create a radical "home away from home" in Harlem and their enthusiastic championing of the pragmatic day-to-day problems of local residents, uptown socialist groups were slow to make their presence felt upon the East Harlem political scene. They were unable until 1916 to translate neighborhood support for their consumer and labor agitations into political power at the polls. Harlem Jews may have demonstrated as good radicals when uptown socialists led rent strikes or initiated protests against the high price of Kosher meat, but they still voted either as good Democrats or Republicans in all district-wide political campaigns. Jewish voting patterns clearly indicate that much of the mass support for uptown socialist groups was ad hoc, based on the attractiveness of a specific pragmatic program advocated by the radicals. Only certain well-circumscribed segments of the uptown Jewish voting public viewed Harlem in "second ghetto" terms; as a northern extension of the ghetto radical political community. As a result, from 1900 to 1914 Socialist Party candidates lagged badly behind the dominant Tammany-backed Democratic candidates and their persistent Republican challengers. Third and fourth party nominees consistently failed to receive more than ten percent of the vote in any single district-wide Congressional battle. The only exception to this voting pattern took place in 1912, when a Progressive Party candidate received approximately one-third of the total vote and ran a close second to the victorious Democratic in a four-man race. The Debs-backed Socialist candidate failed to capitalize on this split within a major party and finished in the accustomed last place, receiving less than ten percent of the vote. Harlem's 16th and its later reapportioned 20th Congressional districts were represented during these years by Jacob Rupert Jr., the local beer magnate, and his successor, Francis Burton Harrison; both loyal sons of Tammany Hall.[43]

Jewish voting patterns differed little from those of the general uptown population. Although more voters in the heavily Jewish Assembly Districts voted the Socialist line than elsewhere, the majority of voters supported the Democratic candidate. Republican incursions into the Jewish, Democratic-controlled Assembly Districts—a common phenomenon on the Lower East Side after 1900—were far less pronounced in East Harlem during this era. Socialist candidates were even less of a serious threat to Democratic hegemony in those early twentieth-century elections.[44]

The failures of the Socialist Party in the political arena may in part be attributed to the inability of even their most consistent and vociferous supporters to vote. Many of the ideologically true backers of uptown radical activities and organizations were newly arrived, unnaturalized aliens, who had no right of suffrage. Many other supporters were newly naturalized Americans who had yet to realize the potential power of a properly cast vote. Socialist leaders were, finally, to blame for not making electoral victory a major goal. Socialist groups contented themselves with political campaigns which they themselves admitted were "of a demonstrative character without any chance of success."[45]

The political fortunes of Harlem's Socialists began to change with the election of 1914. In that year, Republican Isaac Siegel succeeded by a narrow margin of some eighty votes in ending fourteen years of Democratic control of the East Harlem Congressional seat. His victory, coming in a year which saw the Republicans gain control of the New York State Congressional delegation, is still quite remarkable because he beat a proven local vote-getter, old-time Harlemite Jacob Cantor, former President of the Borough of Manhattan. Siegel's victory was fashioned through his capturing of the predominantly Jewish 24th and 26 Assembly Districts by over 150 votes, which offset Cantor's victories in the predominantly Italian neighborhoods. Of equal importance was the fine performance of the Socialist candidate who received over 1,000 votes in the Jewish district. Tammany's grip on the uptown electorate and especially its Jewish component seemed to be on the wane.[46]

The most important outcome of the 1914 Congressional elections affecting uptown Socialists did not occur in Harlem. It took place on the Lower East Side where labor lawyer Meyer London became the first Socialist Party candidate to be elected to any office in New York City. This victory was achieved due to the unstinting efforts of his supporters, through continuous house-to-house electioneering, to convince downtowners of the value of having an individual of Russian-Jewish birth, sensitive to labor's needs, in political office. Harlem Socialists learned from this victory that through concerted efforts, their candidates could succeed in defeating major party candidates in heavily Jewish working-class areas. And early in 1916, Harlem Socialists met to draw up plans for duplicating London's Socialist Party victory in Harlem, touching off a spirited intraethnic debate over what type of Jewish representative was best qualified to serve his coreligionists in Congress.[47]

Harlem Socialists understood that the size of their electoral registration rolls would have to be dramatically increased if they hoped to defeat both Siegel and the Tammany machine candidate. Late in January 1916, party officials attempted to deal with this problem by establishing a Socialist Party Naturalization Committee, which was clearly mandated to make citizens out of aliens who would "have the right to take part in the elections this year." Naturalization classes were held at the Workmen's Circle's Labor Lyceum to help immigrants pass their citizenship tests.[48]

In February 1916, the Harlem Socialist Party organized a 20th Congressional District Campaign Committee, founded on the model of London's successful Lower East Side organization. Uptown leaders directed an early effort to canvass the neighborhood to alert socialist sympathizers of the great electoral battle ahead. A similar district-wide canvass was taken early in July to ascertain the strength of the party's electoral appeal.[49]

These early organizational activities, were, however, only important adjuncts to the crucial problem facing party leaders—that of selection of a candidate like Meyer London; one possessed of charismatic qualities who could represent effectively the Socialist cause. In selecting such a candidate, uptown leaders looked to the Lower East Side and convinced Morris Hillquit, renowned defender of labor causes and former unsuccessful Socialist candidate on the Lower East Side, to move to Harlem and run as their candidate for Siegel's seat. Hillquit accepted the Socialist designation late in July, 1916, and uptown party members immediately began to work for his election.[50]

Hillquit's candidacy received an early boost in September when five major New York unions—some with branches in Harlem—agreed to participate actively to help elect the Socialist candidate to Congress. Leaders of the ILGWU, Cap Makers', Furriers', and Bakers' Unions, and the Jewish Socialist Federation decided to sell 25,000 stamps valued at ten to twenty-five cents each to their memberships to help finance the Hillquit campaign. They also agreed to compile detailed membership lists to be used by campaign workers in canvassing Harlem's working-class population. Several weeks later, three other Harlem labor groups voted to back Hillquit, as uptown labor groups began to close ranks behind the Socialist candidate.[51]

Following the strategy used successfully in London's victory on the Lower East Side, Hillquit's advisors deemphasized the ideological differences between their candidate and his two "capitalist" major-party opponents. Abandoning the demonstrative character of previous campaigns, Hillquit's workers concentrated on the practical side of politics, twice canvassing those who had voted previously to increase Socialist Party electoral registration. When Hillquit did attack the incumbent, his criticisms were directed at Siegel's voting record on issues directly affecting the immigrant community.[52]

Uptown Socialists were particularly critical of Siegel's approach to the Burnett Literacy Test Bill of 1915. Recognizing the growing strength of restrictionist sentiment in the United States Congress, Siegel and his fellow Jewish Congressman, Adolph Sabath, had drafted an amendment to this anti-immigration act providing that all refugees from religious persecution be exempted from the proposed literacy test. These efforts, done in conjunction with Louis Marshall of the American Jewish Committee, were characterized by Socialist opponents as doing "great harm to the immigrant by easing the way for passage of the bill." The Siegel-Sabath amendment was ultimately defeated and the Burnett Bill was passed without serious modifications. Jewish agitation, did, however, according to one historian, "confirm President Wilson in his opposition to the bill." Wilson vetoed the measure and thereby delayed its final passage until 1917. New York's Socialist press, nevertheless, harangued their local East Harlem Congressman for the insufficiency of his efforts on behalf of immigrants. In leading the chorus of critics, Hillquit demonstrated that he had developed a heightened sensitivity to Jewish group issues since 1908, when he was defeated on the Lower East Side due in part to his support of the general socialist and labor restrictionist position on the immigration question so crucial to many downtown voters.[53]

Siegel's stance on "Jewish" issues was also criticized by his Democratic opponent, Bernard Rosenblatt. Tammany Hall's candidate was well-known in uptown Zionist circles for his service as Honorary Secretary of the Federation of American Zionists. This American-born Columbia University-educated lawyer was also president of the Zion Commonwealth Inc., and a member of the newly formed executive committee of the American Jewish Congress Organizing Committee. An intensely nationalistic Jewish leader, Rosenblatt charged that Siegel had "no definite principles in matters Jewish" and that while he supported "every humanitarian move in favor of Jews," Siegel was not "fully aware of the needs of the Jewish people." He further accused Siegel of "taking orders" in Jewish affairs from "men like Louis Marshall" who "do not express the needs and interests of the Jewish masses." While not directly criticizing Siegel's performance on the immigration question, Rosenblatt was, nevertheless, moved to comment "that Siegel's activities . . . found him lacking in independent judgment."[54]

Rosenblatt's supporters were even more critical of his Socialist Party opponent. They characterized Hillquit as a "well known socialist lawyer and able labor advocate who was more or less indifferent to matters Jewish, being an acknowledged representative of class interests." Rosenblatt, in their opinion, was the only candidate "with a clear conception" of the questions "facing the Jews" and the "personal power to advocate them."[55]

Siegel, for his part, was not without his own weapons in defending himself against these political attacks. He presented himself to the voters as the man most intimately acquainted with the local needs of East Harlemites and as the "Jewish" candidate best prepared to lead their community within the mainstream of American political life. His supporters depicted Siegel as a self-made man who was born in New York City in 1880 and received his law degree from New York University in 1901. This son of Russian-Jewish immigrants was appointed Special State Attorney General in 1901 and gained his first elective post when he defeated Cantor in 1914.[56]

Siegel asserted that his opponent was a political "carpetbagger" imported from the Lower East Side, who had little knowledge of the problems facing uptown Jewry. He further contended that Hillquit's advocacy of economic and social policies inimical to American ideals made him an ill-advised choice to represent an immigrant community in the halls of Congress Siegel's supporters argued that it was important "that Jewish voters send a Jewish representative to Congress from a Jewish quarter who is an American, a man in whom Americanization is solidly engrained with the spirit of the land." They warned that the sending of a man to Congress who "desires to overturn the system of society and whose chief goal is to destroy the order upon which this government is built" would certainly cast doubts upon "the patriotism of the American Jews." One critic of Hillquit suggested that this election was a fundamental struggle between the "respectable element" and the "dirt-slingers and trouble makers" within the immigrant Jewish community. With specific reference to Siegel's performance on the immigrant issues, his supporters warned that if the Congressman's naturalized constituents failed to return him to his seat, it would indicate to some Americans that his immigrant district supported the imposition of a literacy test.[57]

Responding to Rosenblatt's contentions that the Congressman was not sufficiently "Jewish" in his outlook, Siegel's supporters repeatedly pointed to the fact that "Isaac Siegel is the only American Jewish Congressman who reads and writes Yiddish." And far from denying their candidate's close connection with Marshall and other members of the American Jewish Committee, Siegel was depicted as the choice of "the best element in American Judaism." Siegel welcomed Marshall's presence at public rallies and constantly solicited his active participation in the campaign. Marshall responded to Siegel's urgings by drafting an open letter of support for his candidacy which was published in several New York Jewish newspapers. Marshall was "shocked" to this particular action by his distress over Zionist contentions that Rosenblatt was "entitled to the suffrage of the Jewish electorate . . . because he is a nationalist."[58]

As this campaign, described by one observer as of "a great cultural-political character," reached its conclusion local newspapers supporting each of the candidates confidently explained why their man was certain of victory. The Socialist *Forward* pointed to the dramatic increase of 42 percent in the number of registered voters in the district as proof of an impending Hillquit victory. Most of these new voters were declared "workers under socialist influence." The newly established *American Jewish Chronicle* counted on Rosenblatt's nationalistic orientation to ensure him the win. And the politically conservative *Morning Journal* declared that Siegel was a "Republican candidate in a Republican year in a district where the younger element, which is majority Republican every year grown stronger." On the day before the election, *The Forward* ran a banner headline stating "Harlem: The Whole Nation Is Watching," indicating clearly that more was at stake in this election than simply a single Congressional seat. Hillquit's supporters hoped that a victory over major party candidates in Harlem would be a harbinger of greater Socialist Party successes throughout the United States.[59]

When the ballots were counted, Siegel emerged as the victor by a small plurality of less than 500 votes over Hillquit and 700 votes over Rosenblatt out of some 12,000 votes cast (see table 1). The incumbent retained his seat, but the Socialist Party made an impressive showing, Hillquit receiving 4,129 votes—close to four times the number attracted to the Socialist Party line in any previous election. More importantly, Hillquit had actually outpolled his two opponents among Jewish voters. He received 35 percent of the vote in the 24th Assembly District and 45 percent in the 26th Assembly District, which included most of East Harlem south of 119th Street, east of Fifth Avenue. Siegel ran second in the combined Jewish neighborhoods and Rosenblatt trailed. Siegel was able to offset Hillquit's plurality in the Jewish election districts by soundly defeating his Socialist challenger in the predominantly Italian 28th Assembly District. Harlem's Italian voters, who according to historian Arthur Mann were generally apathetic to local Harlem politics until Fiorello LaGuardia "stirred them up" in the early 1920s, constituted only one-third of the district's eligible voters. But their votes proved to be decisive because they gave Siegel a 900 vote margin over Hillquit which offset the Socialist's triumph in Jewish areas. When the votes were analyzed it became apparent that Hillquit had won the battle for the Jewish vote but had lost the electoral war.[60]

Two years later, after an unsuccessful bid in 1917 to capture the New York mayoralty, Hillquit once again challenged Siegel for his Congressional seat. This time both major parties, in the words of Hillquit, "quietly laid aside all pretense of rivalry" and supported Siegel as a Fusion candidate. The 1918 election was in many ways a carbon copy of the earlier contest, with Siegel dominating the non-Jewish electoral districts. He defeated Hillquit by a more than two-to-one margin, while Hillquit held, and even increased, his strength in the Jewish areas (see table 1). The new "Jewish" 17th Assembly District gave Hillquit a plurality of almost 700 votes. The Socialist candidate gained 58 percent of the vote in the Jewish neighborhoods, scoring a second decisive victory for his party.[61]

The two combatants met a final time in the 1920 Congressional election and the now familiar pattern was once again repeated. Siegel defeated Hillquit by some 3,700 votes among Italian voters, offsetting the Socialist victory by 700 votes in the Jewish areas.

TABLE 1.
Hillquit vs. Siegel in New York City's 20th Congressional District, 1916–1920

1916 ELECTIONS

	SIEGEL	ROSENBLATT	HILLQUIT
24th A.D.	734 (28%)	942 (37%)	915 (35%)
26th A.D.	1641 (34%)	1115 (21%)	2107 (45%)
28th A.D.	1984 (42%)	1695 (36%)	1036 (22%)
30th A.D.	175	139	71
Soldier vote	8	16	—
Total	4542	3907	4129

1918 ELECTIONS

	SIEGEL	HILLQUIT
15th A.D.	273	415
16th A.D.	73	63
17th A.D.	1695 (42%)	2337 (58%)
18th A.D.	6204 (69%)	2737 (31%)
19th A.D.	445	338
20th A.D.	501	84
Soldier vote	226	31
Total	9417	6005

1920 ELECTIONS

	SIEGEL	HILLQUIT
15th A.D.	419	657
16th A.D.	67	102
17th A.D.	2406 (43%)	3178 (57%)
18th A.D.	8381 (64%)	4651 (36%)
19th A.D.	600	578
20th A.D.	729	275
Soldier vote	3	1
Total	12605	9442

TABLE 2.
Election Returns in Harlem's 20th Congressional District, 1922

	LAGUARDIA	FRANK	KARLIN
15th A.D.	197	302	342
16th A.D.	55	65	84
17th A.D.	1133 (20%)	2706 (47%)	1962 (33%)
18th A.D.	6124 (44%)	5239 (38%)	2498 (18%)
19th A.D.	339	333	274
20th A.D.	640	309	100
Total	8492	8324	5260

In 1922, Siegel retired from Congress and Fiorello LaGuardia was nominated by the Republicans in his stead. LaGuardia gained election to Congress after a bitterly contested fight with Democratic candidate Henry Frank (see table 2). The Socialist, William Karlin, ran a poor third, losing many of Hillquit's supporters in the Jewish electoral districts and receiving little backing elsewhere. The Jewish district went back over to the Democrats as Frank polled nearly one-half of the total vote in a three-way race. LaGuardia, like Siegel before him, ran to victory on the heels of his great popularity among Italian voters.[62]

Hillquit's several strong challenges to major party hegemony in East Harlem, though monuments to effective political organization and inspired electioneering, did not, as we have begun to see, fundamentally alter the long-term fortunes of the Harlem Socialist Party. Uptown Socialists never succeeded in establishing a truly powerful ghetto radical political community in East Harlem (see table 3). The party's apparent dramatic growth and electoral successes from 1916 through 1920 were in actuality illusory, stemming more from Hillquit's

TABLE 3.
The Socialist Party's Congressional Vote in East Harlem by percentile, 1910–1922 (16th and later 20th C.D.)

1910	no candidate
1912	8% in a 4 man race
1914	12% in a 3 man race
1916	31% in a 3 man race
1918	39% in a 2 man race
1920	43% in a 2 man race
1922	23% in a 3 man race.

HARLEM'S RADICAL SECOND GHETTO ORGANIZATIONS

1897–1917

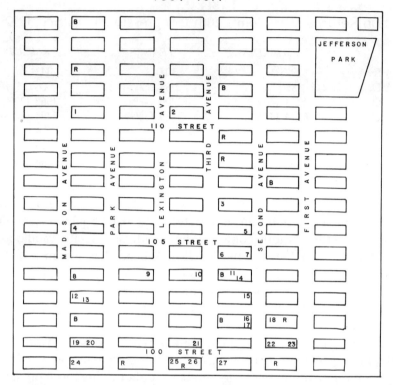

Map 5. Harlem's Racial Second Ghetto Organizations, 1897–1917
Source: Kehillah of New York, *Jewish Communal Register Of New York City 1917–1918*, 1918. Map by L. Salit.

R represents one or more tenement houses struck during 1904 or 1908 rent strike.
B represents location of struck bakeries in 1904 Baker's strike.

1) 1666 Madison—Workmen's Circle School (1906).
2) 1786 Lexington Ave.—Industrial and Agricultural Cooperative Association Inc. (1915).
3) 1915 Third Ave.—Branch #2, A.R. meeting hall (1901)
   —protest meeting during meat strike (1902).
4) 52 E. 106th St.—Cooperative lodging house (1915).
5) 243 E. 105th St.—Socialist Territorialists (1908).
6) 209 E. 104th St.—Headquarters 32nd A.D. Socialist Party (1901).
7) 241 E. 104th St.—The New York Cooperative offices (1902).
8) 46 E. 104th St.—Harlem Naturalization League (1914).
9) 106 E. 104th St.—Jewish Socialist Organization of Harlem (1909).

10) 143–145 E. 103d St.—Labor Lyceum (1910).
11) 210 E. 104th St.—Robert Owen Club (1903).
      —Brisker Radical Benevolent Association, Br. #87
        A.R. (1905).
      —Poalei Zion (1905).
      —Polish Social Democratic Party (1905).
      —Bakers Union #305 (1906).
      —Br. #36, A.R. (1907).
      —N.Y. Cooperative Shop.
12) 64 E. 103d St.—Mass meeting during 1906 meat boycott.
13) 53 E. 102d St.—Socialist Verein Poalei Zion Uptown (1906).
14) 227 E. 103d St.—Painter's Club (1904).
15) 220 E. 103d St.—Bakers Union #305 (1908).
16) 102d St./Second Ave.—Open-air meeting of Label Agitation Com-
      mittee U.H.T.
17) 239 E. 101st St.—Robert Owen Club (1903).
18) 302 E. 102d St.—1904 rent strike center.
19) 60 E. 101st St.—Harlem Bund (1904).
20) 72 E. 100th St.—Harlem Socialist Educational Club.
21) 250 E. 101st St.—Branch #2, A.R. meeting hall (1900+).
22) 101st St./Second Ave.—Site of 1910 meat riot.
23) 317 E. 100th St.—Rent strike site (1910).
24) 100th/Madison—Headquarters of 1906 meat boycott.
25) 200 E. 100th St.—Branch #2, A.R. meeting hall (1900+).
26) 201 E. 100th St.—Cooperative Grocery (1902).
27) 1799 Third Ave.—Local 1101 Uptown Painters and Paperhangers
      Union.

special personal appeal rather than widespread new voter acceptance of the Socialist Party platform. Hillquit's remarkable showings were not translated into a general uptown electoral shift to the left, as evidenced by both his consistently running far ahead of the other members of his ticket and the inability of local Socialists to transfer his electoral strength to future Congressional candidates. In 1916, for example, Hillquit gained more than a third of the Jewish vote while the Socialist Party presidential candidate polled only 1,376 votes out of 7,700 cast in the predominantly Jewish area. And in 1922, Karlin failed to hold the allegiance of Hillquit's so-called Socialist voters and finished far behind LaGuardia and Frank. The momentum of Hillquit's candidacy could not be transferred to any less glamorous replacement.[63]

In 1924, the Socialist Party elected a representative to Congress, Fiorello LaGuardia. But this formerly Republican incumbent's victory was really a triumph for his own independent Progressive policies and not for the program of the local Socialist Party. LaGuardia's electoral popularity did little to help either the Socialist presidential candidate or the Progressive Party candidate, Robert La Follette, in the Jewish districts. Both ran far behind the Democratic candidate John W. Davis, who garnered close to 60 percent of the Jewish votes in East Harlem. By 1924, those Jews remaining in East Harlem were moving in the direction of the Democratic party in both local and national elections.[64]

East Harlem's Socialist Party members felt at least an illusion of ascendency during the Hillquit era. In Central Harlem, the electoral impact of radical organizations was almost totally negligible. In that area, from 1900 until the close of the uptown Jewish era in 1930, no radical party candidate ever polled more than five percent of the total votes cast. The upwardly mobile, acculturated Jewish residents of Harlem's 17th and later reapportioned 19th Congressional Districts joined with their non-Jewish neighbors in voting either Republican or Democratic. Indeed the influence of a uniquely "Jewish vote" seems to be minimal, as witnessed by the absence of Jewish major party candidates until after 1920 and the lack of any noteworthy political debates centering around issues specifically of interest to Jewish voters. The Socialist Party established only a token presence west of Fifth Avenue and was never a significant factor in that district's political life.[65]

The failure of Harlem Jewish Socialists to build a permanent "downtown" political base within either uptown neighborhood graphically underscores a most basic perception about the very nature of Harlem Jewish life; those who conceived of uptown as a "second ghetto" community constituted but one well-circumscribed segment of a much larger uptown Jewish settlement.

Indeed, in all areas other than politics, those who thought in radical or practical terms of transmitting and preserving transplanted European and downtown ideas and institutions in Harlem lived an almost separate existence from other Harlemites. Their concerns were fundamentally different from those of the affluent, acculturated Jews who made up Harlem's other "second-settlement" community. The question, for example, of how to preserve and transmit radical ideas born in Europe and fashioned within the ghetto were relevant only to those who had yet to fully internalize the basic political conservatism of America. The problems of building Harlem-based unions and of strengthening city-wide labor organizing efforts were also significant only to that subcommunity of less economically mobile individuals who still defined themselves as part of the working class. Harlem's businessmen, manufacturers and professionals may have been concerned with the uptown union movement, but only to the extent that boisterous labor agitations disturbed their business or social lives. Rent strikes, meat protests and the like were, similarly, crucial only to the poor tenement dwellers. Lenox Avenue Jews were unconcerned; again except to the extent that such activities threatened the holdings of those landlords and butcher bosses who may have lived in that community. In fact, one might even suggest that there existed distinct geographical borders to the "second ghetto" corresponding closely but not exactly to the limits of the uptown Jewish working-class section, located east of Third Avenue and south of 105th Street, beyond which downtown influences rarely reached. For all other Harlem Jews, labor problems, socialist agitations and consumer protests were not pressing neighborhood concerns.[66]

Despite its limited numbers and circumscribed influence, the very existence of a Harlem "second ghetto" community is, nevertheless, significant. It graphically underscores the impact of the complex ghetto removal process upon the nature of uptown communal life. The history of this radical subcommunity, composed of those who migrated not primarily out of social choice but out of economic necessity, argues once again that one may not automatically predict either homogeneous economic distribution nor simple social description for areas of second settlement in American cities.

chapter 4

Harlem in Its Heyday—The Two Communities

2: Solving the Problems of Americanization

While one segment of uptown leadership was striving to build a second ghetto community rooted in transplanted European and downtown ideas and institutions, another fundamentally different group of communal workers was attempting to deal with the problems caused by the rejection of these same old-world and ghetto values by the majority of Harlem Jews. The founders of Harlem's second community of acculturated Jews recognized that most immigrants had migrated to Harlem out of their "conscious resolve" to break both the economic and social bonds of the ghetto. And they noted that for most, resettlement represented, as one contemporary described it, "a station on the main line of progress towards entering the great body of American citizenship." These Harlem-bound Jews were committed to rapid acculturation and perceived ghetto ideas and institutions as barriers to be overcome in the quest to become part of general society.[1]

This new elite leadership of businessmen, builders and real estate operators and their modern-thinking East European clerical supporters shared the general enthusiasm for rapid acculturation and worked to expose all Jewish Harlemites to the values of America. But they were also troubled by what they perceived as a pernicious by-product of the immigrant's struggle to become part of general society; the equation of Judaism with outdated ghetto culture and the willingness to discard religious practice in their zeal to become Americans. And these leaders were convinced that the problem of alienation from Judaism was destined to get worse among the next generation of American Jews who did not even feel their parents' minimal nostalgic attachment to a Judaism rooted in old-world traditions and customs. Reports of scandalous Christian missionary successes among uptown Jews was evidence enough for them of the dimensions of the problem.

The new elite leadership initiated a twofold response to this dilemma, emphasizing above all else that acculturation—the process of adopting the speech, dress, politics, work, and lifestyles of the majority culture—did not require assimilation—the abandonment of one's own unique religious heritage and one's basic self-perception as a Jew. They assisted leaders of the German-Jewish community in establishing the Harlem Federation, uptown's one large settlement house. There they affirmed the value of acculturation while emphasizing the consistency of the principles of good American citizenship with the moral principles of Judaism. They also worked with the Germans in reordering the focus of Jewish education through modern talmud torah system. There, through institutions like the Uptown Talmud Torah and the Rabbi Israel Salanter Talmud Torah, first efforts were made to separate the essence of traditional Judaism from its old-world shell. Here in Harlem, there began on a neighborhood-wide basis the process of creating an American form of Orthodox Judaism, acceptable to those intent upon becoming one with general culture.[2]

These joint German–East European efforts also marked a new era in intraethnic relations, as elite segments of the immigrant community were accepted as full partners in Jewish communal work. Both groups clearly understood that the acculturation process brought with it both rewards and challenges to the immigrant Jew. It was in Harlem that the amalgamation of German-East European ideals of communal service and the emergence of an American Jewish approach to maintaining group cohesion first took shape on a neighborhood level.

These activities clearly demonstrate the inaccuracy of another generalized concept of the nature of urban immigrant life. The Harlem Federation and the talmud torah movement both testify that, at least in New York, each step of the acculturated Jew away from the ghetto did not represent a major milestone in the "process of assimilation." The desire to maintain Jewish group cohesion did survive ghetto outmigration and was felt strongly by Harlem's subcommunity of acculturated Jews. Their history argues strongly that to the extent that areas of second settlement were conducive to rapid Americanization, they were also hospitable to the maintenance and even to the strengthening of Jewish identification.[3]

The need to create institutions that emphasized that acculturation did not necessitate abandonment of Judaism first became an issue for communal discussion and activity in December 1903, when Harlem Jewry was shocked by newspaper revelations describing the widespread success Christian missionaries were enjoying among neighborhood youth. Missionaries who had achieved a measure of success among ghetto children "driven to the streets by congestion and the unsanitary conditions of the tenements" were now reportedly "driving stakes in Harlem" and were "saving souls in a new district with the usual display of affection for the Hebrews." Conversionary conquests in the upward-moving Jewish district were advanced, according to contemporary observers, not by the physical poverty of a ghetto existence but by the apparent inability of newly acculturated immigrants, divorced from a Jewish identity rooted in the ghetto traditions of the past, to live comfortably as Jews with their American cultural present and future. Local newspaper editorialists pilloried Jewish leaders for not acknowledging the existence of acute social problems among these new Harlemites and for failing to create suitable Jewish cultural alternatives in Harlem for the immigrant civilization left behind on the Lower East Side. One critic pointedly accused communal leaders of being so intent on studying "ghetto conditions that they were apt to lose sight of that portion of the Jewish community which has emancipated itself therefrom and migrated to a more desireable part of Manhattan. We have regarded them as healthy minded, normal individuals who need no uplift." Another noted that although the ghetto had many physical problems, "the concentration of so many Jewish institutions in that quarter, kept alive a Jewish spirit and a Jewish feeling in that district. But uptown, the greater spread of Jewish inhabitants brings them in closer contact with outside influences, especially with the younger generation, and this has to be counterbalanced by really Jewish influences."[4]

Those surveying the local communal scene early in 1904 found few institutions then in existence specifically designed to meet this new challenge of fitting Judaism to America. Observers noted, at one extreme, institutions like the Russian American Hebrew Association, the

Chesterfield Club and the S.E.I. Club—organizations brought to Harlem by those well on the way to complete acculturation into American society—that promoted and extolled an almost totally uncritical acceptance of the virtues of Americanization. At the other extreme were dozens of small landsmanshaft synagogues and tiny cheders—second ghetto institutions—transplanted by the unacculturated segment of uptown Jewry, that continued to foster and to teach an old-world form of Judaism, oblivious to the impact Americanization was making on the immigrants and their children.

The Russian American Hebrew Association, which had been formed originally on the Lower East Side in 1890 by Dr. Adolf Radin, Rabbi of the People's Synagogue of the Educational Alliance, first appeared uptown in 1896. Dr. Radin, a native of Neustadt, Poland, was a product of both Eastern European erudition and Western European secular scholarship. He received his rabbinic training at the famous Volozin Yeshiva in Poland and his academic degree from the University of Berlin. A thoroughly "enlightened" East European Jew, Radin emigrated to the United States in 1884 and immediately began a career dedicated to "civilizing and Americanizing" his fellow immigrants.[5]

The People's Synagogue was the main vehicle for his efforts. He conducted traditional services there, using Hebrew, English and German as the languages of prayer and homiletic discourse. Yiddish, the native language of his prospective congregants, was disdained as a foreign cultural influence. The Russian American Hebrew Association was conceived as a logical adjunct to his synagogue. Its purpose was to provide "prominent Russian Americans" with the opportunity to hear lectures and to participate in public discussions and debates on a variety of contemporary issues and literary themes. All meetings were conducted in English.[6]

Radin's efforts met with only limited success on the Lower East Side. Most Russian immigrants were uncomfortable in, and suspicious of, any synagogue where Yiddish was not used. Furthermore, most of the topics debated at these meetings were outside the pale of immigrant interest.

In 1895, Radin, still active on the Lower East Side, moved uptown and became affiliated, on a limited basis, with a small German congregation, Tikvath Israel. A year later, he interested a group of his uptown congregants in joining with several newly arrived East European Jews in creating an uptown branch of the nearly defunct downtown

Association. In 1897, Harlem members heard a variety of speakers including such important Reform leaders as Rabbi Kaufmann Kohler of Temple Beth-El, Rabbi Rudolf Grossman of Temple Rodef Sholom, and Dr. David Neumark of Temple Israel. Each lecturer upheld the virtues of rapid acculturation, speaking on such pointed topics as "The Mission of the Russian Jew in America" and "The Influence of the Puritans in this Country."[7]

During the next few years, two other former Lower East Side organizations sympathetic to the goals of Radin's Association moved to Harlem. In 1901, the Chesterfield Club, a social organization composed of "a number of the most prominent residents of the Upper East Side" and numbering in its ranks some of the best-known businessmen in the section, moved its clubhouses from East Broadway to upper Madison Avenue. A year later, the S.E.I. Club of the University Settlement, a society formed by "a dozen lawyers, as many public school teachers, successful salesmen and young men in other business activities" decided to transfer its program of "debates declamations and readings" from the Lower East Side to Harlem.[8]

Although it may be unfair to accuse Dr. Radin and the others of being oblivious to the tide of disaffection from Judaism that was quickly surrounding them, it is certain that none showed the imagination to deal effectively with the problem on a large-scale basis. Even the Jewish Endeavor Society, created in 1901 specifically "to instill religious zeal and the love for Jewish learning" among the Jews of Harlem, failed to meet the religious educational needs of the Americanized uptown population. This society ambitiously sponsored classes in Bible for young adults and prevailed upon prominent uptown rabbis of both Reform and Conservative-Orthodox denominations to lecture to its members. The society received a measure of local support in its early years and attracted by March, 1902, a dues-paying membership of 350. But only forty students enrolled in the Bible courses.[9]

Harlem's many small landsmanshaft synagogues and cheders were similarly ill-quipped to inspire real allegiance to Judaism among the masses of uptown Jews. The perpetuators of the cheder educational system and the landsmanshaft religion that supported it—relics of the East European shtetl—were undoubtedly concerned with inculcating a love for Judaism among the American-born children of immigrants.

Still they were doomed to fail because of the old-world medium of their religious message.

The basic Jewish educational institution of the East European shtetl had been the cheder. In the cheder, the Jewish private elementary school, most Jewish boys received their first formal exposure to the Hebrew language and to biblical and rabbinic texts. The melamed, the poorly trained, poorly paid and poorly motivated cheder teacher, was also charged with providing the boys with the basic general educational skills—primarily arithmetic—to enable them to work, albeit on a limited basis, along with their gentile neighbors. Jewish girls were excluded from this system of primary Jewish education. They acquired the barest rudiments of general and religious education at home from their parents.

Those few cheder boys who showed the greatest intellectual promise and/or were the scions of the shtetl's most affluent families continued their education at the yeshiva. There, they were exposed to an intensive study of the Talmud and rabbinic texts. These schools provided the Jewish communities of Eastern Europe with their leading scholars and religious leaders.

The talmud torah was the community-run Jewish "public school" established to educate indigent children and orphans who could not afford to pay the nominal cheder tuition. The talmud torah curriculum included only the most elementary Hebrew and biblical studies. Since talmud torah students rarely, if ever, went on to the yeshiva, a greater educational emphasis was placed on preparing these students to move in the hostile gentile outside world. Talmud torah children learned the basics of the local languages and studied arithmetic in greater depth. Some talmud torahs even instructed their students in a usable trade or craft. Poor Jewish families strove mightily to avoid having to submit to the humiliation of having to send their sons to the charity-sponsored talmud torah.

Through the cheder, yeshiva and talmud torah, children of the East European shtetl were socialized into a traditional society; a society that placed the highest premium on religious learning and that showed only slight concern with integration with other ethnic and religious groups in general society.[10]

This type of Jewish educational system had little chance of surviving transplantation to America. Most Jewish immigrant parents wanted their children to learn American ways and become part of general society. They looked to the universal free system of public education as the most efficacious means of achieving that goal. The East-European cheders and yeshivas, which taught only Jewish values, were symbols of that past when Jews lived apart from general society. Most immigrants showed little enthusiasm for the perpetuation of such institutions in America.[11]

In stressing the value of public education for their children, many immigrant parents overlooked the fact that great Americanizing institutions were not designed for religious education. Their own religious commitment was expressed through a "landsmanshaft religion," a one-generation continuation of ritual practices based on nostalgia and the social element of synagogue life, institutionalized through the immigrant chevrah. A religion fashioned around small European-style synagogues was especially important to downtown Jews and to the unacculturated segment of uptown Jewry because it afforded the opportunity for immigrants to worship in their previously accustomed manner among Jews from their own old home town or village. The various social and religious activities offered by the chevrah provided the religious immigrant with the same measure of social stability in making the difficult adjustment to America afforded the secular or radical Jew by the Socialist debating or discussion social club.

Landsmanshaft religious organizations had far less appeal to those uptown Jews seeking to break with the immigrant past. Those acculturated Jews who still felt moved to attend services worshiped in the splendid sanctuaries of Congregations Ohab Zedek, Kehal Adath Jeshurun, and in other multinational congregations where old-world social and family ties were not strongly emphasized.*

The children of immigrants—even those of the most unacculturated newcomers—showed little real interest in the landsmanshaft religion

---

* Many newly affluent Jews living in the uptown second-settlement community attended new types of large "multinational" congregations established uptown instead of the small landsmanshaft chevrah congregations which were so much a part of ghetto Jewish life. Congregations Ohab Zedek and Kehal Adath Jeshurun were two of the largest and most famous multinational congregations composed of Jews from Central Harlem who had left downtown congregations at the same time and arrived uptown around 1905. The Harlem Ohab Zedek synagogue, which maintained close relations with the Lower East Side, was renowned for its famous Rabbi Philip Klein, a Yiddish-, German- and Hungarian-speaking rabbi famous for his talmudic erudition—who served both uptown and downtown congregations—and Rabbi Bernard Drachman, its English-

practiced by their parents. Though undoubtedly many were cap-
tivated by the stories of the old country, told before and during services, most of the ritual practices based on old-world traditions were
unintelligible to the American-born generation. They felt none of the
nostalgia for the European past. Their general education instructed
them to look forward and to adopt the totality of American ways and
values. Their Jewishness could not be expressed through their
parents' form of religion.[12]

   Those unacculturated parents concerned with this problem placed
the job of instilling a love for Judaism among their American-born
children in the unsteady hands of a fellow immigrant cheder melamed. These teachers operated their schools in their own homes or
rented lofts. One Harlem melamed used a real estate office as a
schoolroom. For a few cents a week, a Jewish child was taught a few
prayers by rote. The untrained functionaries who ran most cheders,
according to one critic, could not and did not understand their students. And as a result most children were "happy to close their Sid-
durs, glad to free themselves from the cheder and their foreign unin-
teresting teachers."[13]

   Most acculturated parents avoided the cheder educational system
completely. Some exposed their children to Sunday and Hebrew
School lessons conducted in the vestry rooms of their new uptown
congregations. Others hired private tutors. Many more regarded Jew-

speaking rabbi, one of the first American-born University-trained rabbis to find a pulpit
in Harlem and serve the needs of the district's upwardly mobile and American-born
Jewish population. For a full discussion of the emergence of an American-born traditional rabbinate in Harlem, see chapter 5.

   Ohab Zedek's most famous religious leader was, however, its cantor Joseph (Yossele) Rosenblatt. In fact, I have found, in questioning former Harlem residents about
"the grandeur of Jewish Lenox Avenue," that respondents invariably point to Cantor
Rosenblatt's high-salaried position and to the magnificent 116th Street synagogue as
symbolic of the affluence of Central Harlem Jews. See Samuel Rosenblatt, *Yossele
Rosenblatt: The Story of His Life as Told to His Son* (New York: Farrar, Strauss and
Young, 1954)

   Congregation Kehal Adath Jeshurun was famous in uptown circles both for the presence of such important new elite leaders as the Cohens on its board of directors and
for its almost decade-long struggle to control the destinies of both uptown and downtown synagogues. The conflict between congregational factions, which twice led to bitter court battles, was over the attempt of Cohen and his followers to liquidate downtown assets and apply them towards the construction of a large uptown synagogue. See
Congregation Kehal Adath Yeshurun M'Yassy v. *Universal Building and Construction
Co.*, New York State Supreme Court, Special Term, pt. 4, January 21, 1910. (Manuscript
copy of Justice J. O'Gorman's decision) and *David Cohen et al.* v. *Congregation Kehal
Adath Yeshurun M'Yassy*, New York State Supreme Court, pt. 4. April 13, 1911 (manuscript of Justice J. McCall's decision.)

ish religious education as a totally unnecessary encumbrance upon their children and provided them with no training whatsoever in their ancestral faith. Turn-of-the-century Jewish religious educational institutions inspired little commitment to Jewish ideals among those of the next generation.[14]

Recognizing the inadequacy of contemporary Harlem organizational efforts to halt disaffection from Judaism was a small, mixed German and East European contingent of communal activists. They dedicated themselves to and worked together for the establishment of communal institutions that reflected a new understanding— Americanization did not require an end to one's Jewishness. The Germans expressed their commitment to preserving and strengthening Jewish group cohesion primarily through the Harlem Federation. The East Europeans placed their faith in a modernized traditional Judaism, which they began to build through the American Talmud Torah.

The beginnings of the Harlem Federation may be traced directly to the horrified reaction of Harlem's German Jewish communal leaders to the newspaper revelations of late 1903. Stung by editorial censures that declared that conversionary efforts were being facilitated by the almost total absence of organized Jewish youth activities uptown, and shaken by a contemporary study of Harlem Jewish youth that estimated that in 1903 7,500 Jewish children were receiving no Jewish instruction whatsoever, making them a ready prey for Christian missionaries, leaders of Harlem's major German congregations met informally late that year at Temple Israel to draft plans for battle. Maurice Harris called upon all Harlemites to recognize the unpleasant truth of these reports, commenting that "there is a worse evil than permitting Jewish children to be converted to Christianity, that is to be taught no religion at all."[15]

Under Harris's personal leadership, local synagogues immediately began sponsoring Saturday afternoon services as a first step in reaching neighborhood youth. Plans were completed, at a subsequent mass meeting held late in January 1904, for the creation of the Hebrew Educational Union of Harlem, to bring a measure of religious training and identification to the estimated three-fourths of Harlem's children who were receiving no Jewish education whatsoever.[16]

The directors of the Hebrew Educational Union were drawn primarily from Harlem's major German congregations, but the Union also included representatives from such city-wide charitable organizations as the Council of Jewish Women and the United Hebrew Charities. East European leaders H. Kaminetsky, Zvi Masliansky and Zvi Malacovsky of the Uptown Talmud Torah also lent their support to the organization's activities. The treasurer of the Union was Mrs. Lillie Cowen, wife of the editor of the *American Hebrew*, which gave constant favorable publicity to the group's plans.[17]

During 1904, the Union succeeded in establishing weekly Saturday afternoon services and religious school classes on a rotating basis at five of the largest uptown synagogues. It may be assumed that the services and instruction conformed to most traditional dictates, as evidenced by the continued participation of the Orthodox congregation, Nachlath Zvi.[18]

These early antimissionary activities alerted German communal workers to a fundamental uptown social problem: the incompleteness of the immigrant's adjustment to American life. Union leaders perceived that the majority of uptown Jews, attempting to act, dress and speak like their gentile neighbors, were unable to find a place for Judaism in their new lives. This social pathology was felt most acutely among Jewish youths who, according to Union people, seemed to believe that the surrender of one's Jewishness, through either conversion or nonaffiliation, was part of the Americanization process. The Hebrew Educational Union decided that the only workable solution to this communal dilemma was the establishment of a large multifaceted Jewish settlement house which would do more than simply provide the linguistic tools and social skills necessary to enter American society and teach the principles of good American citizenship. It would also foster the "grand moral principles of our faith, principles of justice, principles of love, principles of righteousness, the underlying principles of Judaism." Daniel P. Hays, president of the Union, articulated the basic outlook of his group when he stated that "a good Jew is necessarily a good citizen." Defining Judaism in simple nondenominational terms as "the observance of certain moral and ethical rules," Hays argued that if the immigrant was taught to regulate "his private life upon the principles of Judaism he will be a good American citizen." The Harlem Federation, founded in April 1905, was dedicated both to acculturation and to the preservation of Jewish group identity.[19]

The Harlem Federation's leadership was drawn primarily from among those already active in the Hebrew Educational Union. Maurice Harris was elected president and Hays served as treasurer. Philip Cowen attempted, both through his newspaper and through private meetings with Harlem B'nai B'rith officials, to convince the uptown branches of this oldest German fraternal organization to take an active role in uptown communal work. Cowen, who was president of the Washington Irving Lodge, went so far as to call a conference of twelve major Harlem lodges in February 1905, to impress upon them the severity of uptown conditions and to gain their commitment to the proposed Federation. Although some lodges did agree to send representatives to the several open mass organizational meetings held later that month, none showed real enthusiasm for communal work. Cowen's valiant attempt to gain wide participation in German-Jewish communal work failed. Temple Israel and her sister congregations were left to continue to shoulder most of the responsibility for supporting their group's communal efforts.[20]

The uptown settlement did succeed, however, in attracting a leading member of the new Eastern European elite, Elias A. Cohen, to its board of directors. Cohen was well known in uptown philanthropic circles for his services to a variety of German and East European communal organizations. A member of East European Congregation Kehal Adath Jeshurun of Harlem, he also served as a director of the German Temple Ansche Chesed. He was a member of the Board of the Uptown Talmud Torah during the same time that he served the Harlem Federation. Cohen, a major link between East European and German groups of communal workers, was elected secretary of the Federation in 1905 and served as chairman of its building committee in 1913. A vocal supporter of this settlement movement, he defended the Federation against charges of inactivity made by the Jewish Defense League of Harlem in 1906. This ad hoc group charged that no serious attempt had yet been made by uptown organizations to combat "the pernicious activities of missionaries" in East Harlem. They called for the establishment of a "Jewish Center" uptown and pledged a nominal sum of fifty dollars towards the goal. Cohen rebutted the charge of inactivity, stating that from its two early centers, at East 100th Street and at Temple Israel headquarters at East 116th Street, Harlem Federation people were "actively working against missionaries."[21]

The Harlem Federation offered its members a wide range of social and educational activities, second in volume only to the downtown Educational Alliance. Its Educational Committee conducted lectures in Yiddish and English and established classes for teaching immigrants English language skills "whether to enable them to find employment and for entering the public schools." An employment service helped clients find work in a variety of areas. The Religion Committee conducted Hebrew classes and ran religious services on Saturdays and Holidays, while the Social Work Committee sponsored club and recreational work. A library was established containing both English and Yiddish books, magazines and newspapers. And a Civic Committee was created to "interest the people in good government, bring them to the knowledge of their rights and duties, awaken an intelligent interest in the community wherein they live and to encourage the assumption of citizenship by those who are not naturalized."[22]

The extensive use of Yiddish in many Federation activities indicated that the settlement house attempted to reach the unacculturated segment of Harlem Jewry as well as those wishing to become Americanized. Harris and his supporters never lost sight of the traditional, paternalistic German-Jewish goal of bringing the light of American ways and values to their unregenerated, newly arrived East European brethren still clinging to their alien immigrant way of life. However, in pursuing their objectives they showed far more sympathy and respect for the cultural baggage of their immigrant clients than did, for example, the founders of the Educational Alliance. The downtown settlement group, in its overwhelming zeal to Americanize recent immigrants, had, during its early years, deemed Yiddish a foreign cultural influence and had excluded it from all its cultural, social and educational activities. This approach alienated many adult East Siders who could never support an institution that disdained their native tongue. It was not until the turn of the century that the directors of the Educational Alliance, in trying to reach this mature segment of the downtown population, granted a grudging approval to the limited use of Yiddish in their institution.[23]

The uptown settlement house, from its inception, provided Yiddish and Hebrew books and periodicals in addition to the normal English fare. Harlem Federation people did not fear that the very use of Yiddish by the immigrant would retard his progress. On the contrary, they believed that Yiddish could be used effectively as a medium for teaching many basic American principles to those of the older generation who were slow to acquire English language skills. The Federation's heightened sensitivity to the recent immigrant's cultural heritage and personal feelings may be attributed both to the recognition by the directors of the problems encountered by downtown settlement groups and to the presence of at least one East European Jew on its original board of directors.

By 1910, the Harlem Federation had 1,100 children attending activities in its adjacent buildings at 105th Street between Second and Third Avenues. The library and recreational facilities were also made available to the neighboring non-Jewish population "justified," according to Federation officials, "by the wisdom of maintaining friendly relations with the considerable portion of Irish and Italian people living in the immediate district." The Federation also received a measure of city-wide recognition when Felix Warburg chose to join it, along with the Hebrew Educational Society of Brooklyn, Yorkville's Young Men's Hebrew Association, and the Educational Alliance, in forming a "deliberative body to devise systematized club work" for the entire New York community.[24]

The new East European elite expressed its dedication to meeting the challenge of combating the disaffection from Judaism among those spiritually removed from ghetto ways through the modern talmud torah. They placed their faith in modern American-style pedagogic methods as the medium for transmitting the eternal messages of the Jewish heritage. The major focus of their ambitious educational plans was the Uptown Talmud Torah; an institution which began as a small, neglected, poorly staffed cheder and which grew to become that district's foremost Jewish social and educational institution.

The Uptown Talmud Torah was founded in 1892 to serve the religious educational needs of the few Russian-Jewish children then living in the vicinity of 104th Street and Second Avenue. Its first principal was Rabbi Joseph Sossnitz, a Russian Jew who immigrated to the United States in 1891 and almost immediately opened a cheder in his own home. Several months later, Sossnitz's school was moved to nearby rented quarters where it was legally incorporated as the Uptown Talmud Torah.[25]

In the first year of its existence, the Uptown Torah received some financial assistance from Reform Jewish leaders Maurice Harris and Kaufmann Kohler of Temple Beth-El, who characterized this cheder as the uptown branch of the Hebrew Free School of East Broadway. Despite this early assistance, the talmud torah was constantly plagued with financial problems. Sossnitz and his successor, Rabbi Moses Reicherson, were frequently forced to commission private fund-raisers to solicit contributions from neighborhood people for their fledgling institution.[26]

The Uptown Talmud Torah was also slow to attract children to its program of Jewish study. By 1902, after a decade of existence, the Uptown Talmud Torah employed only four teachers to instruct less than 200 school children. Its poorly ventilated three-story school building with its inadequate sanitary facilities did little to attract students. Its poorly trained, Yiddish-speaking faculty, who taught only the "Aleph-Beis [alphabet], Siddur [Prayerbook] and a bit of Chumash [Penta-teuch]" was incapable of reaching and effectively influencing the younger American-born generation.[27]

The financial and educational problems of the early Uptown Talmud Torah undoubtedly compounded the frustrations that its second principal, Rabbi Moses Reicherson, experienced. A noted author and grammarian in Eastern Europe, Reicherson was identified by that contemporary observer of immigrant life Hutchins Hapgood as the typical "submerged scholar." Hapgood depicted him as a man who "no matter what his attainments and qualities" were was unknown and un-honored "amid the crowding and material interests of the new world . . . his moral capacity unrecognized by the people among whom he lived."[28]

Reicherson was born in Vilna in 1828, and was a student of the famous Russian-Jewish Maskil Yehudah Leib Gordon. While a teacher in his home town, Reicherson wrote eleven books on Hebrew grammar and literature. He was also credited with translating the works of the German playwright Gotthold Ephraim Lessing and the Russian folkwriter Krilow into Hebrew. He migrated to the United States in 1892 to be near his son and settled in Harlem. He soon realized that there were few employment opportunities available for Hebrew gram-marians in New York, but nevertheless he continued to write about Hebrew grammar for a Chicago-based periodical, Regeneration. He received no pay for these efforts, "the editor being as poor as him-self." His major means of support was his position at the Uptown Talmud Torah which paid him a salary of five dollars a week. When Reicherson died in 1903, one eulogist reflected with sorrow on the tragedy of this highly trained Hebraic scholar who died a "grammar melamed in the Uptown Talmud Torah." [29]

The fortunes of the talmud torah changed dramatically during the administration of Reicherson's successor, Zvi Malacovsky. Malacovsky, himself a Russian immigrant, was one of the first of his generation to recognize the inadequacy of the cheder and to offer a workable program for making Judaism attractive to American Jewish youth. Malacovsky argued that the Jewish religious community had not the money, the staff, nor the desire to create a Jewish parochial school system. Immigrant parents, he observed, were almost totally committed to the public school system and would not support any Jewish educational program that advocated separatism. A transplanted cheder system built along East-European lines was clearly doomed to failure.

Malacovsky also understood that for most Jewish youths, religious education was a noncompulsory, parttime pursuit, supplementary to their general education. For children to choose to study about their faith, a curriculum would have to be devised which would be entertaining as well as informative. He argued that although it was impossible to "make a Hebraist" out of each Jewish child, every talmud torah student could be taught to love his religion and to follow its precepts.

Malacovsky's theories on Jewish education found practical expression in the new, modern educational program of the Uptown Talmud Torah. He designed a three-level system for educating American-born students. Students with no prior Jewish education entered at the first level where they were taught "Jewish history, morals and the achievements of the Jewish people" while being introduced to the Hebrew alphabet. All instruction was, of course, conducted in English. Towards the end of the first level, students began to be exposed to "Hebrew words and phrases" and ultimately to basic religious concepts. The second level began by the faculty evaluating the performance and capacity of each student. The weaker students would continue to be taught "the dogmas of our religion" in English, with little emphasis placed on acquiring a fluency in Hebrew. The stronger students would be encouraged to acquire a greater proficiency in Hebrew. Religious classes were conducted completely in Hebrew, using the "Ivrith b'Ivrith" method.

The third stage would attract only the "5 percent" desirous of entering a seminary or rabbinical school. They would receive intensive preministry instruction, preparing them for a career as the leaders and teachers of the next generation of American Jews. Malacovsky wrote of this latter group: "It is worth for this five percent alone to open this new school system. They will be the pride of the Judaism of the future." Malacovsky perceived his system as realistic and economic, recognizing both the needs and the limited assets of his contemporary Jewish community.[30]

Malacovsky's modernization plans were actively supported by most members of the Talmud Torah Association, a committee headed by a real-estate man, Louis Wolf, which began raising funds for the school during Reicherson's last years. In February 1904, Wolf announced that the association had undertaken to solicit funds to acquire an adjoining house on 104th Street for the 250 students attending the newly reconstituted school. Malacovsky joined Wolf in appealing "to the rich Jews of Harlem" who were still supporting "downtown chevrahs" to remember the Talmudic dictum that "the needs of the poor of your city take precedence over those of any other place" and to transfer their allegiance and financial support to the Uptown Talmud Torah.[31]

While Wolf and his group were attempting to raise money for their new school building, a second group of East European uptown communal workers was planning to establish its own major Jewish center uptown. The Harlem Educational Institute was formed in October, 1904 with the goal of building up a social, educational institution "somewhat along the lines of the Educational Alliance" for their less-than-fully acculturated uptown brethren. David and Elias A. Cohen headed a league established to raise funds for the new organization.[32]

In February 1905, leaders of the Talmud Torah Association and the Educational Institute, recognizing that neither organization was succeeding in accumulating sufficient funds to begin its own separate building program, decided to pool their assets and merge their plans in a new Uptown Talmud Torah Association. The new organization would be both "the school where Judaism and Hebrew is taught" and "the center of social and educational endeavors" in Harlem. Such a merger would "give the talmud torah movement a new dignity and win it a larger measure of support from neighborhood people. The social activities of the educational institute would be conducted in frank recognition that work done for Jews shall be Jewish and . . . that the spirit of Judaism should pervade all the efforts and activities." In conducting its Americanization activities, the Harlem Educational Institute, like the Harlem Federation, would show greater sensitivity to the needs and habits of its constituency, a sensitivity deemed missing from older social service institutions. "Here," one editorialist wrote, "will be none of that 'non-sectarianism' that mars the value of our institutions."[33]

David Cohen was elected head of the new organization, which was composed of, according to a newspaper group biography, "leading representatives of the Jewish race in Harlem." Those who worked with Cohen were "men over 50 years of age who have been in this country 25–35 years and who from early youth trained to be intensely Orthodox, yet so thorough is their Americanization that they saw at once the possibility of a combination of the Hebrew school with the modern educational institute with all its accessories." In May 1905, the new Uptown Talmud Association purchased a plot of land at 111th Street and began soliciting funds for its uptown center.[34]

Buoyed by this new leadership, the Uptown Talmud Torah experienced dramatic growth over the next few years. The modern teaching methods employed by Malacovsky and his successor Ephraim Ish-Kishor succeeded, by the end of March 1908, in attracting some 700 students to an expanded program of classes and social activities. Ish-Kishor, former principal of London's Garden Street Talmud Torah and founder and grandmaster of the British Zionish Order of Ancient Maccabees, became principal in June 1907, when Malacovsky moved to Brooklyn. Ish-Kishor's Zionist orientation was quickly expressed through the founding of a Hebrew-speaking group, Hovevei Ivrith, and a Zionist youth group, Jehudia, in 1908. Under Ish-Kishor's leadership, the talmud torah became, over the next decade, the foremost uptown center for Zionist youth activities, housing some nine of fifteen branches of the Harlem Young Judea.[35]

The Talmud Torah Association, the financial arm of the institution, also grew stronger, speeding construction of the new uptown social and educational center. By March 1908 the Association could boast of a dues-paying membership of 1,300: 600 regular members, 400 in the Young Folks' League and 300 in a Ladies Auxiliary. The Association was also assisted, in February 1908, by Rev. H. P. Mendes of the midtown Spanish and Portuguese Synagogue and Yorkville's Rabbi Moses Zebulun Margolies who pledged their support for the plans. German philanthropist Jacob Schiff also expressed his commitment to the talmud torah's program by joining the Association's board of directors and by donating five thousand dollars to its building fund.[36]

In March 1908, the Uptown Talmud Torah initiated a plan for the standardization of curricula and materials used in New York's largest Hebrew Schools. Elias A. Cohen outlined the plans in a letter to fellow board member Louis Marshall. Cohen called for the establishment of a city-wide board consisting of representatives of East Broadway's Machzikei, Talmud Torah, the Brownsville and Bronx Talmud Torahs, the Hebrew school of Yorkville's Young Men's Hebrew Association as well as those of the Educational Alliance and the various orphan asylums. The board would establish common grades and a common curriculum and would collate common "Jewish-English" books which would be copyrighted and sold to Jewish communities throughout the United States. The income from such sales would be used to help support the proposed educational system. Such a system of grades, curriculum and books would make it possible for children moving from one part of the city to another to adjust quickly to a new Hebrew school. Cohen also proposed that the teaching staffs of these institutions be composed of Jewish Theological Seminary graduates, "into which the senior classes of the larger institutions will graduate." This plan gave practical city-wide application to Malacovsky's early plans and would in turn serve as one of the bases of the New York Kehillah's Bureau of Jewish Education standardization program, inaugurated two years later.[37]

Not all members of the Uptown Talmud Torah's board of directors shared Cohen's enthusiasm for modernization. Many of the older members—especially those who had been members of Louis Wolf's original Talmud Torah Association—were fearful that these younger East European members who constantly advocated further program and curriculum changes shared little of their dedication to strict Orthodoxy. They were wary of the presence of such German Reform Jews as Marshall and Schiff on the board of directors—they certainly could not be trusted to adhere to traditional dogmas. Rabbi Moses Zebulun Margolies's position on that same board did little to allay the fears of the older members. Those who opposed Cohen's modernization plans often voted as a unit, blocking efforts to expand association activities.[38]

This organized opposition was a constant frustration for Cohen. Once, after a particularly difficult and unsuccessful fight to gain approval for a plan to have each Harlem synagogue represented on the talmud torah's board, he angrily denounced those dissenting members as "reactionaries" who through their "blind, unreasoned prejudice based on 400 years of ghetto life" are never able to understand "that nobody had any designs whatever upon their beloved Orthodoxy."*

The simmering factional conflict within the Uptown Talmud Torah first attracted public attention in January 1910, when Jacob Schiff was asked by members of the board of directors to assume a ten thousand dollar second mortgage on the newly constructed Harlem Hebrew Institute building. Schiff acceded to their request and took over the mortgage for a period of ten years, free of interest, on the two conditions that the newly established Teachers' Institute of the Jewish Theological Seminary, which was then based at the Harlem Hebrew Institute building, be allowed to continue to occupy classroom space free of charge, and that, more importantly, "the methods of teaching at the Harlem school meet with the approval of a committee set up by the Teachers' Institute." Schiff demanded that the Uptown Talmud Torah receive annual certification in writing from the trustees of the Jewish Teachers' College Fund and the principal of the Teachers' Institute attesting that the highest educational standards were being maintained at the school. Schiff was quick to state that he had no quarrel with the Orthodox content of instruction but insisted that the methods of instruction "conform to approved modern methods and ideas of pedagogy and hygiene and maintain at all times in your building, activities looking to the Americanization of our Jewish youth."[39]

Schiff's certification demand was rejected by the majority of board members. They feared that such a formal agreement would constitute the first step in "the subordination" of the Uptown Talmud Torah to the Schiff-financed Conservative Teachers' Institute. They also felt that such an annual report would be a personal source of humiliation to the school's leadership. The board communicated its thanks to Schiff for his generous financial offer but clearly indicated the unacceptability of the certification condition.[40]

It remained for a select three-man committee composed of Harry

---

* There were at this time thirty-five members of the board of directors. Again due to the absence of Uptown Talmud Torah papers we are unable to determine how members were appointed or elected and which members voted for and against modernization efforts. My impression from reading Cohen's brief description of his opponents is that they, like himself, were drawn from the at least moderately affluent segment of uptown society. I do not think it was simply a case of the affluent voting for modernization efforts and the poor objecting to them.

Fischel, Louis Marshall and Max Podell, secretary of the Uptown Talmud Torah, to arrange a compromise between Schiff and those fearful of his influence. After several meetings with board members and the personal intercession of Marshall with his friend and fellow communal worker, Schiff decided to modify the certification condition. It was agreed that it would not be necessary for the talmud torah to submit to a demeaning yearly examination. Instead, it was proposed that the Teachers' Institute be permitted "from time to time, not more frequently than once a year" to study the school's teaching methods. If the Teachers' Institute found any deficiencies in the school's educational policies, the school would be granted a six-month period to make any recommended changes. This compromise partially allayed the board members' fears of outside domination while granting to Schiff his desired institutional commitment to maintaining the highest standards of pedagogy at the Uptown Talmud Torah.[41]

With its financial security assured by this compromise, the Uptown Talmud Torah experienced over the next few years further growth. By 1911, the school was running thirty-eight different classes for boys and four classes for girls. It was estimated that 8,000 neighborhood people regularly used the institution's social, cultural and athletic facilities. In 1912, the number of boy's classes rose to forty-eight, servicing 1,707 children. That year also saw the organization of a children's congregation and the inauguration of a breakfast program for poor neighborhood children. The Hebrew Institute received an additional financial boost from Schiff in 1913, when the philanthropist donated twenty-five thousand dollars earmarked for new classrooms and administrative offices.[42]

The only noteworthy event dampening the spirits of those who controlled the institution was the death in 1911 of their president and early leader, David Cohen. His position was more than adequately filled by the well-known Jewish builder and philanthropist, Harry Fischel, who like the Cohens was a leading member of that newly affluent and Americanized group of East European communal activists who had made their fortunes in New York's real estate industry. Fischel, according to his sympathetic biographer and son-in-law Rabbi Herbert S. Goldstein, arrived from Russia in 1885 "practically penniless, and at times faced starvation because of his refusal to desecrate the Jewish Sabbath." Armed with an abiding faith in God, Fischel quickly overcame his difficulties to become a leading New York businessman and Jewish communal figure. Goldstein characterized his father-in-law as "the East European Jacob Schiff."[43]

Fischel was indeed renowned for his participation in a variety of both German- and East European-run institutions. As a board member of the German Hebrew Orphan Asylum and the Hebrew Sheltering and Guardian Society, he was instrumental in convincing these institutions to begin observing Jewish dietary laws. He served the downtown Machzike Talmud Torah and was one of the principal founders of the Yeshiva Rabbi Itzhak Elchanan. His major contribution to the Uptown Talmud Torah was its financing in 1913 of a "rich man's Annex" at 115th Street and Lenox Avenue.[44]

It was Fischel's perception that Jewish communal workers, in their zeal to serve the readily apparent needs of the poor and semiacculturated of the community, had overlooked the spiritual needs of the most affluent and Americanized segment of Harlem Jewry, the rich Jews of Lenox Avenue. He believed that not enough effort had been given to convince the rich "balabatim" of the value of a talmud torah education for their children. Other observers joined with Fischel in noting the hypocrisy of those Jewish educational activists who were so concerned with the future of Judaism among the poor but were "negligent when it comes to their own children's Jewish education." They permitted their children to become, in the words of one contemporary, "respectable ignoramuses."[45]

Fischel outlined his plan for a "rich-man's Annex" in an open letter to Harlem Jews in October 1913. "This building," Fischel announced, "was built for the purpose of filling a long-felt want for a school to give proper Jewish instruction along the most modern lines to the children of the so-called 'balabatim'—that is men whom God has given sufficient means to pay for the instruction of his children. We have selected this site on 115th Street, near Lenox Avenue, because it is centrally located and within reach of all between 110th and 125th Streets and because we know that the residents of this section are well able to pay this small sum for the instruction of their children." Fischel saw the importance of a "high" $3 per month per student tuition fee as a means of attracting those individuals who would object to sending their children to a "charity school." Under his initiative a Jewish private school was established in the heart of Central Harlem.[46]

Fischel's administration also saw the Uptown Talmud Torah establish and maintain close connections with Kehillah's Bureau of Jewish Education. This agency, created in October 1909, was given a mandate to improve and standardize the pedagogic methods used in all of New York's Jewish schools. The forward-looking members of the talmud torah board who had worked long and hard for educational reforms in their own school welcomed the Bureau's city-wide initiatives. The Uptown Talmud Torah was one of the first schools to affiliate with the Bureau, agreeing to pay the minimum salary rates to duly licensed teachers and receiving in return financial help from the Bureau. Fischel himself convened a meeting in his own home of the presidents of the five largest talmud torahs in Manhattan in October 1911, to convince them to commit their institutions to the new Bureau. He succeeded in allaying the fears of the more conservative representatives who were concerned that the new curriculum proposals "might conflict with Orthodox Jewish belief." He convinced them to modify their demand that each affiliated school be given veto power over all curriculum changes. They supported Fischel's proposal that only a two-thirds majority was needed for any reform to become operative. Fischel and his Harlem followers committed their institution further to the Bureau of Jewish Education by allowing for the establishment of preparatory girls classes, offering American Jewish women for really the first time a systemized religious education, and extension classes, to serve the needs of those children and young adults who for a variety of reasons were unable to attend regular talmud torah classes. The Bureau seemed to be the fulfillment of Elias A. Cohen's 1908 dream of a unified and standardized "parochial system."[47]

Although Fischel was successful in allaying the fears of the leaders of the five largest talmud torahs in Manhattan, he was soon to find out that members of his own board had greater reservations against the Kehillah's educational agency. Once again, those who saw themselves as the guardians of strict Orthodox Jewish tradition were outspoken against the imposition of questionable modern educational techniques in their school. They did not share the new elite's belief that the old-world shell of Orthodox religious educational practices could be removed without endangering the essence and the future of traditional faith. Born and raised in a foreign environment, these board members could never be convinced of the propriety of American educational methods. They were outraged, for example, by Fischel's decision to permit the placing of a piano in the children's synagogue and the showing of motion pictures in a religious institution. One dissenting member took independent action against the "modernizers" by ripping out the wires on a newly purchased slide machine, earmarked for use in teaching Bible stories to children. Such an activity, in this unidentified individual's view, violated the Second Commandment of creating "no graven images."[48]

More moderate dissenters also protested what they saw as "the autocratic methods" used by Fischel in connecting the school with the Bureau of Jewish Education. Fischel was pointedly accused of turning over control of the Harlem institution to his Kehillah friends. These dissenters and their supporters claimed that the Bureau of Jewish Education had abandoned its announced program of establishing model experimental schools and was intent on fostering "experimental methods" in existing schools. The Bureau's leadership was accused of being tyrannical and of having on its side the power of monied philanthropists who had little conception of the real needs of the community. The opposition called for the end of Kehillah control over neighborhood schools, leaving "the people of moderate means to work out their own solutions, to blunder and look for remedies in their own way."[49]

This controversy over community control of Jewish education peaked in February 1914 when Fischel asked for a vote of confidence from his board. When he failed to receive overwhelming support, Fischel resigned his post in dramatic fashion at the annual public meeting of the Uptown Talmud Torah.[50]

Appeal's from supporters like Schiff, board member Otto Rosalsky and Judah Magnes, Chairman of the Kehillah, failed to change Fischel's mind. He communicated his frustrations in a letter to Schiff written a week after his resignation. He offered no apologies for the necessary use of a strong hand in leading the board when he wrote that "were it not for these autocratic methods, which I was compelled to use, it would have been impossible to connect our institution with the Bureau of Jewish Education and to accrue the benefits of their advice and cooperation and to accomplish so much for the thousands of children who have derived the advantages of a Jewish education."

He charged that his opponents were "of the old-fashioned" type who believed that the only way to give children a Jewish education, is by teaching them in the same way as they were taught twenty-five years ago in Russia. And it is the same men who have always held back the progress of the institution at all times. It was only by means of these 'autocratic methods' that I was able to take the institution out of chaos, and transform it to an up-to-date Talmud Torah run along the most modern and efficient system."[51]

Fischel was replaced as president of the Uptown Talmud Torah by Henry Glass who also served as president of Congregation Ohab Zedek; a man undoubtedly more acceptable to the dissension-ridden board. Fischel remained active at the school, continuing as a member of its board of directors.[52]

Rabbi Schmarya Leib Hurwitz, founder and principal of the Rabbi Israel Salanter Talmud Torah, shared Fischel's dedication to the harmonization of Judaism with American ways and experienced similar opposition in trying to institute modern pedagogic practices in his uptown school from those who feared that practical innovations threatened the continuity of Judaism. Rabbi Hurwitz migrated to the United States in 1906 and almost immediately earned a considerable reputation within the ghetto as an able preacher, often attracting packed audiences to his Sabbath and Holiday services. In 1908, Hurwitz left the Lower East Side to assume an uptown pulpit at Harlem's Congregation B'nai Israel Salanter Anshe Sameth, having been recruited by real estate operator Joseph Smolensky, the president of the congregation, who offered him a lucrative contract, thus securing Hurwitz's financial future and sparing him, according to one account, "from the poverty which most Rabbis find themselves in."[53]

Soon after arriving in Harlem Rabbi Hurwitz became aware of the problems of uptown Jewish education. He noted that those children living along the outer ridge of the major Harlem Jewish concentration, north of 118th Street, were not being adequately serviced by institutions like the Uptown Talmud Torah which was located in the heart of the uptown settlement. He saw thousands of Jewish children growing up without the benefit of a Jewish education and felt there was a critical need for a neighborhood talmud torah in the vicinity of East 118th Street.[54]

Rabbi Hurwitz communicated his findings to his patron Smolensky, who agreed to help him establish a talmud torah under the congregation's auspices. Together, they prevailed upon the congregational board of directors to allocate temporary classroom space within the synagogue building and in December 1909, the Rabbi Israel Salanter Talmud Torah opened its doors to uptown children.[55]

By 1910, some 350 children were attending twelve different, separate boys' and girls' classes in their own newly renovated school building adjacent to the synagogue. There they were exposed to a curriculum closely resembling that of the Uptown Talmud Torah. Ivrith b'Ivrith language system was used to teach everything from the basic alphabet to the most advanced Talmudic studies. Rabbi Hurwitz also organized a children's congregation at the synagogue to supplement the students' regular classroom training. But Rabbi Hurwitz also recognized the need of a standardized curriculum for New York's constantly moving Jewish school age population. He often characterized New York Jewry's residential mobility as a "plague" against Jewish education. "You begin with a child," he complained, "and when he is about to go to a new higher subject, he is gone elsewhere." He understood that a set uniform city-wide curriculum would ensure the continuity of Jewish education. Under Rabbi Hurwitz's guidance, Salanter Talmud Torah became one of the early members of the Bureau of Jewish Education. Rabbi Hurwitz supported the Bureau's "model school" program and permitted the establishment of a boy's preparatory junior high school on his school's premises.[56]

Rabbi Hurwitz's advocacy of modern pedagogic methods and his support of the Kehillah's educational system brought him into conflict with the more conservative members of his congregation who feared the Bureau's "reformist" tendencies. He was stung by criticism of his plans and programs which he perceived as "strictly Orthodox." Realizing that the "present synagogue had the wrong atmosphere" for modern Jewish education, Rabbi Hurwitz severed his ties with the Congregation B'nai Rabbi Israel Salanter Anshe Sameth in 1911, but he did retain his close connection with Joseph Smolensky, who agreed to assume the financial burdens of the new independent institution. With its monetary base secured, the talmud torah continued to grow. By 1915, the school enrolled more than 800 boys and girls in thirty-two different classes.[57]

Those Harlem Jewish parents who viewed the modern talmud torah movement as a threat to the continuity of traditional Jewish religious practices had, after 1907, the option of sending their children to one of the two local all-day Jewish schools, the Yeshiva Toras Hayim or the Harlem Yeshiva (also known as the Talmudical Institute of Harlem).

The first attempt at establishing a yeshiva uptown was undertaken in 1907 by members of two local congregations, Beth Hamidrash Ha-Gadol of Harlem and Beth Knesset of Harlem, who organized and operated Yeshiva Rabbi Elijah Gaon M'Vilna out of a public hall on Madison Avenue. They hired Rabbi Moses Sterman of Suviak, Russia as Rosh Yeshivah (Dean) and gave him a mandate to create a school on the European model, which would show that "American boys can learn Gemara as well as European boys."[58]

Rabbi Sterman's mandate was quickly called into question in 1908, when an insurgent religiously liberal group of financial backers attempted to gain control of the school. They wanted instruction to be conducted in English and insisted that girls be granted admission to the Yeshiva. Classes in Talmud, the keystone of the European Yeshiva educational system, were to be kept only "for appearance's sake." Much greater emphasis was to be placed on biblical, Hebraic, and general studies. These proposed modifications were totally unacceptable to the original founders of the Yeshiva, who subsequently split with the insurgents and reestablished their "European" Yeshiva, Yeshiva Toras Hayim.[59]

For the first three years of its existence, Yeshiva Toras Hayim held its classes at Beth Hamidrash Ha-Gadol of Harlem. The tone of education offered at the school is best illustrated by an advertisement for instructional personnel that appeared in the local Yiddish newspaper specifying that teachers "must be able to teach a blat [page] of Gemara [talmud] and keep order in the classroom." In 1912, now boasting of more than 400 students, Yeshiva Toras Hayim built its own educational center at 103rd Street and Lexington Avenue. The yeshiva received financial assistance from the Beth Hamidrash Ha-Gadol and from a small chevrah congregation, the Bressler Synagogue, established and run by Rabbi Noah Zeev Bressler, who was also Dean of the new yeshiva.[60]

The liberal wing of the Yeshiva Elijah Gaon M'Vilna reconstituted itself as the Harlem Yeshiva. Dropping the demand that girls be included in the school, backers joined with leading uptown figures like Rabbis Bernard Drachman of Ohab Zedek and H. Kaminetsky of Uptown Talmud Torah in creating a school where children "learned Jewish and English subjects together."[61]

The founders of the Harlem Yeshiva did not share the prevailing view within Jewish educational circles that the public schools and the talmud torahs could successfully coexist. They argued that the "after-public school" nature of the talmud torah, with all its modern pedagogic methods, could never "go beyond teaching the fundamentals of Judaism." They believed that the next generation of Jewish teachers and leaders could arise only from among those exposed to an intensive yeshiva education.[62]

These educational leaders did not, however, advocate a policy of total Jewish separatism similar to that of the old European yeshiva or the local Yeshiva Toras Hayim. They understood that this next generation of leaders would have to be rooted in American values as well as Jewish tradition. The Harlem Yeshiva's curriculum reflected this appreciation of the impact America had made upon their community. Half a day was spent studying traditional texts and the other half was devoted to general studies. An hour of physical training was also instituted as part of the daily program. Dr. Alexander Brody, a local Jewish public school principal, was hired to run the yeshiva's general studies program. His religious counterpart was Rabbi Moses Sterman, who apparently followed the liberal wing of the old Yeshiva Gaon M'Vilna in coming over to the Harlem Yeshiva. This institution, along with its sister schools, Rabbi Jacob Joseph Yeshiva of Henry Street, Yeshiva Rabbi Chaim Berlin of Brownsville and Yeshiva Torah Vo-Daat of Williamsburg, were the forerunners of the contemporary modern yeshiva-Jewish day school movement.[63]

The conflicts between Harlem's new elite East European leadership and some of the people whom they hoped to serve—so dramatically seen in Fischel's resignation from the Uptown Talmud Torah, in Hurwitz's disputes with his immigrant congregation, and in the splits within the Yeshiva Elijah Gaon M'Vilna—signify the one major area where the histories of uptown's two basically separate subcommunities intersect. It is here that the ultra-Orthodox segment of the second ghetto community fought those who argued that a Jewish identity based on old-world values and institutions had little chance of surviving the Americanization process. Even more significantly, it is here out of this and other local disputes that the divisions within contemporary Orthodoxy were to a great extent first crystallized. Harlem's new elite supported the idea that American educational methods can and must be applied to traditional studies. They recognized the impact American conditions of freedom and opportunity had made upon the Jew and sought means to perpetuate what they saw as the essence of traditional Judaism. This American Orthodox point of view ultimately found its most profound expression in institutions like Yeshiva University. And it is not at all coincidental that David Cohen and Harry Fischel—the foremost spokesmen for the new elite—were intimately involved with the founding of this standard-bearer of contemporary American Orthodoxy.

The other, European-style Orthodox position—most clearly identified institutionally in the Harlem experience by Yeshivas Toras Hayim—also survived but with a most limited constituency. The point of view that the faith of the fathers need not change to accommodate America was later articulated by those who opposed the founding of Yeshiva University. It finds contemporary expression—with only the slightest modifications—among certain separatistic Hasidic groups and among the students and teachers of a number of geographically and culturally isolated centers of advanced torah study. Thus the Harlem Jewish experience, that demonstrates that European ideas and institutions can survive the crucial first transplantation out of the ghetto, challenges us to determine whether and how old-world values have persisted—if only among ultra-Orthodox groups—for several generations and through subsequent Jewish resettlements.[64]

chapter 5

Harlem Jewry and the Emergence of the American Synagogue

During the 1920s and 1930s a new form of Jewish communal life was fashioned by second-generation American Jews residing in newly constructed outer-city neighborhoods. Living on the outskirts of immigrant centers, these Jews had no need for ghetto "self-improvement" institutions; they had, after all, acquired far more than the basic rudiments of Americanization. The native-born, public school educated, Americanized Jew had outgrown those communal institutions specifically dedicated to hastening his entrance into American society.

These second-generation Jews had not, however, outgrown, at least in the view of concerned Jewish leaders and lay people, their need for those immigrant-directed institutions that forcefully emphasized that one could achieve complete Americanization without surrendering one's Jewishness. In fact, they needed these institutions more than ever. The old fears that Americanized Jews would perceive Jewish tradition as totally inconsistent with American values seemed all too real to a new generation of communal leaders struggling with the dilemmas of assimilation and intermarriage. Their present apprehensions were specifically predicated upon their unhappy perception that many of their fellow Jews, having internalized the values and goals of their native land, stood ready to discard their ancestral religious identity as a foreign cultural influence standing in the way of full assimilation. They also recognized that many Jews, seeing no cultural difference between themselves and other Americans, and un-challenged in many areas by anti-Semitism, felt no compelling reason to restrict their social and marital contacts.

In counterattacking the forces of communal disintegration, subur-ban Jewish leaders realized that institutions that emphasized that complete Americanization did not equal loss of Judaism, would have to play the key role in perpetuating Jewish identity. But this crucial concept would have to be more fully developed and the base of its appeal broadened, if ethnic cohesion were to withstand assimilation. Communal leaders recognized that such efforts as the modern talmud torah movement, which had begun the job of harmonizing Judaism with Americanization, were inadequate because they reached only limited numbers of one segment of Jewish society. New forms of Jew-ish communal life would have to be developed if the challenge of communal reorganization was to be effectively met.[1]

The major bulwark against assimilation and intermarriage created by concerned Jews in these new neighborhoods was the Jewish center-synagogue. Inspired by the teachings of Jewish thinkers such as Mordecai Kaplan, these Jews looked to their reorganized syna-gogues as the key to the perpetuation of Judaism in America. They learned from Kaplan that the modern synagogue could continue to be more than just a home for worship and sacred study. It could and should be a social agency providing its members with a feeling of eth-nic togetherness. Ancillary recreational activities—new to the age-old history of the synagogue—could, according to Kaplan's philosophy, "rally all the Jews in the neighborhood whether they were religious or irreligious." It was hoped that once within the confines of the syna-gogue, individuals' social interests would broaden to include spiritual matters. Most important, the Jewish center would provide the young people of the community with a Jewish context for their own social gatherings. These modern synagogues sponsored youth groups, so-cial clubs, dances, athletic events and other attractive synagogue ac-tivities that brought Jewish young adults together. The Jewish center-synagogue represented the most profound attempt to present Jewish traditions within an American cultural context.[2]

The Jewish center concept that flourished during the 1920s and 1930s was first adumbrated almost a generation earlier among for-ward-looking Jewish leaders working both in Harlem and to a lesser extent on the Lower East Side. Men like Henry Morais and Jacob

Dolgenas of Harlem's Congregation Mikveh Israel and downtown communal workers like Albert Lucas and the founders of the Young Israel synagogue all sought ways of making synagogue life more attractive and responsive to the children of immigrants who felt uncomfortable in their parents' synagogue. As early as 1905, they sponsored youth synagogues and advocated the acceptance of certain subtle changes in the traditional approach to religious services in the hope of making Judaism more palatable to those unable or unwilling to relate to the old forms of synagogue life.

Although most of these early youth synagogues did not survive longer than a few years, they served as models for several of Harlem's largest German and East European congregations. By 1910, these congregations had quietly reformed themselves by adopting means similar to those used in the youth synagogues to attract young people to their services. In implementing changes in synagogue life, uptown congregations looked to graduates of the Jewish Theological Seminary for spiritual leadership. The election of young American-born traditional rabbis, committed to reaching their acculturated coreligionists, to prestigious German and East European pulpits marked a significant milestone in the establishment of the Conservative movement as a major force in an emerging American Jewish community.

Foreshadowing later Jewish center activities in the social sphere were the founders of the Harlem Young Men's Orthodox League, Harlem Hebrew League and the Harlem YMHA. They sought to help that segment of Jewish society which had become, in Kaplan's own terms, "sufficiently Americanized by the middle of the first decade of the century to look for something other than Americanization." These leaders sponsored the development of a variety of social and cultural activities within their institutions which were also directed at strengthening the religious identity of those becoming estranged from Judaism.[3]

The greatest effort in both these areas was Herbert S. Goldstein's Institutional Synagogue, established in Harlem in 1917. Rabbi Goldstein, a contemporary and colleague of Kaplan, applied many of the Jewish center concepts in an effort to reach a disaffected segment of uptown youth. For Goldstein, like Kaplan, the synagogue was the center of Jewish communal life; his dream was to integrate the sanctuary, study and social halls and gymnasium within an Orthodox Jewish atmosphere attractive to an American constituency. Goldstein's early efforts acted as an ideal experimental laboratory for the Jewish center concepts that blossomed during the next generation. Harlem was, thus, not only hospitable to efforts to maintain and strengthen Jewish identification among immigrants and their children, but was also the place where the instrumentality for preserving Jewish group cohesion among future generations was first fashioned.

The earliest adumbrations of the Jewish center movement date back to the turn of the century and to a group of Harlem synagogues expressedly constituted to serve the needs of American-born Jewish young adults. The first, Beth Ha-Knesset Ha-Gadol, was organized in December 1896 by fifty men, all of whom, according to newspaper reports, were thirty-seven or younger, who had been born in New York City and had recently migrated from the Lower East Side. They held their first meeting at the Harlem Lyceum (107th Street and Third Avenue), soon purchasing a church at the corner of 109th Street and Madison Avenue, which they converted to a synagogue.[4]

Six years later, responding to what was perceived to be a need for a "large well constructed Orthodox synagogue," Rabbi H. P. Mendes of the Spanish and Portuguese Synagogue and Rabbi Bernard Drachman of Congregation Zichron Ephraim joined with local Harlemites in establishing Congregation Shomre Emunah at 121st Street and Madison Avenue. The organizers of this synagogue promised services conducted according to "Orthodox ritual in an impressive decorous manner." They pledged to their prospective Americanized constituency that the unsightly noise, commotion and blatant commercialism that attended the immigrant landsmanshaft congregation would find no place in the up-to-date Orthodox synagogue. In 1904 a second modern congregation, Congregation Mount Sinai, was established in Central Harlem at 118th Street and Lenox Avenue. This congregation was organized along lines similar to the German Conservative-Orthodox synagogues of the late nineteenth century, offering to its members Orthodox ritual, mixed seating and a weekly "sermon in the vernacular." These two congregations hoped to attract acculturated, English-speaking East European Jews who wanted to retain a modified traditional form of prayer, while eliminating some of the obvious immigrant trappings of worship.[5]

The first Harlem congregation specifically organized to attract what its leadership called "the rising generation in Israel" was Congregation Mikveh Israel, founded in 1905. This synagogue offered uptown young people decorous Orthodox Sabbath and Holiday services conducted by two English-speaking, University-trained ministers. Both Henry S. Morais and his assistant, Jacob Dolgenas, emphasized the importance of active congregational participation in the prayers and encouraged congregational singing. Recognizing that many young people were uncomfortable in synagogues where cantors droned on in solo recitations of the prayers, Morais instructed his cantor to be a true "servant of the community" by singing simple melodious prayers which could be easily followed by worshipers. Lay people were encouraged to join in singing the prayers, thereby making traditional forms of prayers more meaningful for all those drawn into the synagogue. Congregational singing also helped synagogue leaders to maintain decorum during services; lay people actively participating in the services had little time for idle gossip.[6]

Congregation Mikveh Israel was also ahead of its time in the admission of two women to its original twelve-member congregational board of directors. Most congregations barred women from synagogue office, relegating them to the leadership of a women's auxiliary or sisterhood. Although services were conducted according to Orthodox ritual, which precluded females from leadership in prayer, Mikveh Israel's women had an important voice in all other synagogue affairs. Contemporary observers applauded Morais' efforts both here and as head of the Young Folks' League of the Uptown Talmud Torah. One writer declared him to be the "only Rabbi in Harlem who stands for principle" and his young supporters to be "Harlem's only hope for the future."[7]

Despite this enthusiastic endorsement, Morais and his followers failed in their ambitious undertaking. Morais' synagogue, like all of these early youth-oriented congregations, was plagued by persistent financial woes arising from having overestimated the numerical and economic strength of that "rising generation of Israel" which it hoped to influence. The majority of Harlem's second-generation Jews had yet to reach young adulthood, leaving Morais' group with a constituency too narrow from which to draw financial support. Congregation Mikveh Israel was consequently never able to raise sufficient funds to move out of rented quarters. Congregation Shomre Emunah likewise saw its dream of erecting a synagogue shattered when a temporary financial recession in 1908 caused its few financial supporters to withdraw their promised monetary assistance from the institution. The uptown youth-synagogue movement first appeared in Harlem about half a generation too early. None of these early forward-looking congregations lasted more than a very few years.[8]

Several of the community's largest congregations more effectively serviced the spiritual needs of Harlem's small but ever-expanding group of American-born young. By 1910, at least four Harlem congregations had appointed American-born, university-educated and Jewish Theological Seminary-trained rabbis to uptown pulpits and charged them with inspiring the new generation. These young rabbis served either as associates of or as replacements for incumbent German or Yiddish speaking rabbis. Jacob Kohn became rabbi of Congregation Ansche Chesed in May 1910, replacing German-born Gustav Hausman who was dismissed for "not possessing the spiritual uplift which a spiritual leader and religious teacher must have" to lead his laity successfully. The new dynamic rabbi soon inspired "a new religious awakening" in the synagogue. He popularized the study of Hebrew by children and adults alike. Kohn's classmate, Benjamin A. Tintner, son of Moritz Tintner, one of Harlem's earliest German reform rabbis, became rabbi of neighboring Temple Mount Zion in 1911. Tintner came to this prestigious uptown pulpit after a three-year tenure as assistant rabbi of the West Side Congregation B'nai Jeshurun. His appointment sparked an immediate upsurge in synagogue membership as many of Tintner's former young West Side congregants followed their spiritual leader and began attending services in Harlem. Bernard Drachman attracted a similar youthful following when he became English-speaking rabbi of uptown Congregation Ohab Zedek in 1909. Drachman worked in close partnership with Rabbi Philip Klein, whose own sermons were most meaningful to the less-Americanized segment of the congregation.[9]

Congregation Anshe Emeth of West Harlem hired on a part-time basis an English-speaking graduate of the Jewish Theological Seminary, Rabbi Julius J. Price. He was given the primary responsibility of preaching to the American-born children of immigrants on the High Holidays, when these young people would be most likely to join their parents in attending services. These several well-conceived personnel moves, which were designed primarily to attract children of immigrants to services, undoubtedly also helped these congregations retain the continued allegiance of their Americanized immigrant members to synagogue life.[10]

The opportunities to minister to the spiritual needs of American-Jewish young adults marked a turning point in the fortunes of the American-born, Conservative-Orthodox rabbi. Earlier, few Jews residing in America identified with the spiritual messages preached by native-born, English-speaking traditional rabbis. Most German Jews had supported the Reform rabbinate which was certainly American and English-speaking but decidedly not traditional. Their late-arriving German immigrant brethren of both the traditional and reform persuasions preferred their own imported European-born spiritual leadership. Immigrant East European Jews were similarly content with their own "landsmanshaft synagogue" Orthodoxy and were suspicious of an "Orthodoxy" preached by clean-shaven, university-educated American rabbis. They looked to their transplanted East European rabbinic leadership to serve their religious needs. American Conservative-Orthodox rabbis of the late nineteenth and early twentieth century found that they had almost no one to preach to. One such rabbi recalled his frustrations when "it seemed for a time that I had mistaken my vocation, that there was no room, no demand in America for an American-born, English-speaking rabbi who insisted on maintaining the laws and usages of traditional Judaism. . . . There were considerable groups of East European, Polish, and Russian Jews in the East Side or Ghetto districts of the great cities, who adhered to the Orthodox traditions of their native lands, but they were Yiddish-speaking and wanted rabbis of that type. They were strange to me and I was stranger to them."[11] The creation of several pulpit positions for American-born traditional rabbis in Harlem promised a more rewarding future for graduates of America's traditional religious seminaries.

The adoption by both German and East European congregations of almost identical policies in attempting to reach a similar Americanized constituency also foreshadowed future American Jewish communal structure. The acceptance of Seminary rabbis in synagogues ranging from the strictly East European Orthodox Ohab Zedek to the formerly staunchly German Reform Temple Mount Zion indicated that, at least in Harlem, forward-looking representatives of all Jewish denominations recognized the need to readjust Judaism to the impact of Americanization. Congregation Ohab Zedek's leaders understood, for example, that a homiletic discourse delivered in the vernacular German or Yiddish had no greater intrinsic holiness than one spoken in English and Temple Mount Zion's people recognized that nineteenth-century Radical Reform principles might be too extreme for formerly Orthodox children of immigrants who desired membership in an American synagogue but who were repulsed by the totally nontraditional forms of Reform worship. And although each denomination would remain, to a great extent, theologically separated, they would be, from this point on, similarly engaged in the fight to construct new, enduring forms of Jewish life acceptable to a native-born Jewry.

These early efforts on behalf of Americanized Jewish young adults reached, however, only that limited segment of the next generation which was still more or less committed to religious life. None of these synagogues ever considered Jewish "missionary" work programs to reach those totally alienated from all forms of Jewish life. And as the numbers of American Jews began to grow during the second decade of the twentieth century, there were thousands of Harlem Jewish young people, whom the talmud torahs were never able to reach or failed to influence, who were growing up with no attachment to Judaism. One contemporary Christian student of American Jewish life described these young people as "the ones who, finding themselves unwilling to maintain the forms of Judaism and having a sort of instinctive dread of other religions are going without any religious expression or experience whatsoever." More ambitious rescue plans had to be drawn up to influence those falling away from Judaism.[12]

The middle of the 1920s saw several similarly constituted rescue organizations established both in Harlem and in the other major Jewish sections of New York. Harlem's Young Men's Hebrew Orthodox League and Hebrew League, downtown's Young Israel synagogue, and Brownsville's Young Men's Hebrew League established synagogues and sponsored social activities on lines similar to Morais' early efforts.

The Harlem Young Men's Hebrew Orthodox League was founded in April 1915, by ten members of the Harry Fischel West Side Annex of the Uptown Talmud Torah, to provide the young adults of the community with an "institution which would create an Orthodox environment and teach the great principles of Orthodoxy." They perceived that even talmud-torah-educated young adults experienced a certain disaffection from Judaism "upon entering academic, professional or business careers." And they understood that once on their own, few Jewish young adults continued to come in contact "during their spare time with a circle that reminds him of his obligations to his faith and people." The leaders of this league believed that they had the intellectual acumen to convince the second generation "that by study, Orthodox Judaism will be found to be entirely compatible with modern ideas."[13]

They inaugurated their program by establishing model youth synagogues at the Annex emphasizing decorum and congregational singing in services conducted by the young people themselves. In the fall of 1914, the new Harlem League conducted a Kehillah-sponsored "provisional synagogue." These provisional synagogues were organized throughout the city to combat the abuses of the "mushroom synagogues" established by private entrepreneurs in public halls and saloons to provide a place for unaffiliated Jews to attend High Holiday services. Many of these entrepreneurs were unscrupulous individuals who hired imposters as rabbis and generally exploited the public for commercial purposes. The provisional synagogues were designed to undercut the market served by "mushroom synagogues" by providing services at reasonable rates under reputable leadership to serve the High Holiday overflow crowd. The selection of the Young Men's Hebrew Orthodox League to serve the Lenox Avenue district of New York represented an early recognition by city-wide authorities of their utility to the uptown community.[14]

Thus established within the community, the Harlem Young Men's Hebrew Orthodox League quickly inaugurated numerous social and cultural activities and planned to maintain its own clubrooms, library, and gymnasium and to hold classes on Jewish topics. Among the lecturers in its early years were Rabbis Jacob Dolgenas, Bernard Drachman and Herbert S. Goldstein. Goldstein, then associate rabbi at Yorkville's Congregation Kehilath Jeshurun, was elected Honorary President of the League in recognition of his constant encouragement of its activities.[15]

A second Harlem-based cultural institution created to attract Jewish young adults back to their faith was organized in September 1915. The Harlem Hebrew League was founded to "make known the ideals of Judaism" to uptown youths. League organizers established a headquarters for "Jewish men under Jewish refining influences" on Lenox

Avenue where social and educational programs were held every weekday evening and on the Sabbath. This league offered its members lectures and debates in addition to its dignified modern Orthodox services. Rabbis Drachman, Goldstein and Morais headed the list of speakers who addressed this youth organization as it began to gain support in the local community.[16]

Uptown efforts to expand the scope of American synagogue life to include social, cultural and recreational activities, in the hope of making Judaism more relevant to neighborhood young people, were paralleled on the Lower East Side by the activities of the founders of the Young Israel Synagogue. These advocates of traditional Judaism created in 1915 a model synagogue on East Broadway run according to the same principles as Morais's 1905 Harlem effort. Harry G. Fromberg, one of the founders of the movement, described their synagogue as a place "where every atom of our time-honored tradition could be observed and at the same time prove an attraction, particularly to young men and women: a synagogue where, with the exception of prayer, English would be used in the delivery of sermons and otherwise." The Young Israel synagogue emphasized congregational singing and decorum, outlawed all forms of commercialism in services, and sponsored a variety of social and cultural activities designed to keep the young people in the synagogue. Late in 1915, a federation of "organizations of young Jewry" composed of Harlem, downtown and Brownsville youth leagues and synagogues was organized "to promote the welfare of Judaism" on a city-wide basis.[17]

For all the energy in this movement the founders of the Harlem Young Men's Hebrew Association still perceived them as too limited in scope and parochial in outlook to serve the majority of its community's young adults. These leaders argued that "Orthodox" Jews represented a relatively inconsequential proportion of the total population. They argued that there were thousands of young people whom the talmud torah never reached. These were young people "who never enter a synagogue and for them there must be some kind of training school" in Judaism. Yorkville's Ninety-Second Street Y, which many East Harlemites did attend, was nevertheless considered geographically inaccessible for the majority of uptown residents. And Yorkville leaders, for their part, were unwilling to expand their own activities to Harlem, describing themselves as an exclusively Yorkville institution. They preferred to support the establishment of a separate

Harlem branch of their National Y.M.H.A. movement. Just such an institution, emphasizing social, cultural and recreational activities and
offering Jewish religious activities on a limited nondenominational
basis was founded at an organizational meeting held at Temple
Mount Zion in 1915. The Harlem Y received the support of several important local rabbinic and lay leaders including Rabbis Benjamin A.
Tintner, Philip Klein and Bernard Drachman, and Representative Isaac
Siegel.[18]

Rabbi Mordecai Kaplan failed to share his uptown colleagues' enthusiasm for the new Harlem Y. This former religious director of the
Ninety-Second Street Y now argued that as presently organized, the
YMHAs were no different from nonsectarian settlement houses, providing social and recreational activities for the youth of their communities in the hope of "keeping them off the streets." Kaplan charged
that there was little that was "distinctly Jewish" in the content of
YMHA programs which would set them off from other community-
service organizations as a bulwark against "the possibility of Jews
becoming assimilated." He characterized the YMHAs as "secular organizations" financed by Jewish money, and called upon the national
movement to either drop the word "Hebrew" from its title and to
openly declare itself a nonreligious organization or to immediately
reconstitute itself as a "distinctly Jewish organization" committing itself wholeheartedly to the battle against assimilation.[19]

Although he doubted that the YMHA would respond affirmatively
to his criticism, Kaplan was not discouraged. For him, the future of
Jewish life in America lay outside the hands of both the secular YMHA
and the religious Orthodox and Hebrew Leagues. Kaplan was convinced that the reconstructed synagogue was destined to play the
crucial role in preserving Judaism in America. He believed that the
primarily secular, social, cultural and recreational activities of the Y
could be effectively merged with modern religious-oriented programs
of the Leagues. The resulting synagogue-center movement would effectively influence the American-Jewish young adult, who had gradu-
ated from the settlements and had outgrown his or her parents' immigrant synagogue culture, to identify with things Jewish. The
synagogue center's social attractions would lure the unaffiliated into a
religious surrounding, where they would be exposed to or reac-
quainted with the beauties, and ultimately, the values of their ancestral faith. It was Kaplan's hope that with time and the proper pro-

grams, many Jews would eventually be drawn to the specifically religious activities of the institution and might ultimately attend their services conducted along the most modern Orthodox lines. Such an institution was to produce committed Jews from among the many religiously estranged young adults.[20]

In fashioning his dream of a reconstructed synagogue, Kaplan drew heavily upon the educational philosophy espoused by his colleague Professor John Dewey of Columbia University. Dewey believed that contemporary modern industrial society had thrust the school, in place of the home and neighborhood, into the role of society's major educative and socializing agent. It was, consequently, the job of modern educators not only to teach the traditional subject matter normally associated with the school but to create within the school an atmosphere conducive both for continued learning and for the personality development of each child/student. For Dewey—and the generation of progressive Jewish educators he trained and inspired—the final judgment on the usefulness of an educational program rested on its success in creating "a desire for continued growth" among its students. Adapting these principles to his proposed synagogue center, Kaplan argued that his new social and recreational activities would create the desired atmosphere conducive for continued identification with synagogue life and would eventually lead to greater interest in studying Judaism.[21]

Kaplan first attempted to put these theories into practice in 1916 when he helped found the Central Jewish Institute organized by leaders of Yorkville's Congregation Kehilath Jeshurun, where he had earlier served as associate rabbi. This congregation and the community it served was an exceptionally good testing ground for his programs to save affluent, Americanized second-generation Jews from assimilation. Kehilath Jeshurun members were drawn from among the most affluent element in the East European community: individuals who had succeeded in less than a generation in achieving a degree of economic advancement comparable to that of the Jews of Lenox Avenue. These Yorkville Jews were described by one official of the Central Jewish Institute as "bourgeois, well-to-do and distinctly conservative in contradistinction to the new Russian immigration which has a strong element of Radicalism and Yiddishism." Religiously, they were depicted as "Orthodox, which implies adherence to Jewish ceremonies and customs and an allegiance to Jewish life." Many were described as the scions of "families which were respected in the social life of the Eastern European ghetto, where learning was the distinguishing class mark."[22]

Their affluent American-born children and their fellow Yorkville friends showed little of their ancestors' commitment to Jewish learning. On the contrary, these young people were observed by the same official to be a "half-baked second generation who knew little of Jewish life, tending to associate it merely with the ceremonies and especially with the prohibitions observed in the home. They are generally indifferent to, if not ashamed of Jewish life." The recipients of a public school education, these proficient English-speakers were also quick to regard themselves "as superior to their parents and everything associated with them." This same student of the community feared that these Yorkville Jews were representative of the disintegration of the ethnic and religious culture in the second generation and recognized the need for an "adequate agency to bridge the gap between the generations, to interpret the old traditions in terms of the new." Yorkville provided Rabbi Kaplan with a ready constituency for his Jewish "rescue" plans.[23]

The Central Jewish Institute represented the first major attempt at amalgamating Jewish social, cultural, and recreational programs with religious educational activities under the auspices of an established Orthodox congregation. Institutional leadership emphasized the "harmonization of Jewish purpose with American life" as its *raison d'etre*. It promoted with equal vigor its program of Jewish studies through a talmud torah and an extension school for "those who cannot be induced to enroll in the intensive work" and a center program whose activities "make for the physical and social well-being of the people who live in the neighborhood." Health and citizenship, it was declared, "are a part of, and not opposed to Judaism."[24]

The Central Jewish Institute was not, however, the truly complete synagogue center envisioned by Kaplan. The single major component missing from its multifaceted program was, ironically, the synagogue itself. Although supported by the leadership of Kehilath Jeshurun and housed in an adjoining building, the C.J.I. lived an almost separate existence from its sponsoring institution. The synagogue failed to coordinate or update its traditional religious practices and rituals with the social and educational activities of the Institute. One critic of this Yorkville movement claimed that it possessed all the elements of a synagogue center "but only externally so. The three departments have no close contact because the synagogue element is not bold enough. The synagogue has not developed its full capacity and its influence is small." In 1918, Rabbi Kaplan, undoubtedly frustrated with the incompleteness of the C.J.I. program, severed his remaining ties with Yorkville's institutions and with the financial assistance of several of Kehilath Jeshurun's most affluent members, who had migrated to the elegant newly developed West Side neighborhood, established the Jewish Center Synagogue at 86th Street between Columbus and Amsterdam Avenues. Now on his own, he was free to create a true synagogue-center program under Orthodox auspices which would serve as a model for hundreds of Jewish center-synagogues organized over the next several decades.[25]

Rabbi Herbert S. Goldstein, founder of Harlem's Institutional Synagogue, shared Kaplan's critique of existing youth organizations and advocated an almost identical synagogue-centered program for attracting young people back to their faith. Goldstein was first directly exposed to Kaplan's philosophy in 1913, when as a senior at the Jewish Theological Seminary he was elected to succeed his teacher as English-speaking minister at Kehilath Jeshurun. He worked in close concert there with Kaplan in the founding and direction of the Central Jewish Institute and learned first-hand of the problems facing those committed to this new form of Jewish communal work. Goldstein first expressed his own dedication to meeting the challenges posed by the new generation of American Jews in June 1915, when he declared that the salvation of "the Judaism of the future" lay solely in the hands of the "young university-trained Orthodox Rabbis" like himself. In a public charge to his American-born, English-speaking colleagues, Goldstein argued that only they could help, for example, the "scientifically-trained, skeptical young Jew, reconcile what he learned in public school and college with the ancient doctrines of his faith." Goldstein believed that only those "reared on American soil, who have breathed the ideals of American democracy, who have been born and bred like other Americans, who have received a systematic scientific, secular education, and who are at the same time deeply saturated with a knowledge and desire of practicing the tenets of our faith," can understand the needs and desires of those eager "to break down ghetto walls . . . to live as their neighbors, their fellow citizens—the Americans." They alone "who have gone through this kind of youth" and remained true to Judaism can meet American Jewish men or women on their own level.

Goldstein called upon all Orthodox Jews to rally around these young zealots and directed established congregations to hire young men to their pulpits who would engage in missionary work among those "who have gone astray, to bring them back to Orthodox Judaism and keep and sustain those who are in the fold."[26]

Goldstein outlined a concrete plan for what he called Jewish missionary work some fifteen months later when he called for the establishment of an Institutional Synagogue to serve second-generation American Jews. In a public letter to New York Jewry published in several local periodicals, Goldstein argued that all existing Jewish institutions were failing to influence young people towards Jewish observance. The relatively few modern educational institutes in existence reached, according to Goldstein, only 15 percent of Jewish youth. The religio-social landsmanshaft synagogues (the so-called "provincial synagogues," that expressed "local European mannerisms") were characterized as "un-American, antiquated and largely responsible for the great gap which now exists between the sons of the founders of the synagogues and the founders." The cheder education system, he declared, was a complete failure for its total inability "to impart to students the true meaning of the Jewish religion, nor inspire in them the proper love of their faith." The talmud torah movement, with which his father-in-law, Harry Fischel, and some of his own closest associates were intimately involved, Goldstein described as a worthy improvement over the earlier system. But he declared it too suffered from some important defects. The talmud torah movement had, he said, failed to overcome its East European roots. As a pauper's school, it failed to attract children of parents who could afford to pay tuition. In addition, the talmud torah movement's approach to Jewish youth was itself not ideal because "it is fractional in its work and divorces the child from the synagogue."[27]

Goldstein expressed similar objection to the Y.M.H.A. movement, characterizing its efforts in the Jewish social field as "partial" because "it only takes the boy off the street and does not give him the education of a Jewish religious environment." Paralleling Kaplan's criticisms published a year earlier, Goldstein also stated that the YMHA's work was "negative" because it "failed to impart positive religion in the minds of the youth. It does not stand for positive religious conviction.''[28]

For Goldstein, like Kaplan the "institutional synagogue-Jewish center" concept represented Jewry's best chance to save a lost generation from voluntarily surrendering its Jewish identity. Goldstein too argued that historically "the synagogue of old was the center for prayer, study and the social life of the community all in one," and suggested that with the proper program, it could once again assume that traditional role. He envisioned a new multifaceted synagogue which would be "a place for study for adults in the evenings and for children in the afternoons." It would be a social and recreational center for young adults where "after plying their daily cares, they could spend a social hour in an Orthodox environment and in a truly Jewish atmosphere." This synagogue would also offer decorus modern Orthodox religious services designed specifically for an American congregation, while "keeping intact the Jewish ceremonies of our people." Goldstein was convinced that "if we desire to perpetuate the ideal Judaism of the past we must so shape Jewish spiritual activity that it will all find expression in one institution." He offered the institutional synagogue as that ideal Jewish social, religious and cultural organization, embracing the best of the synagogue, talmud torah and YMHA.[29]

Goldstein submitted that he had both history and practicality on his side. From a purely financial standpoint it would be cheaper for local Jewish communities to build one large institutional synagogue, combining all the activities of a large congregation, talmud torah and YMHA, than to support each separately. He also reasoned that the individual Jew could, for a little higher membership fee in the institutional synagogue, derive the benefits of three Jewish institutions. The three-in-one synagogue centers would have the additional advantage of making it possible for all members of a family to participate in their own age-group activities within the same religious institution and thereby bring back to family life "that religious unity and enthusiasm which is sorely lacking today."[30]

Rabbi Goldstein's ambitious proposals for reviving Jewish youth were well received by the leaders of both the Harlem Young Men's Hebrew Orthodox League and the Harlem YMHA. Late in 1916, these men considered amalgamating their organizations to reach the youth of their neighborhood. The Harlem League, the smaller of the two organizations with only thirty-five members on its rolls, was almost immediately taken by Goldstein's concepts; it decided several weeks after this published pronouncement to reorganize the organization and to "push with vigor its campaign for the establishment of a real Jewish center in Harlem." The League, which previously sponsored only religious and cultural activities, now announced its intention to construct a gymnasium and organize a library to attract a wider segment of uptown Jewry to its organization. The Harlem YMHA, seventy-five members strong, expressed its support of Goldstein's idea in April 1917, when it agreed under the leadership of its new president, Representative Isaac Siegel, to join Harlem League officials in inviting Rabbi Goldstein to coordinate uptown youth work. The Rabbi was given the mandate of "bringing the message of Jewish Religious Revival to (Harlem) youth" through existing youth organizations reconstituted as the Institutional Synagogue.[31]

Representative Siegel's leadership in the Harlem YMHA and his subsequent presidency of the Institutional Synagogue was the second instance of his direct involvement in local religious affairs. Almost a decade earlier, in 1908, Siegel had led a group of young protestors against Congregation Ohab Zedek, accusing this leading uptown synagogue of conducting organizational "business" on the Sabbath. Siegel's group claimed that on a given Sabbath several young men had attempted to gain admittance at the 116th Street sanctuary and were told by congregational leaders that only worshipers holding admission "tickets" could enter the synagogue. Siegel's young men were allegedly told that tickets could be purchased at a cigar store located across the street from the synagogue. Siegel publicly condemned this open commercialism and this obvious desecration of the Sabbath practiced by the religious "hypocrites" of Ohab Zedek.[32]

Siegel's charges, which were published in a local Jewish periodical, were answered in print by a Mr. D. Berliner, an officer of the congregation. Berliner counterclaimed that admission tickets were "authorized solely to preserve order and decorum" in the services and vigorously denied that tickets were sold on the Sabbath. According to Berliner, tickets were needed to "keep back the mob of young men struggling to enter and the young dandies who came in merely to ogle women in the balcony."[33]

Berliner's defense failed to move one contemporary editorialist who condemned Ohab Zedek for failing to recognize that a synagogue "has something more to do than to engage a chazan with a beautiful voice." "Where is the Rabbi?", this critic asked. "Where is the Hebrew and Religious School? What is the new Hungarian congregation doing for the community?" The editorialist went on to declare that the "Jewish community expects more" from its synagogues and commended Siegel for bringing this problem to public attention. Ohab Zedek's decision in 1909 to appoint Bernard Drachman to its uptown pulpit may well have been directed, to some extent, by communal pressure to modernize its approach to synagogue life, arising from this incident.[34]

It is interesting, however, to note that Siegel deemed it inappropriate or impolitic to point to this early involvement in communal affairs when attacked by Rosenblatt as a "non-Jewish" representative in the fiercely contested 1916 Congressional elections. It is possible that the candidate of the then "respectable element" in uptown Jewry did not want at that point to remind his most consistent supporters that he had once openly criticized the policies of one of Harlem's major religious establishments. By the same token, it is possible that Siegel's reawakened interest in communal activities may be attributed in part to his desire to still critics of his "Jewish" record. Whether the Congressman's involvement in the Institutional Synagogue project was pietistic or political, it was Siegel who assumed the presidency of the merged organizations and who accepted the responsibility of contacting Rabbi Goldstein to invite him to assume the new Harlem pulpit.[35]

Rabbi Goldstein accepted the call of uptown Jewry in April 1917, as an exciting challenge, making only two major requests of Harlem leaders: that he be granted life tenure as rabbi and leader of the Institutional Synagogue, and that the synagogue's constitution indicate that "no innovation in traditional Judaism may be inaugurated" into the synagogue's ritual "if there be one dissenting vote at a meeting of the corporation." His position thus secured, Goldstein immediately made plans for creating what he described as a "Jewish revival movement" in Harlem.[36]

The new synagogue leased a private house near 116th Street and Lenox Avenue, described by Goldstein as the "heart of the most distressing Jewish conditions in the United States," for a synagogue, club and schoolhouse. Goldstein announced plans for conducting "monster rallies" throughout Harlem to attract thousands of young people to his movement. He proposed the leasing of local theaters on Sunday mornings for services and lectures to reach "the large mass of young men and women who cannot be reached on Sabbath." In a related move, Goldstein suggested that Institutional Synagogue leaders approach leading Orthodox Jewish merchants in Harlem to solicit jobs for Jewish young people who themselves wished to keep the Sabbath.[37]

Goldstein's Institutional Synagogue received an early spiritual boost in May 1917, when Henry S. Morais voiced his public support for this contemporary "youth synagogue." That same week saw the new project obtain its greatest financial assist when an anonymous supporter donated a five-story building at 116th Street between Lenox and Seventh Avenues as a home for Goldstein's Jewish center-synagogue-school complex.[38]

The new movement, through its Sunday revival meetings and its diversified program of youth activities, quickly gained the support of neighborhood people. By September 1917, after only five months of existence, the Institutional Synagogue attracted some 1,200 people to its Rosh Hashanah services, held at a public hall in Central Harlem. In January 1918, the synagogue reported a membership of 2,000 dues-paying members supporting thirty-one clubs and eight religious classes housed at the 116th Street building. A month later, the Institutional Synagogue, in conjunction with the Jewish Sabbath Association, opened a Harlem branch of the Association's Employment Bureau. Goldstein subsequently attempted to convince all Jewish shopkeepers in Harlem to close their stores on Saturday, in order to "arouse a Jewish spirit" in the neighborhood.[39]

The Institutional Synagogue's most ambitious program remained its Jewish "missionary" work expressed through frequent "monster rallies." Mount Morris Theater, located only one-half block away from the synagogue, was the usual location for these meetings which often featured lectures by United States Senators, Congressmen and well-known local and national Jewish figures. Rabbi Goldstein explained the underlying purpose of these revival meetings when he declared that "every community needs an occasional soul-stirring re-awakening and a revival of a religious interest from time to time. At our regular religious services we attract only those who are habitual synagogue-goers, but we must reach the wavering as well. This can only be done through revival meetings."[40]

The Institutional Synagogue absorbed more than its share of criti-

cism during its early years. The most frequently heard charges contended that this Orthodox institution was "elitist" in nature and was
simply a recast, improved Harlem Hebrew League, of use only to
those of that particular religious persuasion. The presence of the
Harlem YMHA leaders on the board of the Institutional Synagogue
apparently made little impression upon those who opposed Goldstein's efforts. Critics echoed the traditional National YMHA contention that "inasmuch as in a community there are young men of
various religious beliefs and some of no religion at all, the problem
cannot be solved by a temple or synagogue." While admitting that in
theory the synagogue was the ideal, dissenters were quick to observe
that "some people are not inspired by that ideal. Shall they come
under no influence at all?"[41]

Critics also noted the Institutional Synagogue's higher "three-in-
one" membership fee as further proof of its fundamentally "elitist"
nature. Goldstein's organization was described by one spokesman for
the Yiddish press as "a private institution for the children coming
from parents not necessarily wealthy, but from those who can afford
to pay for instruction." Membership rates at the Institutional Synagogue, critics contended, "were prohibitive to the wage earner."[42]
Those who felt that the mass-oriented revival movement was not
within the true spirit of Judaism also censured the new Harlem movement, and those who preferred rabbis to play a less activist role in
community social problems deplored Rabbi Goldstein's decision to
"resign as a minister of an established congregation to donate his entire time and energy to Billy Sundayism." Rabbi Goldstein was advised
to "concentrate on religious education" and leave "sensationalism"
to Christian evangelists.[43]

Rabbi Goldstein responded by asserting that his movement was
primarily religious and was pointed towards bringing the unaffiliated
into the synagogue, and leading those ignorant of Judaism towards
the house of study. Goldstein also argued that there was nothing
novel or radical in the concept of "Jewish revivalism." The prophets
of old and the itinerant preachers of the East European settlement
were all "revivalists" and all operated within the fabric of Jewish tradition. He asserted that his movement had both Jewish history and
modern ministerial techniques on its side.[44]

In considering Rabbi Goldstein's Institutional Synagogue and the
other early youth organizations that operated both in Harlem and in

the adjoining communities as forerunners of the Jewish Center movement of the 1920s and 1930s, one immediately notes that as early as
the 1910s, religious leaders were aware that rapid, complete Americanization brought with it profound challenges to the continuity of
Jewish life in this country. They understood that even young adults
who had been exposed as children to some Jewish education were
not immune to the pressures imposed by general society to assimi-
late; to conform totally to majority cultural values. They feared for
those Jews but even more so for those children of immigrants who
received no training in Judaism and who were growing to maturity as
Americans oblivious of the traditions of their people. And although
American Jews still constituted but a relatively small proportion of
their predominantly immigrant community, they understood that
these people were the first wave of a second-generation American
Jewish society that would grow to full maturity in later decades.

The Central Jewish Institute, the Jewish Center and, of course, Harlem's Institutional Synagogue, which operated under Orthodox auspices, represented the first concerted efforts to deal with these problems and served as workable prototypes for later Conservative Jewish
synagogue centers established in the soon-to-be constructed outlying
neighborhoods by second-generation Jews. The Harlem and Yorkville
youth organizations also influenced later communal developments by
providing a forum for the emergence of the American-born or educated, university-trained, traditional rabbi as a dominant force in communal life. Men like Drachman, Morais, Kaplan and Goldstein represented the vanguard of a new generation of traditional American
Jewish rabbis dedicated and equipped to tend to the spiritual needs
of the American Jewish community. Jewish Theological Seminary
teachers and rabbis who had made so little impact on the immigrant
ghetto population found a small but enthusiastic group of followers
within the Americanized segment of Harlem's German and East European communities. These rabbis and their successors were destined
to become even more important factors in the life of their communities in the years to come. Many of the lessons learned in these uptown Orthodox institutions were readily applied to suburban Conservative congregations.

A high level of cooperation existed between the founders of the
Conservative movement and their contemporary modern Orthodox
counterparts. Indeed, it is often difficult to differentiate between the

two. Both stood for traditional Judaism and preached similar messages to their Americanized congregants. A study of the early careers
of Rabbis Herbert S. Goldstein and Mordecai M. Kaplan is highly in-
structive in this area. Before entering the Seminary and earning his
rabbinic degree from this American rabbinic institute, Goldstein was
ordained as an Orthodox Rabbi by Rabbi S. Jaffee of Beth Ha-Midrash
Ha-Gadol of Norfolk Street. Armed with this dual ordination, Goldstein was a logical choice as an English-speaking assistant rabbi under
Rabbi Moses Z. Margolies, a leading East European Orthodox Rabbi
who was sensitive to American problems and values. Margolies, it will
be remembered, was a director of the Uptown Talmud Torah and
supported local and Kehillah-sponsored efforts to update Jewish educational practices. Named to his post at Kehilath Jeshurun, Goldstein
succeeded Rabbi Kaplan, a fellow Seminary graduate, who had not
earned Orthodox ordination prior to his rabbinic appointment but
who nevertheless was deemed qualified to minister to an important
traditional congregation. Margolies and Kaplan and, later, Margolies
and Goldstein apparently worked harmoniously in the Yorkville pulpit. And they all seem to have cooperated successfully in the founding of the Central Jewish Institute, as the senior rabbi undoubtedly
regarded both men as traditional rabbis and as skilled communal
workers. The differences in their rabbinic training does not seem to
have been a point of conflict among the three.

Both Goldstein and Kaplan severed their ties with the Kehilath
Jeshurun community to establish similarly constituted youth-oriented
synagogues in Harlem and on the West Side. Both institutions were
organized and maintained according to traditional Orthodox guide-
lines. It is therefore interesting to observe, in retrospect, that the
"Jewish Center-Institutional Synagogue" concept, which found its
first expression within an Orthodox context controlled by Seminary-
trained rabbis, ultimately gained its greatest acceptance within the
Conservative movement.

A final, enduring similarity between early modern Orthodoxy and
Conservative Judaism may be seen from an examination of Rabbis
Goldstein and Kaplan's later careers. Although Goldstein and Kaplan
would ultimately go their separate theological and denominational
ways, the former as a leader of both the Union of Orthodox Jewish
Congregations of America and Yeshiva University, the latter as the
founder and leader of the left-wing Conservative Jewish Reconstruc-

tionist movement, both remained united in their continued commitment to leading and inspiring that emerging heterogeneous group of
modern Jewish religious leaders who sought, through similar homile-
tics and almost identically constituted socio-religious institutions, to
serve the spiritual needs of a truly American Jewish community.

Chapter 6

The Decline of Jewish
Harlem, 1920–1930

Two basic theoretical paradigms have been generally offered to describe and explain the racial transformation process in American cities. The first, sociologist Ernest W. Burgess's invasion-succession theory, argued on the basis of 1920s Chicago, and by analogy for other American cities, that blacks, like the immigrants before them, entered the city into areas of first settlement (zones in transition), displacing earlier arriving foreign groups then in the process of relocating to better residential areas on the periphery of the urban centers. Burgess believed that the black migratory experience was basically similar to that of other urban ethnic groups and suggested that the residential segregation of newly arrived blacks was a result of their present low-socioeconomic position. Inherent in this theory is the implication that with the passage of time and the achievement of greater economic power, blacks too would be able to depart run-down ghettos for better housing elsewhere in the city.[1]

Other groups of scholars have recently offered a second more detailed analysis of the neighborhood transformation process. Both Otis Dudley Duncan and Beverly Duncan in their study of Chicago of the 1940s, and Karl E. Taeuber and Alma F. Taeuber in their examination of ten American cities in the 1950s, have argued that neighborhood population turnovers proceed through four very distinguishable stages. The first stage, *penetration*, occurs when blacks first move into a previously exclusive white neighborhood. These blacks are of relatively high socioeconomic status compared to the total black population. When the number and percentage of blacks becomes—in the words of the Duncans—"significantly great," and includes those of significantly lower socioeconomic status, a second stage is reached: *invasion. Consolidation* coincides with a further increase in black population and is accompanied by a significant decrease in white population. The final stage, *piling-up,* occurs when the area becomes almost exclusively black. The Duncans argued additionally that the rate of racial succession "may be quite variable, i.e. the complete process may take only a short while or may occur over a long period of time." And the Taeuber's noted, with more specific reference to Burgess's economics-based theory of residential segregation, the existence of a "dual housing market" in changing areas of many cities fostered by the racial descrimination imposed by the "all-white" housing covenant. These "gentlemen's agreements" maintain real estate prices at artifically high rates in deteriorating areas and prohibit the out-migration of most blacks with the economic resources to escape the ghetto.[2]

The process of racial displacement in Harlem was fundamentally different from that suggested by Burgess. The early turn-of-the-century black incursion into Harlem was obviously, to begin with, into an area of second and not of first immigrant settlement. It emanated not from outside the city but from the Tenderloin and other run-down areas of Lower Manhattan. And it closely paralleled the migration to Harlem of upwardly mobile Jewish immigrants from the Lower East Side. Furthermore, the arrival of blacks uptown was not preceded by the beginnings of immigrant out-migration nor did their settlement spark an exodus of Jews and other ethnic groups to other neighborhoods.

The similarities between the experiences of the black and those of his Jewish Central Harlem immigrant neighbor, so important to Burgess's theory, ended after World War I. Then newly affluent immigrants and their second-generation American children were able to flee a deteriorating Harlem for suburban areas. Harlem's earliest black settlers were trapped in the district by economics and racism. They were soon joined by thousands of new Southern blacks who took the places of the existing whites.

Harlem's history is more properly analogous to the Duncan-Taeuber theoretical pattern. It differs only—and significantly—in the very protracted time-span between the black penetration of Jewish areas, which began in 1905 and progressed very slowly, and the latter three stages, which took place more than a decade later. Until World War I, Harlem's blacks were, for the most part, concentrated in their own enclave in the new Harlem community in close proximity to other ethnic groups, and made only minor incursions into the white areas. The black take-over of Jewish Harlem began after the end of World War I.

World War I was the crucial point in the history of twentieth-century Harlem. Until the war, uptown—despite its densely populated tenement district and its less than elegant pre-1900 brownstone flats—remained an area attractive to those seeking to improve their living conditions. After the war, Harlem quickly became a neglected inner-city ghetto, housing only those who were, for whatever reason, incapable of fleeing to newly constructed outlying areas. The basic causes of this shift were the pronounced physical deterioration of Harlem under the impact of severe wartime overcrowding and wartime building restrictions that precluded builders from providing new housing for an expanding urban population and allowed landlords to exploit this temporary housing shortage.

Early in this century, Harlem—and to a lesser extent Yorkville and the West Side—had begun serving as population safety-valves from overcrowded downtown areas. Several years later, Brownsville and Williamsburg joined uptown in providing major residential alternatives for Manhattan's tenement dwellers. And before the war, New York, still attracting thousands of new settlers yearly, had maintained its residential equilibrium by limited construction in newer sections of Brooklyn and in Queens and the Bronx. The growth of these outer-borough areas was facilitated, as residential construction had been in earlier periods, by the extension of mass transit lines to previously inaccessible sections of Greater New York. By 1917, subway lines had brought most sections of the outlying boroughs within reasonable commutation time of Manhattan.[3]

Most prewar observers of the New York real estate scene shared the expectation that the slow but on-going development of new neighborhoods would continue to offset at least partially any further large increment in population. Tenement House Department officials prophesized that New York's tenement population would continue to disperse itself until Manhattan ceased being the residential hub of an emerging multicentric metropolis.[4]

The start of World War I put an abrupt end to this first generation of urban population relocation. Wartime governmental restrictions on all but essential construction brought tenement building almost to a standstill. New housing starts were also severely curtailed by what one governmental official described as "the exceedingly high price of materials, the delay in obtaining them" and the scarcity of skilled laborers. "Extremely abnormal conditions resulting from the great European conflict," he further observed, "rendered building almost prohibitive."[5]

The cessation of construction occurred at the very moment when the city—due to an unexpected mass influx of population—needed more than ever a resurgence in new housing construction. The war industries established within the major urban centers were attracting hundreds of thousands of workers, many of them black, from the hinterlands of America, and New York received more than its share of the migrants. The city's population rose by more than 600,000 between 1915 and 1920. Overcrowded Manhattan, which since 1910 slowly had been losing population, quickly acquired an additional net population of 146,000. These new settlers, like millions before them, competed with the existing population for the limited housing available. The relatively few new apartments constructed before the war were quickly occupied. New York's prewar residential equilibrium was soon shattered and tenement and apartment house dwellers throughout the city were once again confronted with seriously overcrowded conditions.[6]

The City's Tenement House Department found, for example, that in 1917 apartments in "new-law" buildings were "unobtainable." "Rents in such buildings," it reported, "were rising and families 'doubling up' (families formerly occupying separate apartments are now living together)." Other governmental agencies observed, two years later, that "over twenty thousands of the houses erected before the new law, which were not in use in 1916 were serving as dwellings in 1919. There are practically no unoccupied apartments that are fit for human habitation."[7]

This home-front crisis was exacerbated by the attempt of New York landlords to capitalize on the increased demand for scarce housing. Armed with the knowledge that most tenants had little option but to pay whatever rents were demanded by them, landlords hiked prices to what a State Housing Commission described as "unreasonable and oppressive" levels. Having no need to do anything to attract tenants, landlords also permitted their tenement properties to deteriorate. Another state survey of postwar housing conditions determined that by 1919, "families were crowded together in dark, ill-smelling apartments, and were unable to find better quarters. In every block were found ill-kept apartments, in fact, certain of them were not kept at all. One tenant said that her shoes had been worn out looking for another apartment."[8]

This study also noted that the housing shortage was causing problems for all classes of tenement dwellers, noting that the "raising of rents resulting from the shortage of houses has affected not only the poor, but a large part of the population even among the moderately well-to-do." "New York's housing capacity," this study conclude, "is very elastic, but the time is near where there will actually be no more room even in the indecently rotten old-law homes."[9]

Harlem was among the most affected sections of the city. Once a safety-valve for excess East Side population, Harlem now had to grapple with its own problems of overcrowding. Central Harlem, for example, experienced a net population increase of some 11,000 people between 1915 and 1920, constituting a percentage increase of more than 15 percent over the prewar period. Uptown housing did not keep pace with the rapid increase in population as only twenty-four more houses were available for residential use in 1920 than were ten years earlier. Harlem's most affluent district was confronted for the first time with a serious housing dilemma.[10]

Central Harlem also experienced the exploitation of money-hungry landlords. Charles Marks, attorney for several tenant groups, including the West Harlem Tenants Association, testified before a Gubernatorial Commission on Housing that in one building, twenty tenants were being forced to pay a "rental increase from $36–$55." "In this case," Marks reported, "no repairs of any kind or nature, have been made of any perceptible kind, excepting absolutely necessary sanitary repairs."[11]

In East Harlem, the era of rent profiteering simply accelerated the deterioration of an already densely populated neighborhood. As early as 1913, the Charity Organization Society declared that the "problems of poverty, need and congestion" in East Harlem were comparable to those which were commonly associated only with the Lower East Side. "All tenements in the area," they reported "are narrow and thickly populated with a poor class of people." Three years later, a study conducted by the Eastern Council of Reform Rabbis determined that "there are worse congested districts in the North East Side than the East Side; only the members of the Eastern Council do not see the evil that are right next door to them. Harlem notably, the West Side, Washington Heights and Brooklyn need very carefully looking after."[12]

East Harlem was severely affected by the housing shortage and by landlord neglect during the war years. A postwar study of a typical East Harlem block revealed a "great number of buildings of the old type that only demolition and reconstruction could make habitable. By that time, those Harlemites with the financial means to escape the overcrowding were well prepared to abandon the old neighborhood and were among those pressing for the revival of construction of suitable accommodations.[13]

The fortunes of Harlemites and other oppressed city dwellers did not improve significantly, however, until February, 1921. The city's Board of Estimate then finally recognized the need to stimulate new home construction and relieve city-wide overcrowding. It passed a tax exemption ordinance highly favorable to builders, providing that "all new buildings planned for dwelling purposes" started or completed between April 1, 1920 and April 1, 1922 would be exempt from almost all tax levies until January 1932. The Board extended the deadline for new construction several times during the 1920s, providing builders with continued protection from taxation.[14]

This bold municipal governmental move sparked a long-awaited resurgence in building projects contiguous to existing rapid transit lines. In the first nine months of 1921, local builders finally overcame their fear of high postwar labor costs and high bank interest rates, proceeding to build nearly ten thousand multiple dwellings and several thousand private homes both in Manhattan and the outlying boroughs.[15]

The first spurt of construction set the building pattern for the rest of the decade. Brooklyn held the lead throughout the 1920s as the site of the most pronounced activity. Some 14,000 apartments were built in previously inaccessible Flatbush, Bay Ridge, and Bensonhurst. More than five thousand apartment houses were built in the Bronx, the majority concentrated along White Plains Road and the Grand Concourse. Long Island City, Astoria and Jackson Heights, similarly, became important new metropolitan neighborhoods as several thousand new houses were erected within close proximity of Queens's mass transit lines. Manhattan lagged considerably behind the other boroughs in the number of new housing starts but its relatively few new luxury apartment houses were as a rule far more expensive than those built elsewhere in the city. Riverside Drive, Washington Heights, Central Park West, and Park Avenue below 96th Street all emerged as new and elegant communities for many of New York's most affluent citizens.[16]

This postwar building boom quickly attracted those eager and able to escape overcrowded conditions away from Harlem and the city's other immigrant and older residential areas to the new sections of town. It also helped set the present-day general demographic profile of the metropolis. Manhattan was established as the home of many of the city's most affluent as well as poorest inhabitants, while the other boroughs became, and remained until very recently, the centers for a variety of middle- and lower-income people.

Although severe overcrowding and the desire of many to avoid paying unfair rents for inferior services precipitated the migration out of Harlem and the other deteriorating metropolitan neighborhoods, it was the generally higher standard of living enjoyed by most workers in the post war period that enabled thousands of city dwellers to make the necessary move. "Labor was never as prosperous as it is today," declared one tenement house official in explaining this exodus from the inner city, "and the American worker has always been desirous of bringing up his family in the best possible surroundings. He has tried to get away from the sordidness and the present prosperity has afforded him an opportunity of which he has taken full advantage." Other contemporaries observed that "since the war, wages have risen and hours have been shortened and the ordinary man expects better accommodations and more enjoyment for his family and himself. He is less easily reconciled to the tenement district and old apartment houses and more eager for what the suburbs offer him." Modern fireproof buildings such as those on the Grand Concourse attracted those able to pay higher rents and many middle- and working-class families responded to the call.[17]

Economically prosperous families were, however, not the only ones to migrate from the inner city. Older sections of the Bronx, for example, offered new housing to former tenement dwellers at rents only slightly above those charged in Manhattan, and well below those prevailing on the Grand Concourse. The some 17,000 housing units built in the 1920s in the Morrisania and Hunts Point sections of the Bronx permitted many working-class families of more limited means to break the bonds of New York's older tenement districts. The deteriorating inner-city neighborhoods continued to house those incapable of escape and absorbed the newly arriving poor.[18]

New York's immigrant Jewish citizens were among the most active participants in this second generation of intracity relocation. As was the case with the settlement of Harlem a generation earlier, both poor and affluent Jews took part in the intracity migration. The higher rents charged for better housing were no real barriers for the many newly affluent, and the more prosperous working-class families. The occupational distribution of immigrant Jews and their children, according to one early urban demographer, underwent a dramatic change during the years prior to the Great Depression. "There was an upward trend in the professions, trades and in the clerical occupations" held by Jews both in New York and elsewhere and a corresponding "downward trend in manufacturing and in the domestic and personal services." This basic pattern of immigrant upward mobility was due, reportedly, both to "the general development of the country and to the successful adjustment of a considerable number of our erstwhile immigrants to the socioeconomic environment of the United States." For prosperous Jews, who during this period also found money for luxury consumer goods and expensive leisure- and vacation-time activities, migration out of the inner city was primarily a question of finding suitable accommodations at a most reasonable price.[19]

Certainly not every immigrant Jewish family shared equally in the decade's prosperity. Not all possessed the economic resources both to move to new better-built homes, while retaining sufficient funds to buy the cars and take the trips advertised in the Yiddish press. One poor young participant in the 1920s' out-of-ghetto movement recalled that his father arranged to borrow money from his boss on the installment plan to afford a new home in residential Brooklyn. Other families relied on pooled family incomes earned by three or more breadwinners to pay higher apartment rents. Whatever the difficulties, escape from the tenements was given the highest priority by Jewish families of every economic class.[20]

The major difference between this and earlier peak periods of dispersion out of the ghetto was that now few Jews were arriving from Europe to replace—or force out—those leaving the old immigrant centers. The start of the First World War had put a temporary halt to mass East European immigration, and the Federal Immigration Laws of 1921 and 1924 made the curtailment of Jewish immigration permanent. Thus, as the old neighborhoods continued to decline and those who had achieved even the most minimal level of economic advancement chose to leave for new areas, no new wave of Jewish immigrants took their place.

Each of the pre-World War I centers of New York Jewish life was consequently, strongly affected by the impact of this outer-borough migration during the postwar years. The Lower East Side, which once housed three-quarters of New York's immigrant Jews and which was, before the war, still home for one-quarter of the city's Jewish population, retained only 15 percent of the total in 1925. Over the next decade, the downtown area lost an additional 60 percent of its Jewish residents, reducing their number to 62,000. The early immigrant settlement of Williamsburg similarly lost close to one-quarter of its settlers between 1916 and 1925 as its population dropped from approximately 123,000 before the war to 105,000 ten years later. Brownsville, on the other hand, continued to enjoy a net population increase through 1925, but at a much slower rate than before. However, its era of ascendancy ended shortly thereafter and by 1930, only 170,000 Jews remained in the *combined* East Flatbush and Brownsville sections of Brooklyn.[21]

The effects of postwar Jewish intracity migration were felt most acutely in Harlem. That community, which numbered approximately 178,000 at the height of the housing crisis, began to lose population as soon as suburban construction was resumed in 1921. By 1923, Harlem's Jewish population had dropped to an estimated 168,000 and Jewish communal observers were already talking of the decline of Jewish Harlem. The Jewish Welfare Board, for example, declared that "the outlook is for a steady reduction of Harlem's Jewish population due to the restrictions on immigration, the desire to better oneself socially as the economic status improves, the influx of negroes [*sic*],

Italians and Spanish-speaking groups." "The Jewish migration from Harlem," was noted, however, as "only at the rate of 1.4 percent annually."[22]

This report greatly underestimated the rate of out-migration, because by 1925—only two years later—another independent communal survey found that only 123,000 Jews remained in Harlem. The settlement had suffered a decline of more than 25 percent over the two years, not the 1.4 percent per annum predicted in 1923.[23]

The steady stream of relocating Harlem Jews increased even more drastically in the second half of the decade. By 1927, Harlem Jewry numbered only 88,000; a percentage decline of over one-third since 1925. Three years later, the Jewish evacuation of Harlem was almost complete. The highest contemporary estimate of Jewish population fixed the number at 25,000. A much later retrospective population study estimated the Jewish population in 1930 at 5,000. Although several thousand Jews continued to live there through succeeding decades and several hundreds still live there today, Harlem's era as a landmark on the Jewish map of New York was over by 1930.[24]

The exceedingly rapid Jewish exodus from Harlem was inaugurated by the same set of forces that would soon lead to the decline of the downtown ghetto and New York's other densely populated old Jewish neighborhoods. The departure was hastened by the postwar black "invasion" of uptown. Blacks were, of course, originally attracted to Harlem during the first decade of the twentieth century for many of the same reasons that motivated Jewish migration. The desire to improve their living conditions and the need to escape the overcrowded and vice-ridden "Tenderloin" district prompted many ambitious black families to seek accommodations in Harlem. Their fears of renewed violence against them by whites, on the scale of the famous Tenderloin Riots of 1900, increased their eagerness to migrate.[25]

Unlike Jews and other immigrants whose choice of uptown accommodations was dictated, in almost all cases, by their ability to pay the higher uptown rents, blacks often found their way uptown blocked by neighborhood protective associations whose members believed that the black migration would automatically lower the value of their real estate holdings. One such organization, The West Side Improvement Association, which some blacks described as "composed in the main by Jews," tried to evict Negroes from the West 90th to 110th Street area. The rationale for such behavior was not "pre-judice against the race," but fear that "their presence in a neighbor-hood would cause the value of property to deteriorate."[26]

Several Yiddish and Anglo-Jewish newspapers strongly condemned the action of these and other protective organizations. *The American Hebrew*, for example, decried the hypocrisy of those individuals who called upon blacks to improve themselves and then denied them a decent place to live. "How are they to become thrifty and indepen-dent and give their children the best education available," one editorialist asked, "if they are not allowed to acquire homes suitable for persons of refinement?"[27]

The Yiddishes Tageblatt, sensing a certain communality of fates be-tween Jews and the persecuted Negro, applauded the efforts of the Afro-American Realty Company which, in 1905 and later, bought up many unoccupied apartment houses and made them available to blacks. In supporting black self-help efforts, Tageblatt writers may well have recalled the problems experienced by some Jews in settling certain parts of uptown. The memory of Irish attacks against im-migrants in the streets of East Harlem, which in 1900 prompted the newspaper to send what they described as a "bitter" protest letter to the local police captain, may have heightened their sensitivity to the present plight of their black neighbors. The newspaper's position on Jewish participation in the perpetration of physical atrocities against Negroes was even clearer. Race riots, in its opinion, were "a terrible pogrom against Negroes" and "a terrible sign for Jews. It shows that the New York people can manifest a great hate for a strange race. For the persecuted Jew to enhearten the persecutors of the Negro is indeed despicable."[28]

Despite vocal—and sometimes physical—opposition from various quarters, blacks succeeded by the end of the first decade of the twen-tieth century in securing a substantial foothold in the northern sec-tions of Harlem. By 1910, blacks had established themselves as the predominant group north of 130th Street, west of Park Avenue. More than two-thirds of Harlem's approximately 22,000 Blacks resided in this section of uptown.[29]

Harlem's blacks lived in housing far superior to anything enjoyed previously by their race in any metropolitan area, and paid dearly for the privilege. Most paid substantially higher rents than whites for their accommodations and many were forced to allocate up to one-third of their incomes to live in what one black contemporary described as "one of the choice sections of Harlem, conveniently and beautifully located, with broad asphalt avenues and streets, modern apartments . . . and admirable transportation to the city."[30]

Despite the high cost of living, which forced some settlers to take in lodgers to meet rent payments, Harlem remained, according to black leadership, "an ideal place to live" for the aspiring black family willing to make sacrifices to reside in a good neighborhood. The uptown black enclave was also apparently a good place to live for the several thousand Jews who had made it their home by 1910. Jews were counted among the many white businessmen who reportedly resided in the black section "for the conveniences it affords them in conducting trade." Other white residents included those who continued to own and maintain the few private homes in the area and those who, reportedly, had "no aversion to Negroes."[31]

Jews remained a recognizable minority within the black neighborhood throughout the next decade. In fact, Jews seemed to have shown a greater degree of persistence than other groups in an area which by 1920 had become overwhelmingly black. The total Jewish presence in northwest Harlem declined only slightly during the prewar years and on some blocks the number of Jews actually rose. When Jews did decide to vacate this uptown area during the 1920s it was not specifically because of their having harbored any special aversion towards living among blacks.*

The massive influx of southern Blacks to the city during the era of the First World War destroyed Black Harlem's residential and racial balance. Entering the metropolitan area in search of work in northern industries, most of these migrants settled in Harlem's Black neighborhood. By 1920, 70 percent of Manhattan's 109,000 blacks resided

---

* In 1920, some 2,260 Jews lived in a North Harlem area which had become almost exclusively Black. Taking the census district with the largest concentration (133d to 140th Street, Fifth and Lenox Avenues) as an example, we find that the proportion of Blacks rose from approximately 50 percent of the total in 1910 to 96 percent ten years later. The Jewish population declined from 11 percent to 3 percent of the total. However, the approximately 450 Jews who remained in the district constituted almost the *entire* white presence in the district. The Jewish presence in the census tract district of 134th to 138th Street, between Lenox and Eighth Avenues, actually increased in the ten year period, which saw the Black percentage of the population rise from less than 20 to 77 percent of the total. Some 730 Jews resided in that district in 1920 where approximately 600 resided there a decade earlier. See Laidlaw, *Statistical Sources for Demographic Studies of Greater New York*, (New York: The New York City 1920 Census Committee, 1923), passim.

between 118th and 144th streets between the Hudson and Harlem Rivers. As rents soared during the wartime and postwar housing shortage, thousands of black migrants "doubled-up" and took in lodgers to meet high Harlem rents. Soon, however, the existing black area was unable to absorb any more new arrivals and as migration peaked during the 1920s, Harlem's black neighborhood began to expand.[32]

Accommodations in other parts of Central Harlem became readily available when widespread building resumed in 1921. As Jews and other white groups began to depart their deteriorating neighborhoods for newer and better sections of Manhattan and the outlying boroughs, their places were quickly taken by the ever-mounting volume of black migration. An additional 175,000 blacks, constituting a net population increase of 115 percent, entered New York City during the 1920s. Desirous of settling among their own kind and restricted economically and socially in their choice of neighborhood, most of these new settlers crowded into the rapidly deteriorating uptown district. There they joined thousands of Harlem's earlier black residents who were also stopped by convention and covenant from seeking the frontiers of suburbia. By 1930, some 165,000 of New York's 328,000 blacks lived in Harlem.[33]

This massive influx of new black settlers more than offset the number of whites leaving Harlem and afforded landlords the opportunity to continue to maintain the housing status quo. Harlem realtors of this era were not at all reluctant to open their doors to blacks. Blacks had always paid high rents for their accommodations and the now greatly increased demand for scarce housing free property owners from any real commitment to improving living conditions. Those landlords who were opposed to black tenancy also capitalized upon the situation. They were able to use the threat of a "black invasion" to extort higher rents from those remaining whites who were either unwilling or unable to leave Harlem, but who were desirous of continuing to reside in segregated surroundings.[34]

This combination of a massive black incursion coupled with the steady deterioration of housing conditions and the continuing high rents charged for now inferior accommodations quickly convinced Central Harlem's remaining upwardly mobile Jews that uptown's "Jewish era" had come to an end. And as each Jewish family left the neighborhood, one or more black families replaced it, furthering the emerging predominance of blacks and promoting in turn the removal of additional Jewish families.

The black take-over of Central Harlem also fundamentally affected the direction of Jewish migration out of East Harlem. East Harlem had never really been a choice residential district attractive to the most upwardly mobile families. As had the ghetto, it had housed many of those awaiting the arrival of good times and the opportunity to settle in better neighborhoods. The wartime housing shortage simply exacerbated already depressed conditions and furthered the resolve of those wanting to escape the tenements.

Under normal circumstances, the resumption of building in 1921 and the early exodus of the most affluent Central Harlemites would have depressed the rentals in that district, enabling less-affluent East Harlemites to migrate to the "better" neighborhood, west of Fifth Avenue. Central Harlem realtors would also have had to improve conditions in their houses if they hoped to attract new tenants from the neighboring area. The curtailment of European immigration coupled with the expansion of suburban housing facilities would have reduced the demand for tenement housing, producing a new "buyers market" in Harlem real estate.

The black incursion uptown eliminated all these possibilities. Landlords never had to lower rents or improve conditions to attract or hold black tenants. Out-migrating East Harlemites quickly realized that they would, paradoxically, have to scrape together more money to afford to "escape" to overcrowded, deteriorating Central Harlem than to migrate to the "suburban" South Bronx. Most took the more logical course of action. Their vacated tenements were soon occupied by New York's newest immigrants—the Puerto Ricans—who began to settle en masse in East Harlem in the late 1920s.[35]*

---

*The history and problems of the so-called "Black Jews of Harlem" lie outside the scope of this present study. These groups, espousing a syncretistic Jewish and Christian theology and advocating a Black nationalist ideology closely linked with Marcus Garvey's "Back to Africa" movement, maintained little if any contact with our white Jewish community of Harlem. As early as July 1933, a study of the "Negro Jews" determined that theirs was, "except for its exploitative aspects, a Negro (movement) and therefore, outside the realm of Jewish social service—except from the broader humanitarian and internationalistic viewpoint." See Edward Wolf, "Negro Jews: A Social Study," Jewish Social Service Quarterly (June 1933), pp. 314–19. See also Howard Brotz, The Black Jews of Harlem: Negro Nationalism and the Dilemmas of Negro Leadership (New York: Schocken Books, 1970).

While it is impossible to determine what percentage of Harlem's Jewish population migrated to which new section of New York City in the 1920s, some indication of the major directions of the dispersal may be discerned through the study of the out-migration of Harlem-based institutions. Although the overwhelming number of Harlem Jewish organizations—especially the immigrant landsmanshaften synagogues and clubs—simply disintegrated as their members exited from the neighborhoods, several of the major Jewish institutions did survive their era in Harlem and were reestablished in the new Jewish neighborhoods on the West Side and Washington Heights of Manhattan and in the Bronx. As a rule, most formerly Central-Harlem-based institutions remained within Manhattan, while most of East Harlem's surviving institutions relocated out of the borough and were reconstituted in various parts of the northernmost borough.

The first institutions to move out of the district were those located on the periphery of the major Central Harlem settlement, north of 130th Street. Congregation Anshe Emeth of 131st Street and Seventh Avenue led the way in 1917 by merging with a new congregation, Mount Sinai of 181st Street and St. Nicholas Avenue. That group was followed to Washington Heights three years later by a neighboring synagogue, The Hebrew Tabernacle, which relocated from 130th Street to temporary quarters on Upper Broadway.[36]

The Hebrew Tabernacle had led a tenuous existence in North Harlem almost from the day it was founded in 1905. Its congregational history reflects the trials of the many small local congregatrions which did not share in the great fat years of Jewish Harlem-bound migration in the early years of this century. Situated away from the major centers of Harlem Jewish life, this congregation always had difficulty attracting members and worshipers. For this synagogue, organizational life was an on-going struggle for existence in a predominantly non-Jewish section of uptown. As early as 1908, for example, the congregation was obliged to hire paid worshipers to maintain daily morning and evening services. Despite these and other financial difficulties, the congregation did grow slowly and was eventually able to erect its own synagogue building. And at one point in its history it even succeeded in enrolling some 400 children in its Sunday School.[37]

By 1918, however, synagogue officials understood that the Tabernacle could no longer survive in North Harlem. In April, synagogue trustees reported that the daily minyan could not be maintained without a substantial increase in the wages paid to daily worshipers. Several months later, they noted that religious school enrollment had dropped off precipitously. Finally, in January 1919, recognizing that "the expenses of conducting services are largely in excess of the (synagogue's) income," Tabernacle membership authorized its trustees to "dispose of our quarters on terms which they deem proper, if opportunities present themselves."[38]

Although the majority of members was in agreement that the synagogue had to be moved, there was much less of a consensus over where the new synagogue should be located. One faction, led by Rev. Edward Lissman, founder, rabbi, life-member and former treasurer of the congregation, sought to relocate the institution along Riverside Drive, south of 120th Street. Another faction headed by board of trustees member Louis Austern, saw Washington Heights as the future home of the Hebrew Tabernacle.

The next year was marked by several complicated congregational intrigues as both Lissman and Austern attempted to devise means of determining the synagogue's future. Austern undertook to negotiate several merger agreements with small Washington Heights groups, while Lissman tried to prevail upon the board to purchase a new site at 83rd Street and Riverside Drive. Neither succeeded in gaining majority support for his program.[39]

Finally, late in 1919, the Austern faction won out, the Hebrew Tabernacle was sold and the congregation moved to temporary quarters at 158th Street and Broadway. Two years later, Washington Heights' newest synagogue was firmly reestablished in a newly altered building on St. Nicholas Avenue. Soon the congregation would once again boast of a religious school enrollment of more than 350 students.[40]

Lissman did not follow the majority of his congregants further uptown. He resigned his lifetime membership and pulpit late in 1920 and established a new synagogue, Riverside Synagogue at 108th Street and Broadway. Bitter over Austern's victory, he called upon his supporters to nullify the trustees' decision by leaving the Tabernacle to help him serve "a needed requirement in the immediate vicinity of Broadway between 105–120th Streets."[41]

Joining Lissman's Riverside Synagogue in serving the growing West Side Jewish community were several of Central Harlem's oldest and most affluent congregations, which followed their members in migrating west of Central Park in the 1920s. Temple Israel, for example, sold its synagogue at Lenox Avenue and 120th Street to a group of Seventh Day Adventists in 1920 and moved to 91st Street between Amsterdam Avenue and Broadway, "following," as Rabbi Harris put it, "the westward drift of our congregants."[42]

Congregations Shaarei Zedek and Ohab Zedek and Temple Anshe Chesed continued their traditions of following their most affluent members to newer sections of Manhattan and also erected large synagogue buildings on the West Side during this period. These three synagogues, it will be remembered, all began as small immigrant congregations on the Lower East Side at different points during the nineteenth century. Each synagogue eventually left the downtown area, following its membership to Harlem, and each established large houses of worship in the Lenox Avenue section of uptown. By 1926 each had followed the Jewish migration out of Central Harlem and had been reestablished in the fashionable area west of Central Park and south of 100th Street.[43]

Three years later, Rabbi Herbert S. Goldstein established a branch of the Institutional Synagogue on the West Side. Alert to the changes in Jewish demography, Goldstein recognized that his constituency of young Jewish men and women was rapidly abandoning Harlem. His goals of instilling "the twin ideals of patriotic Americanism and Judaism" would be best continued among the young people of Manhattan's new Jewish neighborhood. Services under his auspices were first conducted in a rented hall at Broadway and 83rd Street in 1927. Two years later, a synagogue center was established at 76th Street, between Columbus and Amsterdam Avenues.[44]

Despite its ever dwindling number of members, its apparently nonexistent dues base, and the resignation of Rabbi Goldstein in 1938, the Harlem Institutional Synagogue continued to operate until 1943. This achievement was due not so much to the great commitment of its remaining supporters to keep the moribund institution alive, as it was to its favorable rental agreement with the New York City Board of Education. In March 1933, the Institutional Synagogue contracted with the Board to rent its schoolroom space for use by a junior high school, at a rate of $10,000 per annum. When, in 1943, a new junior high school was built in Harlem, The Harlem Institutional Synagogue lost its last major source of income and its building was sold.[45]

The first East Harlem Jewish institution to follow its constituency to a new section of New York was the Rabbi Israel Salanter Talmud Torah, which in 1923 removed from its original home at 114th Street and Madison Avenue to Washington Avenue in the South Bronx, where it was renamed Yeshiva Rabbi Israel Salanter of the Bronx. This particular institution was destined to continue following the generational migrations of Bronx Jewry. In 1940, the Salanter Yeshiva moved to Webster Avenue in the Tremont section of the borough. And in 1970 the then declining Yeshiva moved to Riverdale, New York, the city's newest Jewish residential neighborhood, where it merged with two other schools and was renamed and reinvigorated as the S/A/R Academy.[46]

Late in the 1920s, Central Harlem's Krakower Simon Schreiber Synagogue moved from its rented quarters at Westminster Hall at 114th Street and Lenox Avenue to Townsend Avenue near the Grand Concourse. There it was joined by East Harlem's Kehal Adath Jeshurun which migrated to nearby Gerard Avenue and 165th Street. This latter religious group soon merged with an indigenous Bronx congregation, Agudath Jeshurun.[47]

Workmen's Circle Branch#2 also responded to the out-migration of most of its members during the late 1920s by shifting the site of its meetings from East Harlem to the Bronx, upholding its oldest tradition of serving members in their own neighborhoods. Branch officials, once leaders of Harlem's most important laboringman's organization, expressed little if any sadness over their decision to leave the old neighborhood. N. Davidoff, chairman of the Branch in 1929, may have best articulated the sentiments of his membership when he noted: "Branch #2 was born in Harlem and we have lived there and grown, when the time came and the majority of members moved away to the Bronx, it was natural that the branch go where the greatest number of members were. Therefore we can see, that although we are growing old, we are keeping up with the times."[48]

This description of the out-migration of the few Harlem Jewish institutions that successfully followed their members out of the deteriorating neighborhood does not, however, presume to suggest that the West Side, Washington Heights and the Bronx were the *only* places that absorbed large numbers of Harlem's Jews. Nor can one say conclusively that these areas took in the majority of the migrants—it is entirely possible that Brooklyn, which showed the most prolific growth during the 1920s, did in actuality attract more Jews from Har-

POPULATION MIGRATION FROM HARLEM

1920 – 1930

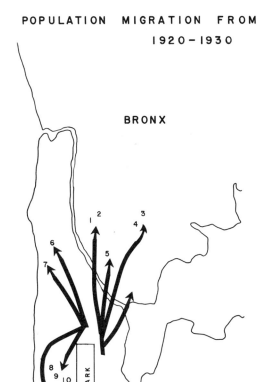

BRONX

QUEENS

Map 6. Population Migration from Harlem, 1920–1930
Source: Works Progress Administration, Historical Records Survey. Inventory of Records of Churches. Jewish Synagogues. Map by L. Salit.

1) Jewish Center of Highbridge
2) Adath Israel
3) Beth David
4) Tifereth Israel
5) Adath Jeshurun
6) Hebrew Tabernacle
7) B'nai Israel Sheerith Judah

8) Shaare Zedek
9) Temple Israel
10) Ohab Zedek
11) West Side Institutional
    Synagogue
12) Mount Neboh

lem. It is also certainly conceivable that many small synagogue groups, landsmanshaften and clubs moved to Brooklyn or Queens and were immediately consolidated with existing organizations in the other boroughs, quickly surrendering their "Harlem identity."

This study does, however, help confirm certain of our impressions about the process and timetable of Jewish migration out of Harlem. Central Harlem institutions, founded and supported by the district's most affluent Jews, were the first to move. Their relocation to the fashionable West Side and Washington Heights indicates that at least some of Harlem's most upwardly mobile residents continued their economic climb in these new middle-class Manhattan neighborhoods.

East Harlem's institutions began to migrate out of their neighborhood at a slightly later date. The presence of former East Harlem organizations in a variety of sections of the Bronx, including the relatively low-rent district of the South Bronx, indicates that East Harlem's less-affluent former residents had achieved the basic level of economic advancement needed to break the uptown ghetto's grip and were able to take advantage of the residential opportunities offered by the Bronx. Their migration from Harlem was, as an anonymous contemporary put it, "not due to economic need. The removal is voluntary and the reason is not gloomy. Jews on the road to bettering themselves and making life more convenient for themselves, moved from Harlem up to the Bronx."[49]

chapter 7

Reflections on
the Harlem Jewish
Experience

This history of Jewish life in Harlem grants long overdue recognition to a once important and until now uncelebrated American Jewish community. But this investigation would be incomplete and its findings valued as of limited enduring import if no attempt were made to indicate what the evidence from this particular local experience contributes towards the understanding of certain basic themes in both American Jewish, urban, and immigrant historiography. The major facets of Harlem's complex communal experience either point out significant lacunae in general historical surveys or question standard interpretations of the most basic aspects of urban immigrant life. Harlem's story deepens our knowledge of the specific processes directing urban neighborhood growth and decay, immigrant settlements and relocations, and internal Jewish communal organization and conflict. And it may suggest new areas for basic future investigation. It is here, on the comparative and analytical levels, that this local communal story ultimately gains its greatest historical significance.

The general historiographical focus of mid-nineteenth-century German-American Jewish life has to date centered either upon the changing communal structure of early Atlantic coast Jewish centers under the impact of large-scale Central European migration or upon the trials and travails of the immigrant peddler—the Jewish component of America's manifest destiny story—who plies his wares in the

Western wilderness and who ultimately succeeds in establishing fo-
cuses of Jewish economic and religious life in most major entrepôt
cities on the road to California. Historians have recognized the absence of substantial communications between the older Eastern
centers and the new pioneer communities of the West. And they have
examined the valiant attempts at national unification initiated by several groups of religious leaders within a dispersed American Jewry.
No one has analyzed, however, the economic life and community-
building activities of those other German Jews who were neither
really part of the seaboard communities nor of the remote midwestern settlements—the Jews of the early, nineteenth-century suburbs.
Indeed, most historians, even those studying specific cities, fail to
mention their existence, let alone examine their problems and contributions. Harlem, New York's uptown suburb, was undoubtedly but
one of many such communities. This present study recognizes that
the beginnings of immigrant migration from the core city to its outlying districts preceded the arrival of both strong intracity rapid transit
links and the late-nineteenth-century new immigrants. And it suggests
the need to examine the histories of comparable Jewish immigrant
groups physically removed from the geographically limited, com-
munications-weak nineteenth-century city.[1]

The emphasis accorded here to Harlem's early German communal
history highlights an often-overlooked aspect of late-nineteenth-century American Jewish life. At present, many discussions of the internal
communal life of the Germans—especially of those Germans residing
in the largest cities—end in 1881. Once the East Europeans begin arriving en masse, the earlier immigrants are often studied almost solely
as members of a community reacting to the new migration. German
Jews are considered either as restrictionists—fearful of what the Russians will do to the good name of American Jewry—or as either self-
serving or genuinely humanitarian philanthropists—working to
Americanize the outlandish foreigners while struggling to keep anti-
immigrant laws off the legislative books. We know a good deal
within this context about the lives and activities of the Schiffs, Mar-
shalls and Warburgs. But what of their less-famous coethnics and
coreligionists? The day-to-day communal life of the average German
Jew is frequently neglected, or discussed only in the narrow context
of their forced removal or replacement in ghetto areas by the newly
arrived poor. Did all the Germans leave the ghetto and quickly assimi-
late? And if not, how did they structure and maintain their own inter-

nal, communal existence? The history of the pre-1900 Harlem German settlement tells a story of persistent ethnic group cohesion and suggests the value of comparable studies of other large non-ghetto communities.[2]

The study of Harlem's several German synagogues, each with its own ritual and underlying theological stance, speaks to the question of the divisions within American Jewish life in this same time period. Most contemporary historiography suggests that with the establishment of the Union of American Hebrew Congregations, the Hebrew Union College and the Central Conference of American Rabbis in 1873, 1875 and 1889 respectively, American Jewry—excepting that segment belonging to the new East European Orthodox immigrant congregations—was unequally divided between a strong unified Reform movement under Isaac Mayer Wise, David Einhorn and Kaufmann Kohler, and a weak, splintered group of traditionalists, led by the Historical School of the old Seminary.[3]

The Harlem experience suggests otherwise. On the local neighborhood level, Reform Judaism was no stronger and no more unified religiously or institutionally than any other group. Only one uptown Reform congregation, Temple Israel, affiliated with the U.A.H.C. and adopted the standard Union Prayer Book. But it broke with the suggested pattern for affiliated synagogues by maintaining the traditional "second day of holidays" and by permitting the wearing of prayer shawls and head coverings during services. Conversely, Temple Mount Zion, Harlem's other large Reform congregation, retained few if any of the old traditional forms and rituals, but never joined the Union. Synagogues declaring themselves traditional also displayed a confusing mixture of Orthodox and Reform practices. Mixed choirs, organs and other instruments characterized the services of several Harlem Conservative-Orthodox congregations, while others with the same self-description pursued the more traditional forms of religious practice. Such evidence from this local community—which suggests the need for comparable work in other geographical areas—indicates that in many localities the power and commitment of particular pulpit rabbis (such as Temple Israel's Maurice Harris), or of synagogue leadership, and not the dictates of any national authority, ultimately determined the nature of synagogue practice.[4]

The detailed saga of turn-of-the-century East European migration from the Lower East Side to Harlem challenges previous assumptions and may contribute to a new and broader understanding of the forces directing intracity migration and underlying the basic character of urban immigrant settlement life. The pioneering works of sociologists Burgess, Wirth and Cressey noted earlier have greatly influenced most analyses of the dynamics of ghetto and out-of-ghetto immigrant life. Their early studies of Chicago's immigrant communities, which they seemed paradigmatic for all American cities, depicted a sharp delineation in economic distribution and social structure between areas of first and second settlement and thus emphasized "uptown" migration as a signal milestone in the changing economic and social life of the new American. In their view, upon arrival in America, the poor and unacculturated immigrant had no option but to settle in the densely populated run-down sections of the city already occupied by his fellow poor coethnics or coreligionists. Though economically impoverished and physically encumbered, the new settler was, nevertheless, to some extent comfortable in his ghetto, surrounded by those of his own kind who were experiencing along with him the common difficulties of adjustment to a strange new world.

Over the course of years, the immigrant, by dint of his hard work or luck, and his exposure, either directly or through his children, to great Americanizing institutions such as the social settlements and the public schools, achieved the economic power and acquired the social confidence to flee the ghetto for better-built second-settlement areas. The growth of urban-suburban rapid transit lines often facilitated the physical move as industrially poor, residentially superior neighborhoods were brought closer to the inner city. The upwardly mobile immigrant fleeing the overcrowded, deteriorated ghetto was able to live uptown and to commute downtown to his work. The poor remained where they were, awaiting their own moment of socioeconomic mobility to join the march uptown.[5]

The newly acculturated, upwardly mobile, second-settlement immigrant quickly demonstrated a fundamentally changed lifestyle. Indeed, an entire immigrant identity rooted in old-world and ghetto ideas and institutions was abandoned uptown as the new settler began to lose social, cultural and religious contact with his fellow coethnics and coreligionists. The second-settlement resident was well on the road to complete assimilation into American society. This situation is illustrated in the Jewish immigrant literary tradition by the sage of David Levinsky, Harlem's best-known Jewish "resident."

But Ab. Cahan's fictional character is not really a typical exemplar of the overall Harlem experience, and that community's history—and indeed that of New York Jewry in general—does not correspond to these generalized theoretical notions about immigrant life. A much less static structure characterized this metropolitan area's immigrant settlement life. A far more complex concert of forces motivated relocation from one area of the city to the next and maintained Jewish identification. Downtown and uptown alike were home, at least after 1900, to both poor and more affluent Jews, and apparently more immigrants moved to Harlem in the hope of financial success than as a sign that they had already achieved this success. And some of the same forces that pushed many of the poor out of the ghetto may well have contributed, ironically, to the persistence there of many of their more affluent fellow immigrants.

New-law tenement legislation, for example, envisioned by well-meaning social reformers as a means of improving the health and living conditions of ghetto inhabitants, inadvertently forced many poor immigrants out of downtown. But these same laws simultaneously encouraged many newly successful immigrant entrepreneurs to remain on the Lower East Side. Ghetto realtors, it will be remembered, quickly recognized the economic profitability of the new building code and created a middle- to high-rent district within ghetto limits. They attracted those successful manufacturers, dealers and shopkeepers who were eager to remain downtown, near their factories or businesses, but who wanted to live in modern apartment houses that reflected their new economic station.

Progressive-inspired public park legislation may have had a similar effect on the economic class composition of the ghetto and of uptown. The condemnation of thousands of tenements to make way for new parks caused many poor Jews either to crowd in with friends or relatives downtown or to seek lodgings outside the ghetto. But these same parks, which improved the physical face of the neighborhood, may well have been a factor convincing the newly affluent immigrant, living in the better-built homes of the Lower East Side and using these new municipal improvements, to remain in the heart of the Jewish section.

The differences between the New York experience and the Chicago-based theory are evidenced, of course, most dramatically by the story of the large numbers of poor and unacculturated Jews who made or who were forced to make Harlem their home. For New York's poor, migration did not mean the predicted resettlement in a new, residentially superior neighborhood built within reasonable commutation time of downtown factory or office. Dumbbell tenements and densely populated streets, so physically reminiscent of the Lower East Side, were the day-to-day realities for the poor, working-class Jews of Harlem's Third Avenue district and elsewhere. For these new uptowners, the building of subways between Harlem and Lower Manhattan played but a minor role in directing the course of their lives. Indeed, the poor ghetto Jews who had to rely on rapid transit to reach their labors—needle trades workers who could find no work in their industry uptown are the best examples—did not remove from the ghetto to Harlem in any large numbers. This evidence ironically indicates, that both for rich downtowners and poor uptowners, the desire to avoid commutation to work played a key role in determining where an immigrant would make his home.

For Harlem's unacculturated immigrant Jews, many but not all of them poor, resettlement uptown was not, as theoretically suggested, indicative either of their adaptation to or acceptance of a new American way of life. The ghetto or downtown Jew's basic family and neighborly institutional response to the social disorientation accompanying early immigrant exposure to foreign American surroundings was the small landsmanshaft synagogue, and literally hundreds of these synagogues existed uptown. This clearly indicates that although a large number of new Harlem settlers may have achieved a high level of acculturation before stepping out of the ghetto, many others had not.

The challenges accepted by Harlem's radicals to recreate what they viewed as the lost atmosphere of the ghetto and to establish and maintain Harlem institutions in close communication with downtown movements and organizations indicates furthermore that many relocating ghetto Jews were neither prepared nor eager to surrender their immigrant identity. They refused to adopt the dominant societal cultural and political norms of their supposed new neighborhood. Their history points out the pervasiveness of local ghetto culture well beyond the geographical limits of the downtown center.

It is clear from the evidence here presented that the Chicago-based understanding of the basic processes of intracity migration and immigrant settlement life cannot be applied to all urban settings. It remains to be determined, however, to what extent New York's experience invalidates Burgess's, Wirth's, and Cressey's predictions for other metropolises. Indeed, one might contend that this country's largest immigrant center, by virtue of its size, its situation as the main port of entry, and the proximity and accessibility of Harlem to the hub of Jewish life, is simply unique, thus causing its immigrant experience to differ from that of other groups elsewhere in America. Certainly given these inherent singularities, it is difficult to state that New York's history typifies the life-course of most American cities. And yet it is apparent that what made this local history so different from what was theoretically expected were not these exceptional factors but a concert of forces which, as noted earlier, New York may well have experienced in common with other places. The pressures placed upon New York's poor ghetto-dwellers by ill-timed urban renewal efforts and well-intentioned slum clearance plans during periods of great migrations into the city, the willingness of poor workers to relocate away from the immigrant hub in seeking their livelihoods and the apparent concommitant desire of both the poor and new-rich immigrants to live where they work, along with the generally recognized predilection of the upwardly mobile to live in the best possible surroundings—all these do not seem to be only part of the particular Harlem-New York Jewish communal story. These influences are, in all likelihood, to be found among other groups in other cities across this country. What this evidence probably points to is the conclusion that neither New York not Chicago nor any other single city can serve as a model for all urban-immigrant conditions. Each area has its unique characteristics while maintaining major elements in common with its sister cities. It is left, however, to future studies of other ethnic groups and localities to finally determine to what extent this present case-study indeed contributes towards a reorientation of our understanding of some of the most basic aspects of immigrant life and historiography.[6]

The history of the institution-building efforts of Harlem's community of acculturated Jews challenges another general conception of the nature of urban immigrant life. This history joins another recent study in questioning the commonly held perception of what Americanization meant to those willing to sever their identification with the immigrant way of life. Upwardly mobile acculturated second-settlement residents—the only variety of uptowners previously noted—traditionally have been depicted as persons on the road to assimilation and the abandonment of their religious and/or ethnic cultural heritage and group identity. The Harlem case-study argues to the contrary and suggests that to the extent that areas of second immigrant settlement were conducive to rapid Americanization they were also hospitable to the maintenance and even to the strengthening of Jewish identification. This detailed examination of the earliest efforts to fashion new social and religious forms for an American Judaism may also suggest that historians now sensitive to the course of the anti-assimilationist communal battle begin their accounts and analyses with the Harlem story.[7]

The account given here of the alliances forged and maintained uptown between German and new elite East European leaders and between those later identified either with the Conservative Movement or with Modern Orthodoxy in beginning the struggle against disaffection from Judaism also gives pause for historical reflection and possible reinterpretation. Most historians of immigration, for example, see the communal interaction between Germans and East Europeans simply in terms of a patron-client relationship. The self-declared culturally superior old immigrant was ostensibly seeking to expose his newly arrived medieval brother to the light of Americanism. The Germans were committed to acculturation and the Russians were the objects of their concern. It is further understood that the patrons accepted without qualification the values of Americanization and showed little concern for the problems of perpetuating the Judaism of their acculturating clients. According to this view, the struggle against assimilation was reserved for the second-generation East European Jew, and the Germans played no role in this latter effort.[8] Only Arthur Goren's masterful history of the New York Kehillah departs from this pattern of interpretation. It points up true German-Jewish concern with the future of Jewish identity in America through their support of institutions such as the Bureau of Jewish Education, a city-wide organization strongly dedicated both to Americanization and to the advancement of Judaism. Harlem's history of great cooperation between Germans and the East European new elite concurs with Goren's analysis and also argues for a new, more sophisticated understanding of Jewish intragroup relations.

Our study clearly indicates that once one group of East Europeans had itself reached a certain level of acculturation, that group became no less committed to Americanizing their fellow immigrants than were the Germans. The job of regenerating the "greenhorn" was not the sole preserve of the old immigrants. And those who arrived in the mid-nineteenth-century wave of migration also seemed not to have harbored any hint of snobbishness or resentment towards those newly affluent and Americanized Russian Jews who sought to share their social welfare concerns. The Cohens and Fischels of Harlem were never viewed by the Harrises and Hayses of that community as their social or cultural inferiors.

Harlem's history additionally demands—as did Goren's study—that all Germans should not be depicted as essentially assimilationists. Those who worked uptown in the talmud torah movement and in the Harlem Federation clearly demonstrated their recognition of the problems of Americanization and their willingness to join the East Europeans in solving them. One might even suggest that this spirit of cooperation, which was so evident in the Kehillah's activities after 1908, was first expressed on the neighborhood level in Harlem several years earlier.

The agreements reached between Harlem's nominally Orthodox East European elite both with the Kehillah and with the leaders of the Jewish Theological Seminary's Teachers Institute—which so infuriated the ultraright wing of uptown Jewry—and the similar approaches to religious services initiated by Rabbi Goldstein in Harlem and Rabbi Kaplan in Yorkville and later on the West Side, raise fundamental questions concerning what were, at that time, the real differences between Conservative Judaism and Modern Orthodoxy. The little historiography presently available on the origins of that brand of Orthodoxy generally associated with Yeshiva University unfortunately views the beginnings of the two traditional American Jewish movements from the contemporary perspective of two separate religious authorities, each with its own seminary, national lay organization, rabbinical leadership and colleagual associations. Modern Orthodoxy was born, according to this analysis, among forward-thinking immigrant Jews who questioned the future viability of the transplanted forms of East European Orthodoxy and who were unfulfilled or dissatisfied with the traditional Judaism offered by what they perceived as the scholarship-poor Seminary brand of Orthodoxy. This supposed on-going split between denominations was formalized with the founding of Yeshiva

University and with the subsequent Modern Orthodox rejection of Seminary overtures to amalgamate their respective rabbinic institutions.[9]

Harlem's history suggests a totally different understanding of these movements, events and issues. The Seminary-Yeshiva split in 1929 did not culminate years of conflict but seems to mark the end of an era of relatively close cooperation between religious groups. This present study suggests that the early Conservatives and the Modern Orthodox had much in common and often worked together as one group in the early decades of this century.

It is known, for example, that the Conservative Teachers' Institute supplied teachers to the Orthodox Uptown Talmud Torah, and one must not forget that the Dean of the Teachers' Institute, Mordecai Kaplan, was appointed by Schiff and was finally accepted by the majority of Uptown Talmud Torah board members as a fitting judge of the quality of the modern pedagogic methods used in the Orthodox Hebrew school.

The relationship between those two similarly trained religious-educational pioneers, Rabbis Goldstein and Kaplan, and their senior rabbi at Yorkville's Congregation Kehilath Jeshurun, Rabbi Moses Zebulun Margolies (RAMAZ), also must not be overlooked. Both of the younger men were Seminary graduates (Goldstein received Orthodox ordination prior to his appointment, Kaplan only after several years in the pulpit) and both were accepted by their older East European rabbinic colleague as qualified spiritual leaders in this major immigrant congregation. Where was the split between Seminary-traditional Judaism and Orthodoxy in this congregation's experience?

Margolies himself is also a truly fascinating figure because he represents a type of immigrant Orthodox religious leader rarely noticed by chroniclers of traditional Jewish life. Here is a clerical counterpart to Harlem's new elite lay leadership; a man steeped in traditional learning who recognized that Judaism had to be harmonized with Americanism, if the faith was to survive under freedom. The biography of this founder of Yeshiva University, who often cooperated with the leaders of the Conservative Seminary, suggests most strongly the need for a new understanding of the early history of these American Jewish traditional religious movements.

Finally, the foregoing sketch of the earliest Black-Jewish relations in an urban setting and the interpretation of the factors effecting immigrant out-migration after World War I provides a basis for future larger-scale investigations of the reasons for Jewish and other ethnic persistence—or lack of same—in racially changing neighborhoods. Although the particular individual and institutional decisions leading to out-of-Harlem migration are often difficult to determine due to the absence of many of the appropriate sources, it is, nevertheless, apparent from those periodical and governmental sources that *are* available that Jewish relocation was not directly due, or especially in response to, the mass arrival uptown of blacks.

As we have noted previously, the exceedingly rapid Jewish exodus from Harlem was part of a general immigrant relocation out of the downtown ghetto and New York's other densely populated Jewish neighborhoods in the postwar years. The black's decision to settle in the deteriorating neighborhood only hastened the departure. Harlem's history strongly argued that Jews did not leave this particular community specifically because of their feeling any special aversion to, or fear of, living among blacks. It was due more basically to their desire and ability to live in the best possible accommodations available to them. It was not the push-out but the pull-to the newer neighborhoods that was critical.

The key piece of evidence supporting this understanding of Harlem Jewish attitudes towards blacks settling in their neighborhood is the exceedingly protracted period between earliest black penetration of uptown, beginning around 1905, and their consolidation in the neighborhood after World War I. As previously described, both upwardly mobile Jews and ambitious blacks sought Harlem's frontiers in the first decade of the twentieth century; each settling primarily in its own well-defined section of uptown. But limited numbers of each group almost immediately penetrated into the other group's enclave. Some blacks could be found in the Jewish Lower Lenox Avenue section of Central Harlem in the prewar years. And even more significantly, in 1910 Jews constituted the largest non-black ethnic group in the uptown district north of 125th Street—this remained so until the close of the First World War. In fact, in one census tract area, the number of Jews actually increased during the same time period in which blacks become the overwhelmingly predominant group in that section of town. It is, therefore, apparent that prior to the First World War, Jews showed no easily recognizable unwillingness towards living with and among blacks, suggesting that the physical deterioration of the neighborhood and the economic and social ability of Jews to seek better accommodations elsewhere were the most important factors directing Jewish removal from New York's first large racially mixed neighborhood.

This final aspect of Harlem's history challenges future researchers of this and other ethnic groups in similar urban neighborhoods to study the forces pulling as well as those pushing white ethnic groups away from emerging black neighborhoods. The history of Harlem Jewry suggests that the dynamics of physical neighborhood decay and of the upward mobility of formerly poor immigrants were more important than was the arrival of black migrants uptown in causing earlier settlers to leave their old neighborhoods for other parts of the city. It is left, however, to future studies to determine the applicability of these findings, for one group and one particular neighborhood, to the understanding of what may well be the truly complex combination of factors underlying the general character of interracial residential encounters in the northern urban setting.

appendix 1

Methodology Used in Studying the 1900 Federal Census of Population Manuscripts

As indicated in note 23 of chapter 2, both the New York City Tenement House Department, *First Report, 1902–1903* and the Bromley *Atlas 1894, 1898* point to the existence in East Harlem of a heavily populated tenement-house district east of Lexington Avenue and a moderately populated mixed tenement and apartment house district west of Lexington.

Using the report of the Tenement House Department further, I was able to determine where the largest concentrations of Jews were located in each district. I found that two relatively well-defined settlements existed in East Harlem. In the Eastern District, I discovered that the ten block area from 97th to 107th Streets, between Second and Third Avenues, besides housing almost one-half of all Russian Jews living east of Lexington, also contained four of the five blocks with the largest Russian-Jewish population in Harlem (both in real numbers and percentage). Most of the early Jewish Socialist and some of the first Russian-Jewish religious institutions were also located there. Turning to the Western District, I found that one-third of all Jews living in the less populous area resided in the area from 105th to 111th Streets, between Park and Fifth Avenues. This area also included several blocks with Jewish populations in excess of 25 to 30 percent of the general population (see map 3). To study the type of Jew and non-Jew living in each of these areas, I chose to study the block(s) with the largest Jewish population(s). In the Eastern District, I studied 101st to 102nd Streets, between Second and Third Avenues. In the Western District, I studied 106th to 107th Streets, between Park and Fifth Avenues.

To check on the validity of my sample, I chose to study, in the Eastern sample area, one corner and one interior house per block, including all different types of construction according to their proportion in the district. For the Western sample area, I decided to study one building of each type, to reflect the diversity of construction in that area. I compared the results from my test sample with the actual block sample and I have indicated in footnotes any significant variation.

The socioeconomic ranking of the some 200 different occupations and job descriptions used in the sample was adapted from the schemes used by Stephan Thernstrom in *The Other Bostonians* (Cambridge, Mass.: Harvard University Press 1972), Appendix B, and Peter Knights, *The Plain People of Boston, 1830–1860* (London, Oxford University Press 1971), Appendix E. Both scholars based their schemes on the earlier work of Alba M. Edwards. See United States, Department of Commerce, Bureau of the Census, *Sixteenth Census of the United States, 1940 Population—Comparative Occupational Statistics for the United States, 1890 to 1940*, by Alba M. Edwards (Washington, 1943).

Both Thernstrom and Knights emphasized the difficulty of determining whether the "merchant" belongs in category I or II. Both rate "merchants" on the basis of the level of taxes assessed against them. I have chosen to place "merchants" who have one or more nonfamily member "servants" in their employ in category I. All others have been left outside the two specific "white-collar" categories and are included only in the general "high and low white-collar" category. Thus, for example, in table A.1, the percentage of high white-collar workers *ranges* from 12 to 17 percent because twenty-six "unclassified merchants" have not been calculated. Although these modifications do not permit simple comparison of these findings with studies based on the more standard "five-step method", comparisons of the aggregate white-collar and blue-collar ranges can be undertaken and are of significant value. Those scholars and students interested in examining the complete range of occupations appearing in my sample are directed to Appendix II of my dissertation, "The History of the Jewish Community of Harlem, 1870–1930," Columbia University 1977, for such information.

In the few instances where the occupation of the head of household was listed as "at home" or "retired", the occupation of the oldest other breadwinner in the family—in most cases the oldest child—was computed. The Russian-Jewish sample also includes the few U.S.-born Jewish heads of households and the similarly few Rumanian Jews who appeared in the population enumerations.

appendix 2

Methodology Used in Studying the 1905 New York State Census of Population Manuscripts

As indicated in note 58 of chapter 2, the printed summaries of the 1910 United States Census of Population appearing in the Laidlaw volumes show that the two largest Jewish settlements in East Harlem in 1910 were centered around those blocks that had been sampled for our study of the 1900 Federal Census manuscripts. Park and Fifth Avenues between 105th and 111th Streets, which had housed one-third of the Jews residing in the "Western District" of East Harlem in 1900, was situated within the census tract bordered by 105th and 112th Streets between Park and Fifth, which in 1910 had the second largest concentration of Jews in all of Harlem. Similarly, 97th to 107th Streets, between Second and Third Avenues, which in 1900 housed one-half of all Russian Jews in the "Eastern District" of East Harlem, continued through the first decade of the twentieth century to be part of the single large Russian-Jewish enclave east of Third Avenue. In 1910, it was part of a census tract bordered by 99th and 104th Streets, between First and Third Avenues, which contained 13,060 Russian Jews, constituting 51.5 percent of the population.

Bromley, *Atlas, 1905* and the annual reports of the New York City Tenement House Department, from 1902 to 1910, indicate that the types of buildings constructed within the two East Harlem districts continued to be of a fundamentally different character during the last stage of the Harlem building boom.

In the area from 97th to 107th Streets, east of Third Avenue, old style—now "remodeled"—tenements remained the predominant form of building. The population density of the five census tracts contiguous to these blocks averaged 385 people per acre. Several of the census tracts in that vicinity showed population densities as high as 637, 583 and 519 people per acre.

In the area from 105th to 111th Streets, east of Fifth Avenue, the previous style of construction was altered by the addition of new-law tenements replacing many private dwellings or built upon previously vacant blocks. The four census tracts contiguous to these blocks showed an average population density of 319 (15 percent less than the Eastern District).

To ascertain the continued existence of two different economic classes in these East Harlem districts, I chose to retain the same sample blocks and the same "test sample" houses from the 1900 study. Bromley's *Atlas 1898, 1905* clearly supports the contention that the Central Harlem neighborhood built in the late 1890s through 1905 contained a type of construction far superior to that in existence in East Harlem. The five-floor, twenty-five-foot front, walk-up tenement so common to East Harlem was almost nonexistent west of 110th Street and Fifth Avenue. Five-story buildings with frontages as large as fifty feet predominated in Central Harlem. Numerous six-story elevator apartments with fifty to one hundred foot frontages were also common. The density of population in Central Harlem south of 120th Street averaged only 258 people per square acre: significantly lower than that of the other district.

As indicated in the text and in note 58 of chapter 2 the only major Jewish concentration within this newly constructed neighborhood was situated between 110th and 118th Streets between Fifth and Lenox Avenues. Some 11,000 Jews resided in that area, constituting about 45 percent of the population. In no other Central Harlem census tract did Russian Jess constitute more than 20 percent of the population.

To study the type of Jew and non-Jew living in this newly created Jewish settlment, I chose to study every third house on 112th to 113th Streets between Fifth and Lenox Avenues (twenty-six houses in all). This block contained the largest percentage of Russian Jews in Central Harlem in 1900. To check the validity of that sample area, I chose to study one corner and one interior house for each block between 110th and 120th Streets between Fifth and Lenox, including all different types of construction according to their proportion in the district.

appendix 3

Tables

TABLE A.1
Occupational Distribution of Heads of Households in the Western District of East Harlem (1900)

	NUMBER	PERCENT
High white collar	53	12–17
Low white collar	184	40–46
Unclassified merchants	26	
Skilled labor	134	30
Semiskilled and service	39	8
Unskilled and menial service	9	2
Unknown	11	2
High and low white collar: 58%		*Skilled and unskilled, etc.: 42%*

SOURCE: Sample data from Federal Census Schedules for Manhattan for 1900.

TABLE A.2
Occupational Distribution of Russian Jewish Heads of Households in the Western District of East Harlem (1900)

	NUMBER	PERCENT
I. High white collar	25	24–34
a) professionals 5 (25%)		
b) major proprietors, etc. 20 (75%)		
II. Low white collar	32	31–41
a) clerks and salespeople 21 (68%)		
b) semiprofessionals 4 (13%)		
c) petty proprietors 7 (20%)		
Unclassified merchants	11	
III. Skilled labor	28	26.5
17 in needle trades (18% of total Jewish population)		
7 in construction trades		
4 in other trades		
IV. Semiskilled and service	1	1
V. Unskilled and menial service	1	1
VI. Unknown	5	5
High and low white collar: 66%		*Skilled and unskilled, etc.:* 34%

SOURCE: Sample data from Federal Census Schedules for Manhattan for 1900.

TABLE A.3
Occupational Distribution of Heads of Households in the Eastern District of East Harlem (1900)

	NUMBER	PERCENT
I. High white collar	12	3.2
II. Low white collar	77	20.9
III. Skilled labor	178	48.3
IV. Semiskilled and service	40	10.8
V. Unskilled and menial service	54	14.6
VI. Unknown	7	1.9
High and low white collar: 24.1%		*Skilled and Unskilled, etc.:* 75.9%

SOURCE: Sample data from Federal Census Schedules for Manhattan for 1900.

TABLE A.4
Occupational Distribution of Russian Jewish Heads of
Households in the Eastern District of East Harlem (1900)

	NUMBER	PERCENT
I. High white collar	5	4
II. Low white collar	33	26.4
a) clerks and salespeople 3		
b) semiprofessionals 2		
c) petty proprietors 28 (84.8%)		
III. Skilled labor	77	61.6
28 in needle trades (36%)		
26 in construction trades (34%)		
13 in cigar making (17%)		
10 in other occupations (13%)		
IV. Semiskilled and service	4	3.2
V. Unskilled and menial service	4	3.2
VI. Unknown	2	1.6
High and low white collar: 30.4%		*Skilled and unskilled, etc.: 69.6%*

SOURCE: Sample data from Federal Census Schedules for Manhattan for 1900.

TABLE A.5
Occupational Distribution of Heads of Households in the Western District of East Harlem in 1905 as Compared With 1900

	1900		1905	
	NUMBER	PERCENT	NUMBER	PERCENT
I. High white collar	53	12–18	41	11
II. Low white collar	184	42–47.6	137	37
Unclassified merchants	26		2	
III. Skilled labor	134	30	149	40
IV. Semiskilled and service	39	8	32	8.5
V. Unskilled and menial service	9	1	10	3
VI. Unknown	11	2	2	.5
High and low white collar:	60%		48%	
Skilled and unskilled, etc.:	40%		52%	

SOURCE: Sample data from Federal Census Schedules for Manhattan for 1900 and State Census Schedules for 1905.

TABLE A.6
Occupational Distribution of Russian Jewish Heads of Households in the Western District of East Harlem in 1905 as Compared With 1900

	1900		1905	
	NUMBER	PERCENT	NUMBER	PERCENT
I. High white collar	25	24–34	35	19–20
a) professionals	5 (25%)		4 (11.5%)	
b) major proprietors etc.	20 (75%)		31 (88.5%)	
II. Low white collar	32	31–41	63	33–34
a) clerks and salespeople	21 (68%)		21 (34%)	
b) semiprofessionals	4 (13%)		7 (9%)	
c) petty proprietors	7 (20%)		35 (57%)	
Unclassified merchants	11		2	
III. Skilled labor	28	26.5	80	43
IV. Semiskilled and service	1	1	5	3
V. Unskilled and menial service	1	1	2	1
VI. Unknown	6	5	2	1
High and low white collar:		66%		53%
Skilled and unskilled, etc.:		34%		47%

SOURCE: Sample data from Federal Census Schedules for Manhattan for 1900 and State Census Schedules for 1905.

TABLE A.7
Occupational Distribution of Heads of Households in Central Harlem (1905)

	NUMBER	PERCENT
I. High white collar	39	23–26
II. Low white collar	72	42–45
Unclassified merchants	11	
III. Skilled labor	34	20
IV. Semiskilled and service	12	7
V. Unskilled and menial service	6	3.5
VI. Unknown	2	1
High and low white collar: 68%		*Skilled and Unskilled, etc.: 32%*

SOURCE: Sample data from new York State Census Schedules for Manhattan for 1905.

TABLE A.8
Occupational Distribution of Russian Jewish Heads of Households in Central Harlem (1905)

	NUMBER	PERCENT
I. High white collar	12	24–36
a) professionals 3 (25%)		
b) major proprietors etc. 9 (75%)		
II. Low white collar	19	39–51
a) clerks and salespeople 17 (89%)		
b) semiprofessionals 1 (5.5%)		
c) petty proprietors 1 (5.5%)		
Unclassified merchants	6	
III. Skilled labor	9	18
IV. Semiskilled and service	2	4
V. Unskilled and menial service	0	—
VI. Unknown	1	2
High and low white collar: 75%		*Skilled and unskilled, etc.: 25%*

SOURCE: Sample data from State Census Schedules for Manhattan for 1905.

TABLE A.9
Occupational Distribution of Heads of Households in the Eastern District of East Harlem in 1905 as Compared With 1900

	1900		1905	
	NUMBER	PERCENT	NUMBER	PERCENT
I. High white collar	12	3.2	8	2
II. Low white collar	77	20.9	106	24
III. Skilled labor	178	48.3	186	45
IV. Semiskilled and service	40	10.8	59	14
V. Unskilled and menial service	54	14.6	46	11
VI. Unknown	7	1.9	12	3
High and low white collar:	24.1%		26%	
Skilled and unskilled, etc.:	75.9%		74%	

SOURCE: Sample data from Federal Census Schedules for Manhattan for 1900 and State Schedules for 1905.

TABLE A.10

Occupational Distribution of Russian Jewish Heads of
Households in the Eastern District of East Harlem in 1905
as Compared With 1900

	1900		1905	
	NUMBER	PERCENT	NUMBER	PERCENT
I. High white collar	5	4	4	2
II. Low white collar	33	26.4	58	33
a) clerks and sales people	3 (9%)		5 (9%)	
b) semiprofessionals	2 (6%)		2 (3%)	
c) petty proprietors	28 (84.8%)		51 (88%)	
III. Skilled labor	77	61.6	91	53
IV. Semiskilled and service	4	3.2	13	7.5
V. Unskilled and menial service	4	3.2	3	2
VI. Unknown	2	1.6	3	2
High and low white collar:		30.4%		35%
Skilled and unskilled, etc.		69.6%		65%

SOURCE: Sample data from Federal Census Schedules for Manhattan for 1900
and State Census Schedules for 1905.

ABBREVIATIONS USED IN THE NOTES

AH	*American Hebrew*
AI	*American Israelite*
AJYB	*American Jewish Year Book*
HS	*Hebrew Standard*
JDF	*Jewish Daily Forward*
JM	*Jewish Messenger*
MJ	*Morgen Journal*
RERBG	*Real Estate Record and Builders' Guide*
YT	*Yiddishes Tageblatt*

Notes

1. THE EARLY YEARS, 1870–1900

1. Real Estate Record Association, *A History of Real Estate, Building and Architecture in New York City During the Last Quarter Century* (New York, 1898), pp. 45–46; *RERBG*, January 17, 1880, p. 53; Moses Rischin, *The Promised City: New York's Jews, 1870–1914* (Cambridge: Harvard University Press, 1962), pp. 6–8.

2. *The 1866 Guide to New York City* (New York: Schocken, 1975), pp. 99–101; Real Estate Association, *History*, pp. 45–46, 55–56.

3. Hyman B. Grinstein, *The Rise of the Jewish Community of New York, 1654–1860* (Philadelphia: Jewish Publication Society of America, 1945), pp. 32–33.

4. "Old Timer's Tale of Harlem's Growth," *Harlem Magazine*, December 1914, p. 14; "Old Timer Writes of Days When Harlem Was a Salt Marsh," *Harlem Home News*, February 16, 1916; William Perris and Henry Browne, *Insurance Maps of the City of New York* (New York, 1876), vol. 8, pls. 164–78.

5. Herbert Manchester, *The Story of Harlem and the Empire Savings Bank* (New York: 1929), pp. 18–19; see also Charles H. White, "In Uptown New York," *Harper's Monthly*, June 1906, pp. 220–28, quoted by Gilbert Osofsky, in *Harlem: The Making of a Ghetto* (New York: Harper, 1966), p. 74.

6. For a discussion of the fundamental institutions associated with nineteenth-century German-American Jewish communities, see Jacob Rader Marcus, "The Periodization of American Jewish History," *Publications of the American Jewish Historical Society* (1959), 47:125–33. See also Marcus, "Background for the History of the American Jew," in Oscar Janowsky, ed., *The American Jew: A Reappraisal* (Philadelphia: Jewish Publication Society of America, 1964), pp. 1–27.

7. *AH*, May 13, 1898, p. 36; May 20, 1898, p. 68; Temple Israel of New York City, *75th Anniversary Journal* (n.p.: n.p., n.d.), n.p.

8. The occupational and residential distribution of the earliest Harlem Jewish settlers was determined from a study of the congregational founders' names provided by periodicals and traced through the New York City Directory. See *Trow's New York City Directory, 1869, 1873, 1876* (New York, 1870, 1874, 1877). There were seven members of the original committee, but only four of those listed in the periodical could be found in the directories for 1869. The starting date of 1873 for Temple Israel is an arbitrary one based on the congregation's "tradition" that the founding of Hand-in-Hand was "not mentioned in the general or Jewish press of the day." See Temple Israel *75th Anniversary Journal*, n.p. In actuality, 1873 was only the date of incorporation. There is a reference to the members of Hand-in-Hand establishing a synagogue in Harlem as early as October, 1869. See *JM*, October 17, 1869, n.p.

9. Maurice H. Harris, *A Forty Years Ministry: Address by Maurice H. Harris . . .* (New York: n.p., 1925), p. 1; *JM*, September 14, 1877, n.p.; September 20, 1878, n.p.

10. *JM*, January 30, 1880, n.p.; *AH*, May 20, 1898, p. 69; see also Constitution and School Regulations of the Shangarai Limud Sunday School Society of Harlem (New York), American Jewish Historical Society. Solomon Carvalho and his son David were descendents of an important nineteenth-century American Sephardic Jewish family. See Solomon Nunes Carvalho, *Incidents of Travel and Adventure in the Far West* (Philadelphia: Jewish Publication Society of America, 1954).

11. *AH*, May 20, 1898, pp. 68, 70.

12. *AH*, May 21, 1880, p. 6; *JM*, December 22, 1882, p. 2; see also Charles S. Levy, "Jewish Communal Services: Health, Welfare, Recreational and Social," in Janowsky, ed., *American Jew*, p. 255.

13. *AH*, August 5, 1881, p. 3. A simple comparison of Hand-in-Hand membership as listed in the Anglo-Jewish press of the day with that of Harlem's Jewish social organizations indicates clearly that religiously oriented uptowners joined the social organizations but that not all Harlem Y and B'nai B'rith members belonged to the synagogue.

14. Alonzo Caldwell, *A Lecture: The History of Harlem* (New York, 1882), pp. 29–31.

15. Independence Day Association of Harlem, *Celebration, 1886* (New York, 1887), pp. 9, 18.

16. Harlem Republican Club, N.Y., *By-Laws and List of Members* (New York, 1892), *passim;* Harlem Democratic Party, N.Y., *Constitution, By-Laws, House Rules, Members* (New York, 1888), *passim*.

17. *JM*, April 29, 1887, p. 2.

18. Harlem Relief Society of the City of New York, *Report of the Relief Committee* (New York, 1893), *passim; AH*, February 20, 1880, p. 9.

19. *YT*, July 6, 1889, p. 1.

20. Real Estate Record Association, pp. 76–82; *RERBG*, August 7, 1886, p. 995; *YT*, February 12, 1900, p. 4; James Blaine Walker, *Fifty Years of Rapid Transit* (New York, 1918), p. 109.

21. *RERBG*, October 8, 1881, p. 941; October 22, 1881, p. 987; May 14, 1881, pp. 489–90; Robert De Forest and Lawrence Veiler, eds., *The Tenement House Problem: Including Report of the New York State Tenement House Committee of 1900* (New York: Macmillan, 1903), vol. 1, *passim*.

22. *RERBG*, November 13, 1883, p. 851; June 16, 1883, p. 235.

23. *RERBG*, January 3, 1880, p. 2; November 8, 1879, p. 896.

24. United States Industrial Commission, *Reports of the Industrial Commission on Immigration*, vol. 1; *Immigration and Education* (Washington, 1901), pp. 470–71; see also Rischin, *Promised City*, pp. 9–10.

25. U.S. Industrial Commission *Reports*, 1:470–71; United States Department of the Interior, Census Office, *Vital Statistics of New York City and Brooklyn Covering a Period of Six Years Ending May 31, 1890*, by John S. Billings (Washington, 1894), p. 100.

26. U.S. Census Office, *Vital Statistics*, pp. 100ff.

27. U.S. Census Office, *Vital Statistics*, pp. 100ff; Real Estate Association, *History*, pp. 107–8; Osofsky, *Harlem*, p. 79.

28. U.S. Industrial Commission, *Reports*, 1:471–76; U.S. Census Office, *Vital Statistics*, pp. 100ff.

29. *AH*, June 4, 1880, p. 33.

30. *AH*, May 20, 1898, p. 68; January 23, 1925, p. 335. A short biographical sketch of Harris' career published in *AJYB* 5(1903): 61–62 indicates that the Emanu-el Theological Seminary, which was for the most part a preparatory school, was, at least in Harris' case, also an ordaining institution.

31. Harris, *Ministry*, p. 3; Moshe Davis, *The Emergence of Conservative Judaism: The Historical School in the Nineteenth Century* (Philadelphia: Jewish Publication Society of America, 1963), p. 143.

32. *JM*, June 27, 1884, p. 2.

33. Temple Israel, *Journal*, n.page; *AH*, November 30, 1894, p. 131.

34. *AH*, January 24, 1890, p. 266. See Davis, *Emergence of Conservative Judaism*, pp. 225–28 and Nathan Glazer, *American Judaism* (Chicago: University of Chicago Press, 1957), pp. 138–39, for detailed discussions of the significance of the Pittsburgh Platform in late-nineteenth-century American Jewish communal life.

35. *AH*, May 20, 1898, pp. 90–92; March 3, 1899, p. 627; see also Temple Israel Sisterhood, New York, "Minutes of Meetings, 1891–93," American Jewish Archives.

36. YMHA of New York, "Minutes of Meetings of the Board of Trustees," meetings of September 7, 1885 and September 21, 1885; "Minutes of Meetings of the Board of

Directors," meeting of December 21, 1898, American Jewish Archives; *AH,* October 22, 1886, p. 171; *JM,* December 22, 1882, p. 2; January 12, 1883, p. 2.

37. Congregation Ansche Chesed, "Minutes of Congregational Meetings, 1876–93"; *AH,* February 15, 1887; *JM,* May 25, 1889, p. 2; *AH,* July 6, 1888, p. 140 and January 11, 1907, pp. 250–51; Interview with Mrs. Cora Kohn, August 17, 1974.

38. *JM,* December 12, 1890, p. 2; *YT,* September 5, 1888, p. 4; *Harlem Local Reporter,* October 1, 1892, p. 1 and September 14, 1895, p. 7.

39. *YT,* August 15, 1890, p. 2, September 19, 1890, p. 2 and July 29, 1892, p. 7.

40. *JM,* August 20, 1897, p. 2 and July 21, 1899, p. 7; *AH,* July 21, 1899, p. 347; Congregation Shaarei Zedek, "Minutes of the Meetings of the Board of Trustees," meeting of May 28, 1899; *One Hundredth Anniversary* (New York, n.p., 1937), *passim.*

41. U.S. Census Office, *Vital Statistics,* pp. 234–37; *YT,* May 5, 1892, p. 2. See also the "Incorporation Papers" of Congregation Nachlath Zvi and the Uptown Talmud Torah on file at the New York County Clerk's Office.

2. THE ARRIVAL OF THE EAST EUROPEAN JEW UPTOWN, 1895–1910

1. Edward A. Steiner, "The Russian and Polish Jews in New York," *Outlook,* November 1902, p. 532; Burton I. Hendrick, "The Jewish Invasion," *HS,* February 15, 1907, p. 14; Gilbert Osofsky, *Harlem: The Making of a Ghetto* (New York: Harper, 1963), p. 88. This widely held view of the rapidly upward-mobile Harlem Jew is reflected beautifully in Abraham Cahan's classic novel of immigrant life, *The Rise of David Levinsky* (New York: Harper, 1960).

2. Alter Landesman, *Brownsville: The Birth, Development and Passing of a Jewish Community in New York* (New York: Bloch, 1971), pp. 40–47, 67–77.

3. Landesman, *Brownsville,* p. 40; Real Estate Record Association, *A History of Real Estate, Building and Architecture in New York City During the Last Quarter Century* (New York, 1898), p. 88; *RERBG,* April 11, 1888, pp. 996–97.

4. Gaylord S. White, "The Upper East Side—Its Neglect and Needs," *Charities,* July 16, 1904, pp. 748–51.

5. American Institute of Electrical Engineers, *The New York Electrical Handbook* (New York: American Institute of Electrical Engineers, 1904), pp. 128–30; *RERBG,* September 16, 1889, p. 402.

6. *Harlem Local Reporter,* November 27, 1890, p. 4.

7. New York State Public Service Commission, First District, *History and Description of the Rapid Transit Routes in New York City* (Albany, 1914), pp. 16–27.

8. "Rapid Transit Progress," *Harlem Local Reporter,* April 18, 1893, p. 4.

9. New York State Public Service Commission, *Transit Routes,* pp. 16–27.

10. *RERBG,* September 17, 1898, September 16, 1899, p. 401. These statistics on Central Harlem's growth pattern were derived from a study of New York land-use maps. See George Washington Bromley, *Atlas of the City of New York, 1894, 1898–99* (Philadelphia: 1894, 1898–99).

11. *RERBG,* October 18, 1899, p. 759. Roy Lubove in his study of tenement house reform in New York City points out that the Tenement House Committee of the Charity Organization Society of New York (COS) considered the recommendations of the City Building Code Commission to be "a distinct step backwards." Lawrence Veiler, a leading spokesman for the COS, complained that the City Commission was composed al-

most entirely of businessmen. See Roy Lubove, *The Progressives and the Slums* (Pittsburgh: University of Pittsburgh Press, 1962), p. 121.

12. *RERBG*, October 22, 1898, p. 572.

13. *YT*, April 19, 1896, p. 3.

14. *RERBG*, August 25, 1900, p. 235.

15. *RERBG*, September 2, 1899, p. 336.

16. New York State Bureau of Labor Statistics, *16th Annual Report, 1896* (Albany, 1896), p. 1046.

17. *Ibid.*, p. 1051.

18. New York State Legislature, Assembly. Tenement House Committee, *Report of the Tenement House Committee of 1894 as Authorized by Chapter 479 of the Laws of 1894* (Albany, 1894), pp. 250–52.

19. *RERBG*, September 16, 1899, p. 40; January 19, 1901, p. 93.

20. Citizens' Union of New York, *Small Parks and Public Piers for the People* (New York, 1897), p. 2.

21. *Map of Public Parks, Boroughs of Manhattan and Richmond* (New York: 1902), *passim*.

22. *RERBG*, August 4, 1900, p. 144.

23. Of the 3,404 Russian Jewish families living in Harlem in 1900, 1,953 (57 percent) lived south of 110th Street and east of Fifth Avenue. Within that area Russian Jews constituted some 12 percent of the general population. North and west of 110th Street, Russian Jews composed less than 5 percent of the population. The southeast Harlem district—where most Jews lived—was divided between a heavily populated area east of Lexington Avenue and a moderately populated area west of Lexington. Sixty-five percent of southeast Harlemites lived in the "Eastern District," 35 percent resided in the "Western District." The Jewish population of Harlem was divided almost equally between the two districts. See New York City Tenement House Department, *First Report.* See also map 5.

Local land-use maps for 1894 and 1898 indicate another significant difference between the districts east and west of Lexington. A comparison of the area from 97th to 107th Streets between Second and Third Avenues, where almost one-half of all Russian Jews living east of Lexington Avenue resided (23 percent of all Harlem Jews), with the blocks from 105th to 111th Streets between Fifth and Park Avenues, where one-third of all Russian Jews living in Harlem's less-populated district resided, shows that the Western District was far less congested and more diversified in its construction. My study of the two districts revealed that a) The Second and Third Avenue area was far more developed than the Park-Fifth Avenue area. All but one of the Eastern District blocks were either 50 to 90 percent or 90 to 100 percent developed. The Western District streets were divided among those of low (0 to 50 percent), moderate and high development. b) More importantly, the types of buildings constructed in the Eastern District were far more uniform in nature than those in the Western District. No fewer than seventeen different types of five-story buildings, most with some sort of semiattached construction, were erected. Many smaller three-story brownstones were also to be found in the latter area. See Bromley, *Atlas, 1894, 1898.*

24. Russian Jews in the Western District also showed a higher concentration in the high and low white-collar categories than did any other ethnic or national group. The Germans and native-born white Americans of native parents ranked second and third in percentage of workers in the highest occupational categories. The Irish were found predominantly in the skilled and semiskilled fields. These findings were derived from sample data from the Federal Census Schedules for Manhattan for 1900.

25. Although the test sample indicates a similar concentration of Jews in the combined high and low white-collar categories, it does show a variance in the individual categories. The test sample indicates a 2 to 12 percent increase in the number of Jews in the highest category and a similar 5 to 15 percent decrease in the lower category. The test sample points to an even more affluent group of Jews living in the Western District.

26. A study of the occupational distribution of the other ethnic-national groups in the Eastern District, derived from sample data from the Federal Census Schedules for Manhattan for 1900, indicates that the Germans showed a degree of economic advancement closest to that of the Russians. Close to 43 percent of German workers were employed in skilled labor. Irish workers were employed primarily in semiskilled and unskilled occupations.

27. *JDF*, November 10, 1907, p. 7; *AH*, August 24, 1906, p. 297.

28. Lucy W. Killough, *The Tobacco Industry in New York and Its Environs* (New York: Regional Plan of New York and Its Environs, 1924), pp. 32–33.

29. *AJYB* (1910), 12:278.

30. De Forest and Veiler, eds., *The Tenement House Problem* (New York: Macmillan, 1903), vol. 1, pp. xiv–xvi.

31. *RERBG*, November 7, 1903, p. 824.

32. *Ibid.*

33. *RERBG*, July 27, 1901, p. 110.

34. *RERBG*, January 5, 1901, pp. 4–5.

35. Mark Wischnitzer, *To Dwell in Safety* (Philadelphia: Jewish Publication Society of America, 1948), pp. 125–27.

36. "Dispersing the Ghetto," *YT*, October 27, 1902, p. 8; see also "The Congestion and Its Relief," *AH*, November 7, 1902, p. 696.

37. It is estimated that some 50,000 people migrated out of the ghetto between 1900 and 1904. See *AH*, October 28, 1904, p. 638; see also Landesman, *Brownsville*, p. 82; *RERBG*, April 9, 1904, p. 782.

38. *RERBG*, January 20, 1900, p. 94.

39. *RERBG*, April 11, 1903, pp. 700–701.

40. *RERBG*, January 19, 1907, p. 145.

41. *RERBG*, August 6, 1904, p. 281.

42. A study of some 143 buildings located between 110th and 113th Streets between Fifth and Seventh Avenues in 1898 provides a good indication of the fundamentally different character of construction in the Central Harlem district. The five-story, twenty-five-foot front tenement, associated with the east of Third Avenue district, is totally absent from the Central Harlem sample. Five-story apartment houses with frontages larger than twenty-five feet predominate. Some have frontages as wide as fifty feet. There were numerous small private homes in Central Harlem; these were uncommon in East Harlem. See Bromley, *Atlas, 1898*. See also *RERBG*, January 6, 1906, p. 1, January 19, 1907, p. 145, and January 4, 1908, p. 1.

It must also be noted that the aforegoing discussion of the various phases in Harlem building activity is in basic variance with Osofsky's earlier presentation in *Harlem: The Making of a Ghetto*. Osofsky wrote of a single continuous building boom from 1898 to 1905. He made no distinction between the 1895 to 1898 spurt and the second era of building between 1903 and 1905. He did not mention the decline in construction between 1898 and 1902, nor did he choose to deal with the 1900 rent war. The building bust of 1906 was nothing new to observers of the Harlem real estate scene.

Osofsky gives one the impression that before 1898, almost all of Central Harlem was empty. The real estate journal and the land-use maps show otherwise. Osofsky over-emphasized the impact of the subways upon Harlem's growth and failed to mention the important changes on the Lower East Side that precipitated the mass migration to Harlem, setting off the post-1900 building boom.

One may also question Osofsky's analysis of the dimensions of the building bust that hit Harlem after 1905. The oversupply of better-grade apartments, of which Osofsky spoke, that facilitated the migration of Blacks to Harlem existed only in that section of Harlem north of 125th Street and west of Fifth Avenue. Confronted with this glut of apartments, northwest Harlem realtors opted to throw open their doors to Blacks, who were willing to pay higher rents than most whites, rather than to engage in widespread cutthroat rent slashing similar to that which had occurred between 1898 and 1900. There was no oversupply of accommodations in other sections of the community.

There was a significant decline in real estate speculation throughout Harlem after 1905. This may be attributed to the emergence of sections of Queens and Brooklyn as alternatives for those seeking to relocate out of downtown. (See Osofsky, pp. 87–91.)

43. Hendrick, "Jewish Invasion," p. 1.

44. Cahan, *David Levinsky*, p.464.

45. *AH*, September 22, 1905, p. 465.

46. Hendrick, "Jewish Invasion," p. 1.

47. *MJ*, April 21, 1911, p. 1.

48. Congregation Anshe Chesed, "Minutes of Board of Trustees Meetings," meeting of October 4, 1907.

49. For a complete consideration of the contributions of the Cohens and other real-estate people to the development of Harlem's Jewish communal life see chapter 4.

50. *JDF*, March 6, 1904, p. 4.

51. *JDF*, March 20, 1904, p. 4.

52. *JDF*, March, 19, 1904, p. 1.

53. *JDF*, March 28, 1904, p. 1 and May 18, 1904, p. 1.

54. Archibald A. Hill, "Rental Agitation on the East Side," *Charity*, April 16, 1904, p. 397.

55. *JDF*, April 18, 1904, p. 2, April 26, 1904, p. 1, and April 29, 1904, p. 1.

56. See, chapter 3 for a full discussion of the 1908 rent strike and the activities of socialist and other radical groups in East Harlem.

57. Walter Laidlaw, ed., *Statistical Sources for Demographic Studies of New York*, (New York: World Council of Churches 1913), 70ff.

58. The printed summaries of the 1910 United States Census of Population indicate that some 24,000 Jews, constituting approximately 60 percent of the general population, resided within the two census tracts lying east of Central Park between 98th and 105th Streets, west of Park Avenue. Contained within these tracts were the two blocks with the largest Jewish populations in the designated "Western District" of East Harlem in 1900. A similar pattern of growth was apparent for the census tract surrounding the largest Jewish concentration in the "East of Lexington District" of 1900. This area bounded by 99th and 104th Streets, contained approximately 13,000 Jews, constituting some 51.5 percent of the population.

The figure of approximately 100,000 Russian Jews was derived from a study of the thirty-two 1910 census tracts lying north of 98th Street on the East Side of Harlem and north of 110th Street to approximately 140th Street in Central Harlem. Some 11,000 Jews living in the four southern census tracts overlapping Yorkville and South Harlem were not included in the above totals. Several hundred Russian Jews residing in the four census tracts lying north of 140th Street were, similarly, omitted from the district totals.

The major Jewish concentrations within the new neighborhood west of 110th Street and Fifth Avenue, were situated between 110th and 118th Streets, Fifth and Lenox Avenues, where some 11,000 Russian Jews resided. These settlers constituted some 45 percent of the district's population. In no other Central Harlem district did Russian Jews constitute more than 20 percent of the population. The largest Jewish settlement north and east of 110th Street and Fifth Avenue was that in the census tract bounded by East 114 and 118th Streets between Park and Fifth Avenues. Some 5,900 Jews resided in that area, numbering 51.5 percent of the population. The next largest census tract was that one located immediately east of 114th Street at Park Avenue. Some 3,800 Jews lived in that area, constituting approximately 25 percent of the population. All these statistics support the assertion that 110th Street and Fifth Avenue was the population center of the Harlem Jewish community. See Laidlaw, *Statistical Sources* and map 4.

59. Laidlaw, *Statistical Sources*, pp. 70ff.

60. Osofsky, *Harlem*, pp. 84–85; (New York City Tenement House Department, *First Report*.)

61. Laidlaw, *Statistical Sources*, pp. 70 ff; see Osofsky, *Harlem*, pp. 70–127 for a full description of the forces which led to the creation of a black ghetto uptown after 1900.

62. The 1910 United States Census of Population indicates that the census tracts lying

west of Third Avenue which housed some 50 percent of all Harlem Jews showed an average density of 319. The districts of 105th to 112th Streets, Park and Fifth Avenues, and 112th to 119th Streets, Park and Fifth Avenues, showed population densities of 481 and 562 respectively. See Laidlaw, pp. 70ff.

A comparison of the land-use maps of uptown areas for the years 1898 and 1905 indicates that most lands that had been vacant in 1898 were covered with new-law tenements in 1905. These maps also indicate that the proportion of three-to five-floor narrow (less than twenty-foot frontage) private dwellings declined from 46 percent of the total in 1898 to 38 percent seven years later. See Bromley, *Atlas 1898, 1905.*

63. The only major variation between the test sample and the actual one in the Western District is to be found within the Jewish high and low white-collar classes. The percentage of high and low white-collar workers in the test sample equals 54.9 percent (only 1.5 percent more than the actual sample.) The variation is to be found within the individual white-collar categories. The percentage of high white-collar workers in the test sample dropped much less drastically than in the actual sample (36 to 32 percent in the test sample, 24 to 34 to 20 percent in the actual sample.) Conversely, the percentage of low white-collar workers in the test sample dropped a bit more precipitously than in the actual sample. The variation in the samples may be due to the large number of "merchants" appearing in the samples who are not easily classified. The drop-off in the test sample's low white-collar categories was, however, among the "clerks and salespeople" group, reinforcing the impression that the most economically advanced were the ones to move out of the district.

64. *MJ,* July 11, 1906, p. 4.

65. *YT,* February 17, 1904, p. 8; *MJ,* July 11, 1906, p. 4.

66. The test sample for Central Harlem showed an even greater concentration of workers in the white-collar categories. Seventy-three percent of all heads of households were found to be employed in the two highest occupational categories. Close to 40 percent were classified in the highest category; some 15 percent more than in the actual sample. These statistics further our assumption that Central Harlem was an economically elite neighborhood.

67. The high level of economic advancement enjoyed by Central Harlem's Russian Jews is further illustrated when these statistics are compared with those of the city-wide Russian-Jewish population. Kessner studied the occupational mobility of Jews in New York for 1905 and found that 46 percent of all heads of households were engaged in the two forms of white-collar work. Central Harlem's percentage of Jewish white-collar workers was between one and one-half and two times as large. See Thomas Kessner *The Golden Door* (NY.: Oxford Univ. Press, 1976), p. 60.

68. *YT,* March 25, 1906, p. 8; *JDF,* October 21, 1904, p. 4.

69. Union Settlement, *Annual Report of the Headworker* (New York: N.P., 1907), p. 8.

70. Ernest W. Burgess, "Residential Segregation in American Cities," *Annals of the American Academy of Political and Social Sciences,* 42:106–7; Louis Wirth, *The Ghetto* (Chicago: University of Chicago Press, 1928), pp. 248–55; Paul Frederick Cressey, "Population Succession in Chicago, 1898–1930," *American Journal of Sociology* (July 1938), 44:61.

71. This Harlem story joins a growing body of American urban historical works in criticizing the applicability of the supposedly all-inclusive Chicago paradigm to a variety of differing locales and group situations. One specific aspect of the urban settlement seen here in Harlem and often noted as missing from the earlier model is the migration of the poor out of the ghetto and even from city to city in search of work. See Stephan Thernstrom, *Poverty and Progress: Social Mobility in a Nineteenth-Century City* (New York, Atheneum, 1970), pp. 85, 198–99; Stephan Thernstrom and Peter Knights, "Men in Motion: Some Data and Speculation about Urban Population Mobility in Nineteen Century America," in Tamara K. Hareven, ed., *Anonymous Americans* (Englewood Cliffs, N.J.: Prentice-Hall, 1971), pp. 17–47; Clyde Griffin, "Workers Divided: Craft and Ethnic Differences in Poughkeepsie," in Stephan Thernstrom and Richard Sennet, eds.,

Nineteenth Century Cities (New Haven: Yale University Press, 1969), pp. 59–61. Kessner, *Golden Door*, that p. 158, shows that the phenomenon of the poor on the move applies to other New York City areas besides Harlem. My work suggests that the other forces directing migration up to Harlem may also be found in other cities and among other groups as well, all in variance from the Chicago-based model.

3. HARLEM IN ITS HEYDAY: 1. THE SECOND GHETTO

1. See chapter 4.
2. *HS*, January 28, 1910, p. 1; Louis Wirth *The Ghetto* (Chicago: University of Chicago Press, 1928), p. 249.
3. Moses Rischin, *The Promised City:* New York's Jews, 1870–1914 (Cambridge, Mass.: Harvard University Press, 1962), p. 87; Arthur Goren, *New York Jews and the Quest for Community: The Kehillah Experiment, 1908–1922.* (New York and London: Columbia University Press, 1970), p. 25; U.S. Census Office *Vital Statistics*, p. 100.
4. Eric Hoffer, quoted in the Preface to Hutchins Hapgood, *The Spirit of the Ghetto* (New York: Schocken Books, 1966), xiii.
5. J. Anapol, "The History of Branch #2 Arbeiter Ring, "*Thirtieth Anniversary Journal, Workmen's Circle Branch #2* (New York: N.P., 1929), pp. 2–8.
6. The *Jewish Daily Forward* was founded in April, 1897 as an outgrowth of a split within the ranks of the Socialist Labor Party over the policies of its leader Daniel De Leon. De Leon, a doctrinaire revolutionary Socialist, tried, during the last decade of the nineteenth century, to capture the allegiance of American trade-unionists away from the moderate American Federation of Labor headed by Samuel Gompers. Failing in this attempt, he organized an opposition radical federation, The Socialist Trade and Labor Alliance. Using the Yiddish newspaper, *Der Arbeiter Zeitung*, as a major propaganda forum, De Leon called upon all S.L.P. members and Socialist-controlled unions to come over to the Alliance. The *Forward* was founded by Louis Miller and Ab. Cahan, leaders of a faction within the S.L.P. which opposed De Leon's attempt to destroy the A.F. of L. See Will Herberg, "The Jewish Labor Movement," *AJYB* (1951), 51:13–14; Ronald Sanders, "The Jewish Daily Forward," *Midstream*, October 1962, pp. 84–85.
7. H. Lang, "A Few Recollections," *Thirtieth Anniversary Journal*, pp. 29–31. Branch #2 was also responsible for the forming of the Zukunft Press Association in 1901 which helped finance the revival of the periodical as a major socialist monthly. The early *Zukunft*, founded in 1892, had suspended publication in 1897. See Rischin, *Promised City*, pp. 120, 227; *JDF*, May 3, 1901, p. 4.
8. Maximilian Hurwitz, *The Workmen's Circle: Its History, Ideals, Organizations and Institutions* (New York: The Workmen's Circle 1936), pp. 36–37; Anapol, "History of Branch #2," p. 2.
9. A. L. Patkin, *The Origin of the Jewish Labor Movement* (Melbourne and London: F. W. Cleshire, 1948), pp. 136–47; Rischin, *Promised City*, pp. 42–45.
10. Patkin, *Origin of Jewish Labor Movement*, pp. 249–61; Rischin, *Promised City*, p. 163.
11. Herberg, "Jewish Labor Movement" pp. 15–16; Hurwitz, *Workmen's Circle*, p. 163.
12. R. Ash, "Greetings," *Thirtieth Anniversary Journal*, pp. 15–16.
13. Hurwitz, *"Workmen's Circle*, p. 167.
14. Ash, "Greetings," pp. 15–16; Anapol, "History of Branch #2," pp. 2–8.
15. Hurwitz, *"Workmen's Circle*," pp. 170–73.

16. Kehillah of New York, *Jewish Communal Register of New York City, 1917–1918* (New York: Lipshitz Press, 1918), pp. 1268–80.

17. Rischin, *Promised City*, pp. 188–89. In 1911, The A. F. of L., under the order of Samuel Gompers, investigated complaints of Jewish workers against the New York Building Trades Council, which had allegedly been spearheading their exclusion from the building trades industry. The A. F. of L. found, in studying the conditions of alteration workers, that they earned on an average only $3.28 a day, as opposed to the $5.00 a day earned by new building construction workers. See Nathan Ausubel, *The Jewish Labor Movement in New York* (New York: Works Progress Administration, n.d.), p. 43.

18. Ausubel, p. 44; *JDF*, September 30, 1907, p. 16 and *Jewish Labor Movement in New York*, June 4, 1912. p. 4.

19. *JDF*, June 21, 1913, p. 3 and July 27, 1913, p. 8.

20. *JDF*, August 29, 1913, p. 8; August 31, 1913, p. 1; and September 8, 1913, p. 8.

21. *JDF*, August 29, 1913, p. 8; March 20, 1914, p. 3, and November 27, 1914, p. 3.

22. *MJ*, April 23, 1915, p. 5.

23. Hertz Burgin, *Die Geschichte fun die Yiddishe Arbeiter Bewegung in America, Russland und England* (New York: United Hebrew Trades 1915), p. 872; H. K. Blatt, *Trade Unions and Labor Movement* (New York: Works Progress Administration n.d.), pp. 38–39; Yossel Cohen, *Jewish Bakers' Union* (New York: Works Progress Administration n.d.), pp. 3–5.

24. Burgin, *Geschichte*, p. 972.

25. *JDF*, January 19, 1904, p. 1.

26. *JDF*, January 28, 1904, p. 1.

27. Burgin, *Geschichte*, p. 872.

28. Cohen, *Bakers' Union*, pp. 3–5; Burgin, *Geschichte*, p. 872.

29. *JDF*, May 17, 1902, p. 1.

30. *JDF*, May 18, 1902, p. 1.

31. *JDF*, May 19, 1902, p. 2 and May 20, 1902, pp. 1–2.

32. *JDF*, June 13, 1902, p. 4; Ausubel, *Jewish Labor Movement in New York*, pp. 2–8.

33. Rischin, *Promised City*, p. 190; B. A. Weinrebe, *Jewish Suburban Movement, Jewish Cooperative Movement* (New York: Works Progress Administration n.d.), p. 3.

34. *JDF*, December 11, 1902, p. 2, and December 12, 1902, p. 5.

35. *JDF*, June 12, 1903, p. 5.

36. *JDF*, July 15, 1903, p. 2.

37. Weinrebe, *Jewish Suburban Movement*, pp. 4–5.

38. *JDF*, January 26, 1904, p. 2, and June 13, 1904, p. 1. Two other smaller cooperative ventures were initiated in Harlem in the immediate pre-World War I period. In March 1915 a cooperative lodging house was established at 52 East 106th Street. One month later, the Industrial and Agricultural Cooperative Association founded a second uptown boarding house at Lexington Avenue and 111th Street. See *Der Tag*, March 18, 1915, p. 3 and April 23, 1915, p. 3.

39. *JDF*, January 1, 1908, p. 1.

40. *JDF*, December 31, 1907, p. 1. It is interesting to note that in the few days between the start of the strike and the calling of the conference three of the five participating organizations were listed in the *Forward* as "the leading spirit of the strike." See *JDF*, December 29, 1907, p. 1; January 4, 1908, p. 8, and January 5, 1908, p. 1.

41. *JDF*, January 6, 1908, p. 1, January 4, 1908, p. 8, and December 29, 1907, p. 1.

42. *JDF*, January 10, 1908, pp. 1, 8, January 11, 1908, pp. 1, 8, and January 15, 1908, p. 8.

43. *The City Record, Official Canvass of the County of New York*, vol. 28, pt. 12 (December 13, 1900), vol. 30, pt. 12 (December 31, 1902), vol. 33, pt. 1 (January 21, 1905), vol. 35, pt. 1 (January 13, 1907), vol. 36, pt. 12 (December 31, 1908), vol. 38, pt. 12 (December 29, 1910), vol. 40, pt. 12 (December 31, 1912), and vol. 42, pt. 12 (December 31, 1914).

44. The predominantly Jewish Assembly Districts in East Harlem between 1900 and 1910 were the 31st and 32d A.D.s running roughly from 96th to 110th Streets, west of

Second Avenue. See Rischin, *Promised City*, ch. 11, for a full discussion of voting patterns among Jews on the Lower East Side.

45. *Der Tag*, November 2, 1916, p. 4; Rischin, *Promised City, pp. 221–22.*

46. *The City Record*, vol. 42, pt. 12 (December 31, 1914). The year 1914 saw the Democrats lose the gubernatorial election as well as control of both houses of the Legislature. It was also a year in which Jews both of the Lower East Side and of Harlem deserted the Democratic Party. And it has been suggested one of the reasons for this defection was the belief held by many Jews that Governor William Sulzer, a great champion of Jewish causes, had been unfairly impeached from office because of his opposition to the policies of Tammany Hall. This anti-Tammany feeling may have provided Siegel with his narrow margin of victory. See Jacob Alexis Friedman, *The Impeachment of William Sulzer* (New York: Columbia University Press 1939), pp. 242–270, Rischin, *Promised City*, pp. 232–33.

47. Rischin, *Promised City*, p. 235; *JDF*, February 20, 1916, p. 2.

48. *JDF*, January 23, 1916, p. 7.

49. *JDF*, February 20, 1916, p. 2 and July 10, 1916, p. 2.

50. *American Jewish Chronicle*, July 27, 1916, p. 377.

51. *JDF*, September 9, 1916, p. 1 and October 19, 1916, p. 9.

52. Rischin, *Promised City*, p. 235.

53. *YT*, April 16, 1916, p. 4; Naomi W. Cohen, *Not Free to Desist* (Philadelphia: Jewish Publication Society of America, 1972), p. 53; Arthur Gorenstein, "A Portrait of Ethnic Politics: The Socialists and the 1908 and 1910 Congressional Elections on the East Side," *Publications of the American Jewish Historical Society* (March 1961), 50:202–38.

54. *American Jewish Chronicle*, September 15, 1916, pp. 602–03 and November 3, 1916, p. 787.

55. *American Jewish Chronicle*, November 3, 1916, p. 787.

56. *YT*, November 8, 1916, p. 1; *Der Tag*, March 28, 1916, p. 609.

57. *YT*, October 26, 1916, p. 4; *MJ*, November 3, 1916, p. 4.

58. *Der Tag*, March 28, 1916, p. 4; Louis Marshall to Isaac Siegel, November 2, 1916, Marshall Papers—American Jewish Archives.

59. *JDF*, October 27, 1916, p. 1; *Der Tag*, October 27, 1916, p. 4; *American Jewish Chronicle*, November 3, 1916, p. 787; *MJ*, November 3, 1916, p. 4; *JDF*, November 6, 1916, p. 1.

60. *The City Record*, vol. 44, pt. 12 (December 31, 1916); Arthur Mann, *LaGuardia: A Fighter Against His Time 1882–1933* (Chicago: University of Chicago Press, 1959, p. 151.

61. *The City Record*, vol. 46, pt. 12 (December 31, 1918).

62. *The City Record*, vol. 48, pt. 12 (December 31, 1920) and vol. 50, pt. 12 (December 31, 1922).

63. *The City Record*, vol. 44, pt. 12 (December 31, 1916), vol. 46, pt. 12 (December 31, 1918), vol. 48, pt. 12 (December 31, 1920), and vol. 50, pt. 12 (December 31, 1922).

64. *The City Record*, vol. 52, pt. 12 (December 31, 1924).

65. *The City Record*, vol. 28, pt. 12 (December 13, 1900), vol. 30, pt. 12 (December 31, 1902), vol. 33, pt. 1 (January 21, 1905), vol. 35, pt. 1 (January 13, 1907), vol. 36, pt. 12 (December 31, 1908), vol. 38, pt. 12 (December 29, 1910), vol. 40, pt. 12 (December 31, 1912), vol. 42, pt. 12 (December 31, 1914), vol. 44, pt. 12 (December 31, 1916), vol. 46, pt. 12 (December 31, 1918), and vol. 48, pt. 12 (December 31, 1920).

66. The geographical dimensions of the radical subcommunity can be seen clearly in map 5. Of the twenty-five houses affected by the 1904 and 1908 rent strikes only nine were located outside the well-defined geographical area. Twenty-six of the thirty-seven known locations of uptown radical organizations (ad hoc and permanent) were similarly situated.

4. HARLEM IN ITS HEYDAY: 2. SOLVING THE PROBLEMS OF AMERICANIZATION

1. *AI*, February 11, 1904, pp. 1, 8.

2. Edward H. Spicer, "Acculturation," *International Encyclopedia of the Social Sciences,* ed. David L. Sills (New York: The Macmillan Company and the Free Press, 1968), 1:24; Robert E. Park, "Assimilation, Social," *Encyclopedia of the Social Sciences,* eds. Edwin R. A. Seligman and Alvin Johnson (New York: The Macmillan Press, 1930), 1:281–83.

3. Louis Wirth, *The Ghetto* (Chicago: University of Chicago Press, 1978), p. 256.

4. *AH*, December 25, 1903, p. 3, January 8, 1904, p. 273, November 4, 1905, p. 631, and December 28, 1906, p. 189; *YT*, December 1, 1903, p. 8.

5. *AH*, February 12, 1909, p. 409; see also Moses Rischin, *The Promised City: New York's Jews* (Cambridge, Mass.: Harvard University Press, 1962), pp. 102–03.

6. *JM*, October 30, 1896, p. 2.

7. *JM*, August 2, 1896, p. 2; *AH*, December 31, 1896, p. 257.

8. *HS*, June 21, 1901, p. 4; *AI*, February 11, 1904, p. 1.

9. *HS*, October 31, 1902, p. 3; *YT*, November 10, 1902, p. 8; *HS*, February 28, 1902, p. 4, and March 28, 1902, p. 5.

10. Mark Zborowski and Elizabeth Herzog, *Life is with People* (New York: Schocken Books, 1962), pp. 88–104.

11. The confidence of the immigrant Jews in the public school system, despite all its own inherent problems and apparent lack of completely modern pedagogic procedures, was clearly noted by muckraker Jacob Riis. "The poorest among them," Riis declared, "make all possible sacrifices to keep his children in schools and one of the most striking phenomena in New York City is the way in which Jews have taken possession of the public schools, in the highest and lowest grades." See Jacob Riis, "The Children of the Poor," in Robert A. Woods et al., *The Poor in the Great Cities* (London: 1896), p. 102.

12. *HS*, September 15, 1916, pp. 1, 3.

13. *YT*, February 5, 1903, p. 7; *HS*, September 15, 1916, pp. 1, 3.

14. See Alexander Dushkin, *Jewish Education in New York City* (New York: Bureau of Jewish Education, 1918) for an excellent account, by a trained educator, of the problems of Jewish education at the turn of the century.

15. *AH*, January 8, 1904, p. 273 and January 15, 1904, p. 293.

16. *HS*, January 1, 1904, p. 8; *AH*, January 8, 1904, p. 273 and January 29, 1904, p. 359.

17. *AH*, January 29, 1904, p. 359.

18. *AH*, February 5, 1904, p. 392 and February 28, 1904, p. 480.

19. *HS*, January 1, 1904, p. 8; *AH*, February 17, 1905, p. 387 and February 10, 1905, pp. 353–54.

20. *AH*, April 17, 1905, p. 616; Philip Cowen, *Memories of an American Jew* (New York: International Press, 1932), p. 106.

21. *HS*, October 19, 1906, p. 3 and October 25, 1906, p. 13.

22. *AH*, April 7, 1905, p. 616 and July 7, 1905, p. 160.

23. Rischin, *Promised City,* pp. 100–03.

24. *AH*, July 7, 1905, p. 160 and April 26, 1907, p. 661.

25. *YT*, May 5, 1892, p. 2. The records of the New York County Clerk indicate that the Uptown Talmud Torah was incorporated on October 22, 1892.

26. *AH*, November 16, 1894, p. 69; *YT*, January 3, 1896, p. 3. The Hebrew Free School Association, a forerunner of the Educational Alliance of East Broadway, was founded in the 1880s by German Jews in the hope of stopping Christian missionary activities among East European Jews on the Lower East Side. See Rischin, *Promised City,* pp. 100–01.

27. *AH*, August 19, 1904, p. 348; Zvi Scharfstein, ed., *Sefer Ha'yovel Shel Agudat Ha'morim Ha'ivrim B''New York* (New York: Modern Linotype, 1944), p. 156.
28. Hutchins Hapgood, *The Spirit of the Ghetto* (New York: Schocken Books, 1966), p. 53.
29. Hapgood, *Spirit of the Ghetto*, pp. 55–58; *YT*, April 5, 1903, p. 1.
30. *YT*, March 27, 1905, p. 4. Malacovsky's views on Jewish education were reprinted in 1906 in the *Hebrew Standard* and thus reached both the Yiddish and non-Yiddish readers of New York's Jewish community.
31. *YT*, February 2, 1904, p. 4.
32. *YT*, February 24, 1905, p. 4.
33. *HS*, February 24, 1905, p. 4; *YT*, May 15, 1905, p. 8.
34. *YT*, May 11, 1905, p. 8; May 15, 1905, p. 8.
35. *HS*, April 26, 1907, p. 4; *MJ*, June 4, 1907, p. 4; *AH*, February 28, 1908, p. 444 and March 27, 1908, p. 527. Unfortunately due to the lack of extant papers of the U.T.T. board of directors, there is no way of determining the reason(s) for Malacovsky's departure from U.T.T. and his replacement by Ish-Kishor.
36. *YT*, March 16, 1906, p. 8; *AH*, February 28, 1908, p. 44.
37. Elias A. Cohen to Louis Marshall, March 31, 1908, Marshall Papers—American Jewish Archives.
38. Elias A. Cohen to Louis Marshall, December 7, 1909, Marshall Papers—American Jewish Archives.
39. Jacob Schiff to the Board of Directors of the Uptown Talmud Torah Association, February 16, 1910, Marshall Papers—American Jewish Archives.
40. Isidor Hershfield, Hon. Secretary, Uptown Talmud Torah to Jacob Schiff, February 23, 1910, Marshall Papers—American Jewish Archives.
41. Louis Marshall to Jacob Schiff, March 5, 1910; Jacob Schiff to Isidor hershfield, February 28, 1910, Marshall Papers—American Jewish Archives.
42. *MJ*, February 6, 1911; *AH*, March 22, 1912, p. 609; *HS*, April 11, 1913, p. 4.
43. Herbert S. Goldstein, ed., *Forty Years of Struggle for a Principle: The Biography of Harry Fischel* (New York: Bloch, 1928), pp. 66–67.
44. *Ibid.*
45. *MJ*, August 11, 1913, p. 5 and October 12, 1913, p. 4.
46. *HS*, October 3, 1913, p. 10.
47. Kehillah of New York, "Minutes of Meetings of the Executive Committee of the Jewish Community (Kehillah) of New York City," meeting of October 10, 1911, Isreal Friedlander Papers—Jewish Theological Seminary Library. See also, Arthur Goren, *New York Jews and the Quest for Community: The Kehillah Experiment, 1908–22* (New York and London: Columbia University Press, 1970), pp. 96–99, 111–19, and Dushkin, *Jewish Education*, pp. 107–09.
48. *AH*, December 5, 1913, p. 152; Alexander Dushkin to Jeffrey S. Gurock, August 4, 1974.
49. *MJ*, February 23, 1914, p. 1 and February 24, 1914, p. 2.
50. *AH*, February 27, 1914, p. 502.
51. Harry Fischel to Jacob Schiff, February 27, 1914, Jacob Schiff Papers—American Jewish Archives.
52. *HS*, March 5, 1915, p. 11.
53. *MJ*, August 7, 1908, p. 5 and August 14, 1908, pp. 7–8.
54. *MJ*, June 5, 1911, p. 5.
55. *MJ*, June 3, 1910, p. 2.
56. *MJ*, June 5, 1910, p. 5 and June 5, 1911, p. 5.
57. *MJ*, September 22, 1910, p. 7 and June 5, 1911, p. 5.
58. *MJ*, October 8, 1915, p. 2.
59. *Ibid.*
60. *MJ*, May 16, 1909, p. 7 and April 4, 1912, p. 8; *Bronx-Harlem Press*, June 21, 1914, p. 5.
61. *MJ*, May 29, 1913, p. 5 and November 21, 1911, p. 8.

62. *MJ*, May 29, 1913, p. 5.
63. *HS*, November 22, 1912, p. 9; *MJ*, March 10, 1914, p. 4.
64. See Aaron Rothkoff, *Bernard Revel: Builder of Modern Orthodoxy* (Philadelphia: Jewish Publication Society of America, 1972), ch. 7, for a discussion of the opposition to the founding of a Jewish university emanating from right-wing elements within the Orthodox community.
Most contemporary ultra-right-wing Orthodox Jews described by sociologist Charles Leibman as "sectarian Jews" arrived in the United States before, during and immediately after World War II and bolstered up what was admittedly a very weak European Orthodox community. I am suggesting here that small numbers of second- and third-generation American Jews—the early opponents of Yeshiva University and those who identified with institutions like Yeshiva Torah Vo Da'at and the Rabbinical Seminary of America—perpetuated forms of East European Orthodoxy in America until the 1940s and perhaps beyond. See Charles Leibman, "Orthodoxy in American Jewish Life," *AJYB* (1965), 66:21–98.

5. HARLEM JEWRY AND THE EMERGENCE OF THE AMERICAN SYNAGOGUE

1. Marshall Sklare, *Conservative Judaism: An American Religious Movement* (New York: Schocken Books, 1972), pp. 66–72. For a complete discussion of the lifestyles of second-generation American Jews in New York City, see Deborah Dash Moore's dissertation, "The Emergence of Ethnicity: New York's Jews 1920–1940" (Columbia University, 1975).
2. Sklare, *Conservative Judaism*, pp. 135–37.
3. Jewish center advocates may have drawn some strength in promoting their nonreligious synagogue activities from the experiences of their Protestant institutional church counterparts who had fought within their own community for the idea that religious and secular activities could be successfully integrated within a church setting. There was, however, a basic difference between these two movements which suggests that the overt influence of earlier Christian upon later Jewish communal workers was minimal. The major impulse behind the institutional church, as Mordecai Kaplan has pointed out, was philanthropic. The well-to-do members of Christian society constructed institutional churches to supply their poor coreligionists with facilities for social and intellectual activities. Their closest parallels in the Jewish experience were such Jewish settlement houses as the Educational Alliance and Harlem's own Harlem Federation. The Institutional Synagogue and the later Jewish community centers were designed to serve both poor and rich Jews, and directed their activities at the acculturated of all economic strata. See Charles Stezle, "The Institutional Church," in Robert D. Cross, ed., *The Church and the City, 1865–1910* (New York: Bobbs-Merrill, 1967), pp. 341–43; see also Mordecai M. Kaplan, *Judaism as a Civilization* (New York: Macmillan, 1934), p. 52.
4. *YT*, December 9, 1896, p. 8.
5. *YT*, March 13, 1902, p. 2; *HS*, March 21, 1902, p. 4; *AH*, June 24, 1904, p. 160.
6. *HS*, April 28, 1905, p. 4, May 26, 1905, p. 4, and April 14, 1905, p. 4.
7. Two women, Mrs. Rivka Banner and Miss Irene Stern, were members of the original board of directors of Congregation Mikveh Israel. See the "Incorporation papers of Congregation Mikveh Israel," on file at the New York County Clerk's Office. See also *YT*, March 25, 1906, p. 8.

8. *HS,* June 29, 1906, p. 4; Bernard Drachman, *The Unfailing Light* (New York: Rabbinical Council of America, 1948), pp. 276–77. Similar small Jewish centers were created by Albert Lucas on the Lower East Side during the same time period. None of these downtown initiatives lasted more than a few years. Lucas and Rabbi Morais were both often mentioned as spiritual antecedents of the Young Israel and Institutional Synagogue.

9. *HS,* April 28, 1911, p. 4, and May 12, 1911, p. 4; Congregation Ansche Chesed, "Minutes of Meetings of the Congregation," meetings of November 30, 1911 and December 29, 1913.

10. *HS,* October 11, 1910, p. 13.

11. Drachman, *Unfailing Light,* p. 167; *HS,* January 7, 1921, p. 10.

12. Archibald McClure, *Leadership of the New America* (New York: George H. Doran Co., 1916), pp. 171–72.

13. *YT,* January 6, 1916, p. 8.

14. *YT,* January 6, 1916, p. 8; Arthur Goren, *New York Jews and the Quest for Community: The Kehillah Experiment, 1908–22* (New York and London: Columbia University Press, 1970), pp. 77–78.

15. *HS,* January 7, 1916, p. 19; *YT,* January 6, 1916, p. 8.

16. *YT,* September 20, 1915, p. 8, and February 10, 1916, p. 8; *HS,* February 11, 1916, p. 16.

17. *HS,* September 29, 1916, p. 4; *YT,* August 30, 1915, p. 8.

18. *YT,* September 18, 1916, p. 8; *AH,* January 29, 1915, p. 343; *YT,* February 26, 1915, p. 8. See also YMHA of New York, "Meetings of the Special Joint Committee Consisting of Members of the Social, Finance and Membership and Neighborhood Committees," meeting of March 14, 1915, for a discussion of the reticence of the 92d Street Y to involve itself directly in Harlem Jewish activities.

19. *YT,* July 19, 1915, p. 8 and July 21, 1915, p. 8.

20. Ira Eisenstein and Ira Kohn, eds., *Mordecai Kaplan: An Evaluation* (New York: Reconstruction Foundation, 1952), *passim.*

21. John Dewey, *Democracy and Education* (New York: Macmillan, 1963), pp. 53, 241–49; see also Goren, *Kehillah Experiment,* p. 120 and Ronald Kronish, "The Influence of John Dewey on Jewish Education," *Conservative Judaism,* Winter, 1976, pp. 49–52.
Many of Kaplan's students, among them Isaac Berkson, Alexander Dushkin, Emanuel Gamoran and Samuel Dinin, who also served as the early leaders of the Bureau of Jewish Education, studied under Dewey and his colleague William Heard Kilpatrick at Columbia University's Teachers College, and received their advanced academic degrees there. See Meir Ben-Horin, "From the Turn of the Century to the Late Thirties," in Judah Pilch, ed., *A History of Jewish Education in America* (New York: National Curriculum Institute of the American Association of Jewish Education, 1969), p. 86.

22. Isaac Berkson, *Theories of Americanization* (Teachers College, Columbia University, 1920, p. 183.

23. *Ibid.,* p. 189.

24. *Ibid.*

25. *MJ,* September 7, 1917, p. 5.

26. *HS,* June 18, 1915, pp. 1, 24.

27. *HS,* September 15, 1916, pp. 1, 3; *AH,* January 18, 1918, p. 322.

28. *HS,* September 15, 1916, p. 24.

29. *Ibid.,* pp. 1, 24.

30. *Ibid.*

31. *HS,* November 24, 1916, p. 7; Herbert S. Goldstein to Jacob Schiff, April 11, 1917, Schiff Papers—American Jewish Archives.

32. *HS,* January 17, 1908, p. 6.

33. *HS,* January 31, 1908, p. 13.

34. *HS,* February 7, 1908, p. 8.

35. See Isaac Siegel to Herbert S. Goldstein contained in the correspondence Goldstein to Jacob Schiff, April 11, 1917, Schiff Papers—American Jewish Archives.
36. Institutional Synagogue, Synagogue Constitution, art. 3, sec. 2; art. 6, sec. 1.
37. *HS*, April 27, 1917, p. 10 and June 11, 1917, p. 12; *AH*, June 11, 1917, p. 29.
38. *New York American*, June 21, 1917, n.p.; *American Jewish Chronicle*, June 18, 1917, p. 56.
39. *MJ*, September 7, 1917, p. 5; *AH*, January 18, 1918, p. 322; *HS*, February 8, 1918, p. 5 and October 18, 1918, p. 5.
40. *AH*, January 18, 1918, p. 322.
41. *YT*, February 19, 1917, p. 8.
42. *Ibid.*
43. *American Jewish Chronicle*, June 15, 1917, p. 163.
44. *Ibid.*, p. 324.

6. THE DECLINE OF JEWISH HARLEM, 1920–1930

1. Ernest W. Burgess, "Residential Segregation in American Cities," *Annals of the American Academy of Political and Social Sciences* 42 (1928):106–08.
2. Otis D. Duncan and Beverly Duncan, *The Negro Population in Chicago: A Study of Racial Succession* (Chicago: University of Chicago Press, 1957), pp. 11, 15, 100; Karl E. Taeuber and Alma F. Taeuber, *Negroes in Cities: Residential Segregation and Neighborhood Change* (Chicago: Aldine, 1965), pp. 24, 164. See Yona Ginzburg, *Jews in a Changing Neighborhood* (New York: The Free Press, 1975), pp. 1–24 for an extensive introduction to the scholarly literature on white-Black relations in a changing neighborhood.
3. Edwin Spengler, *Land Values in New York in Relation to Transit Facilities* (New York: Columbia University Press, 1930), pp. 19–24.
4. New York City Tenement House Department, *Seventh Report, 1912–14* (New York: Martin Brown Press, 1912–14), pp. 66, 121.
5. *Idem, Eighth Report, 1915–16* (New York: Martin Brown Press, 1915–16), p. 18; *Ninth Report, 1917* (New York: Martin Brown Press, 1917), p. 11.
6. Walter Laidlaw, ed., *Population of the City of New York 1890–1930* (New York: City Census Committee, 1932), p. 82.
7. New York City Tenement House Department, *Ninth Report*, p. 11; New York State Reconstruction Commission, *Housing Conditions: Report of the Housing Committee of the Reconstruction Committee of the State of New York* (Albany: J. B. Lyon, 1920), p. 9.
8. New York State, Commission of Housing and Regional Planning, *Report of Commission of Housing and Regional Planning to Governor Alfred E. Smith and to the Legislature of the State of New York on the Present Housing Emergency, December 12, 1923* (Albany: J. B. Lyon, 1924), p. 14; New York State Reconstruction Commission, p. 21.
9. New York State Reconstruction Commission, pp. 10–11.
10. Walter Laidlaw, ed., *Statistical Sources for Demographic Studies of Greater New York* (New York: The New York City 1920 Census Committee, Inc., 1923), *passim.*
11. New York State, Commission of Housing and Regional Planning, p. 14.
12. *MJ*, February 25, 1913, p. 4; *YT*, May 9, 1916, p. 8.
13. New York State, Commission of Housing and Regional Planning, p. 38. The attempt of landlords to maximize their profits at tenement-dwellers' expense was

strongly resisted by tenants through a series of state-wide postwar rent strikes conducted on a far larger scale than those seen in New York a decade earlier. Housing
conditions reached their nadir in 1920 when the New York State Legislature declared a
"public emergency" existing in housing.

14. *RERBG,* March 5, 1921, p. 295.

15. *RERBG,* September 3, 1921, p. 295. See also *RERBG,* January 3, 1920, pp. 21–22 and
January 1, 1921, p. 4 for discussions of labor problems and monetary difficulties that
faced builders in the early postwar years.

16. New York City Tenement House Department, *Tenth Report 1918–1929* (New
York: Martin Brown Press, 1929), pp. 36–49.

17. *Population, Land Values and Government: Studies of the Growth and Distribution
of Population and Land Values; and of Problems of Government, Regional Survey of
New York and its Environs* (New York: Regional Survey of New York and its Environs,
1929), 2:62. See also *RERBG,* March 18, 1922, p. 329 and March 20, 1926, pp. 8–10.

18. New York City Tenement House Department, *Tenth Report,* pp. 36–49; *New York
City Market Analysis* (New York: *The New York Herald Tribune, Daily News,* and *New
York Times,* 1933), *passim.* This latter study indicated that by 1930 the "estimated annual median family housing expenditure" for a family in the Morrisania or Hunts Point
areas of the Bronx ranged from approximately $2,600 to $3,200. Residents in the area
paid only slightly more than the Manhattan median rent. The cost of living on the
Grand Concourse was estimated at $3,750 per annum.

19. Nathan Goldberg, "Occupational Patterns of American Jews," *Jewish Review*
(1943) 3:162–186. Goldberg's study of immigrant Jewish upward mobility was based on a
variety of sources including a 1920s federal census monograph on the economic status
of immigrants and their children (based on that decade's census manuscripts, which
are presently unavailable to scholars), and several independent Jewish surveys of a variety of cities. None of these studies focused specifically on the economic life of New
York's Jews, but one can assume that that city followed the general national pattern.

More detailed examinations of both general New York Jewish immigrant mobility and
the specific Harlem communal picture, on the scale done in chapter 2 for the turn of
the century community, are not easily done due to important lacunae in the available
source materials. Federal census manuscripts for 1910 to 1920 are closed to scholars by
law. The 1925 State census manuscripts are available but they enumerate only an individual's place of birth, and not also that of his or her parents (as do the federal manuscripts). This makes study of second-generation American Jews very difficult. The only
sample that conceivably could be done would be among those second-generation Jews
still living with their own parents.

It is, of course, possible to demonstrate as we have done—through an examination
of the cost of living in different parts of the city, that both poor and rich Jews were able
to leave Harlem for accomodations elsewhere. See above, n.18. But determining the
actual income or basic economic structure of mid-1920s Harlem Jewry is not possible
given the available sources.

In lieu of truly substantive data on New York economic mobility, I have been forced
to rely primarily on—in addition to the aforementioned government reports on labor—
what may be described as impressionistic indices of wealth to illustrate the economic
advance of immigrant Jews and their children. In this context, I believe, such evidence
as the advertising by such groups as car menufacturers, ocean-liner owners and resort
operators in the Yiddish press—the traditional chronicler of immigrant poverty and
laboringmen's problems—is significant. And although it is not possible to determine
how many Jews responded to these commercial appeals, it is, nevertheless, noteworthy
that, beginning in the 1920s, Jews are being viewed as consumers of luxury items and
the like.

20. See *YT,* June 2, 1922, pp. 2–3 for typical examples of automobile advertising. By
that year, automobile ads were almost a daily feature of several of New York's Yiddish
newspapers. See also *YT,* May 11, 1919, p. 2 and June 9, 1922, p. 2, and Harold Jaediker
Taub, *Walforf in the Catskills: The Grossinger Legend* (New York: Serling Publishing

Company, 1952) for advertising and discussions of the growth of Jewish resort areas in response to the desires of upwardly mobile Jews to escape the city summer. Michael Gold, in *Jews Without Money* (New York: Horace Liveright, Inc., 1930), p. 215, discusses the difficulties encountered by the poor seeking relocation out of the ghetto.

21. Bureau of Jewish Social Research, *First Section: Studies in the New York Jewish Population. Jewish Communal Survey of Greater New York* (New York: Bureau of Jewish Social Research, 1928), p. 8; C. Morris Horowitz and Lawrence J. Kaplan, *The Estimated Jewish Population of the New York Area 1900–1975* (New York: Federation of Jewish Philanthropies, 1959), pp. 133, 209, 239. The figures presented here on the Jewish population of New York and of Harlem for the years 1916 through 1930 are only rough estimates of their true numbers. Since the United States and New York State census tabulations do not enumerate "Jews" as such, it is impossible to determine Jewish population on the basis of such governmental documentation. This problem has caused Jewish demographers and communal leaders to devise several less-than-scientific self-survey techniques for estimating the number of Jews in a given city or minor subdivision. See Sophia M. Robison, *Jewish Population Studies*, Jewish Social Studies Publications, no. 3 (New York: Conference on Jewish Relations, 1943), pp. 1–10 for a complete discussion of the several techniques and their methodological limitations.

Despite the problems with these "unofficial" systems, such techniques as the "Yom Kippur school absence method" and the "death-rate method" have been used extensively by Jewish demographers in the several major Jewish population studies undertaken over the last decades. Accordingly, the results of the Bureau and of Horowitz and Kaplan are presented here simply in the hope of giving some measure of quantitative perspective to the otherwise well-documented history of the important demographic shifts that affected the New York and Harlem Jewish communities in the postwar decade.

22. Jewish Welfare Board, *Preliminary Study of the Institutional Synagogue* (New York: Jewish Welfare Board, 1924), *passim*.

23. Bureau of Jewish Social Research, p. 8.

24. Jewish Welfare Board, *Study of the Institutional Synagogue in Relation to Harlem, N.Y.C.* (New York: Jewish Welfare Board, 1938), p. 33; Horowitz and Kaplan, *Estimated Jewish Population*, pp. 156–61. As of July 1974, the only synagogue in Harlem dating its existence from the 1910s is Congregation Tikwath Israel of 113th Street between Lexington and Third Avenues. Services are held at this institution on Sabbaths and Sundays and are attended by the few elderly Jews who live in the nearby housing projects.

25. Seth M. Scheiner, *Negro Mecca: A History of the Negro in New York City 1865–1920* (New York: New York University Press, 1965), p. 26.

26. *Ibid.*, p. 30.

27. *AH*, December 16, 1911, p. 168.

28. *YT*, August 6, 1906, p. 4; *YT*, September 7, 1900, p. 1. H. Lang of the Arbeiter Ring recalled that at the turn of the century "the streets of Harlem to us immigrants were foreign. In the streets around us lived many Irish and we were often attacked by them." See Lang, "A Few Recollections," *Thirtieth Anniversary Journal*, Workmen's Circle Branch #2 (New York: The Workmen's Circle, 1929), pp. 29–33. See also *YT*, August 1900, pp. 1, 4 and May 11, 1906, and *JDF*, July 7, 1903, p. 1, for discussions of "pogroms" against blacks.

29. Laidlaw, *Statistical Sources*, pp. 70ff.

30. National League on Urban Conditions among Negroes, *Housing Conditions among Negroes in Harlem, N.Y.C.* (New York: Poole Press Association, 1915), pp. 8, 13.

31. *Ibid.*, pp. 7, 13–26; see also Gilbert Osofsky, *Harlem: The Making of a Ghetto* (New York: Scribner's, 1963), p. 111.

32. Scheiner, *Negro Mecca*, p. 20.

33. Osofsky, *Harlem*, pp. 128–30.

34. *Ibid.*, p. 139; New York State, Commission of Housing and Regional Planning, p. 16.

35. New York City Market Analysis, *passim*. See also Lawrence Royce Chenault, *The

Puerto Rican Migrant in New York (New York: Columbia University Press, 1938), *passim*.

36. *HS*, August 17, 1917, p. 12.

37. Hebrew Tabernacle, "Minutes of Congregational Meetings, 1908–1919," American Jewish Archives.

38. *Ibid*.

39. Hebrew Tabernacle, "Minutes of Meetings of the Board of Trustees," meetings of March 24, 1919, October 27, 1919 and November 14, 1919.

40. *Idem*, Minutes of Meetings of the Board of Trustees," meeting of December 5, 1920.

41. *Idem*, "Minutes of Congregational Meetings," meeting of April 27, 1922.

42. Works Progress Administration, Historical Records Survey, Inventory of Records of Churches, Jewish Synagogues, New York City Municipal Archives.

43. *Ibid*.

44. *Ibid*.

45. The source of the discussion of the Institutional Synagogue's agreement with the New York City Board of Education is an untitled document, apparently a bill of sale or foreclosure, between the Institutional Synagogue and the Bank of New York, dated April 12, 1943. The document reviews in great detail the history of the agreement and the reasons for the present sale. This document is part of an uncatalogued collection of Institutional Synagogue papers housed at Yeshiva University.

46. Works Progress Administration, Historical Records Survey.

47. *Ibid*. 30th Anniversary.

48. *Journal*, Workmen's Circle Branch #2, pp. 21, 22, 24–25.

49. Federal Writers Project, Yiddish Writers Group, *Die Yiddishe Landsmanshaften fun New York* (New York, I. L. Peretz Writers Union, 1938), pp. 114–115.

7. REFLECTIONS ON THE HARLEM JEWISH EXPERIENCE

1. See Rudolf Glanz, *Studies in Judaica Americana* (New York: KTAV 1970), Jacob R. Marcus, *Memoirs of American Jews, 1775–1865*, 3 vols. (Philadelphia: Jewish Publication Society of America 1955) and American Jewish Archives, *Essays in American Jewish History in Commemoration of the 10th Anniversary of the American Jewish Archives* (Cincinnati) American Jewish Archives 1958) for examples of continent-wide-looking historiography. Glanz, in "German Jews in New York City in the Nineteenth Century," in *Studies*, pp. 123–52, fails to note the uptown settlement's existence. This exemplifies how early Harlem German history has been overlooked by scholars of New York Jewry. It should be noted, however, in fairness to earlier historians of other localities, that I cannot be sure whether their failure to discuss the history of Harlemlike suburbs, divorced from but in close proximity to the centers of their own Eastern seaboard Jewish areas, was due to the simple nonexistence of such outposts elsewhere in America or to their not having searched for them. It is painfully clear, however, that until recently American Jewish communal historians have not been particularly sensitive to the methodology of and issues raised by urban history—such as the process of intracity migration and the relationship between city growth and the course of Jewish group experience—in studying their specific locales. See Henry S. Morais, *The Jews of Philadelphia: Their History from the Earliest Settlements to the Present Time* (Philadelphia, The Levytype Company, 1894), Morris A. Gutstein, *The Story of the Jews of Newport* (New York: Bloch 1936), Isaac M. Fein, *The Making of an American Jewish Community; The*

History of Baltimore Jewry from 1773–1920 (Philadelphia: Jewish Publication Society of America, 1971) and Charles Reznikoff and Uriah Z. Engelman, *The Jews of Charleston: A History of an American Jewish Community* (Philadelphia: Jewish Publication Society of America 1950).

2. See Irving Aaron Mandel, "The Attitude of the American Jewish Community towards East European Immigration as Reflected in the Anglo-Jewish Press 1880–1900," *American Jewish Archives* (1950), vol. 7., and Zosa Szajkowski, "The Attitude of American Jews to East European Jewish Immigration (1881–1893)," *Publications of the American Jewish Historical Society* (1951), vol. 40, as examples of these types of discussions of the reaction of the Germans to East European migration. The tendency to overlook or downplay, post-1881 German communal history, as noted in the text, is particularly true with reference to studies of America's two largest cities, New York and Chicago. These housed in their heyday close to 45 percent of the country's Jews, and obviously experienced the most significant immigrant incursions. Rischin, in Chapter 6 of his *The Promised City*, exemplifes the omission by historians of New York Jewry of the internal communal life of the intracity migrating German Jew in the late nineteenth century. Landesman, writing on Brownsville, mentions that settlement's first German-Jewish families, but does not attempt to explain in city-wide terms why they came. More importantly, he does not search for German-Jewish families in the extant New York State Census of Population manuscripts for Kings County for 1892, which he used to trace East European incursions into Brooklyn. We cannot tell from his work whether Germans moved to Brownsville ahead of or with East European Jews in the 1880s and 1890s and whether they retained their Jewish heritage. See Landesman, *Brownsville: The Birth, Development and Passing of a Jewish Community in New York* (New York: 1971), chs. 3 and 4. Hyman L. Meites' early *History of the Jews of Chicago* (Chicago: the Jewish Historical Society of Illinois, 1924), Philip P. Bregstone's subsequent first-person history *Chicago and its Jews* (Chicago: n.p., 1933) and Morris A. Gutstein's *A Priceless Heritage: The Epic Growth of Nineteenth-Century Chicago Jewry* (New York: Bloch 1953) predictably share this lack of recognition of the significance of post-1881 German communal life. And Louis Wirth's *The Ghetto* (Chicago: University of Chicago Press, 1928), an earlier and by no means historically complete sociological study, only notes in passing the creation of a "Deustchland" by German Jews who fled the invasion of the inner city by East Europeans.

Interestingly enough, our questions on what became of the German communities in the twentieth century are considered and partially answered for Chicago by a 1960s study of "Lakeville," an unidentified Chicago suburb. This examination of contemporary levels of Jewish affiliation discovered several groups of third- and fourth-generation German Jews still belonging to the several local Jewish institutions, continuing to identify (at least minimally) with their ancestral faith. See Marshall Sklare and Joseph Greenbaum, *Jewish Identity on the Suburban Frontier* (New York: Basic Books 1966).

Historians of smaller communities that witnessed more limited incursions of East European Jews and consequently experienced much less of an out-migration of German Jews, have been more sensitive to and successful in telling the internal history of older immigrant communities. Stuart Rosenberg's study of Rochester's community, for example, devotes almost equal space to the German and East European experiences between 1870 and 1925. See Stuart Rosenberg, *The Jewish Community in Rochester, 1943–1925* (New York: Columbia University Press, 1954), parts two and three.

3. See Nathan Glazer, *American Judaism* (Chicago: University of Chicago Press, 1957), pp. 57–59, Moshe Davis, *The Emergence of Conservative Judaism: The Historical School in the Nineteenth Century* (Philadelphia: American Jewish Historical Society, 1963), pp. 311–13 and Herbert Parzen, "The Early Development of Conservative Judaism," *Conservative Judaism* (1947), vol. 3, for this type of understanding of the structure of late nineteenth-century American Jewish life.

4. This analysis agrees in many ways with Leon Jick's provocative recent discussion of the nature of Reform Judaism in nineteenth-century America. Jick argues that the Pittsburgh Platform was not that most significant milestone in the evolution of American

Reform Judaism, as others had previously depicted it. Rather, it was to a great extent an ideological expression or justification of the ritual changes already instituted by reforming groups in America without the "authorization" of the so-called national leaders such as I. M. Wise, Einhorn or Kohler. Indeed, Jick contends, the changes in doctrine and belief implied in these ideological reforms were often not even noted by contemporaries. Harlem's history certainly supports this thesis, as the Pittsburgh Platform had a limited impact on this local community's religious life—except possibly in the area of philanthropy. I would even take Jick's argument one step further and suggest that this ideological statement was ignored not only because some Jews had reformed or were reforming on their own, but also because others continued to resist the more radical forms of change being there expressed. The victory of the reformers over the traditionalists which Jick postdates to the last third of the nineteenth century may well have remained incomplete beyond that era. I also believe that Jick's attempt to downplay the importance of the clergy in determining synagogue change may be—if the case of Harris and Temple Israel is at all paradigmatic—a bit overstated. See Leon A. Jick, *The Americanization of the Synagogue 1820–1870* (Hanover: University Press of New England 1976).

5. See Sam Bass Warner, *Streetcar Suburbs: The Process of Growth in Boston, 1870–1900* (Cambridge: Harvard University Press, 1962), chs. 2 and 3, for an example a historical study that emphasizes the importance of rapid transit in creating new suburban neighborhoods settled by upwardly mobile individuals. Warner found for his particular city that migration to areas of second settlement and beyond meant a breakdown in ethnic cohesion. These areas, he argued, were settled by income and not by ethnic group and he noted that the physical arrangement of the suburbs discouraged individual participation in community life.

6. As indicated previously, one particular process noted in the Harlem Jewish story— the migration of the poor out of the ghetto in search of work—has been studied extensively by historians and appears to apply to a variety of city and group contexts. See above, chapter 2, n. 71. Whether the other forces causing Harlem's history to differ from what was theoretically predicted are to be found elsewhere during this same time period remains to be studied. Our conclusions indicating the probability that no one urban experience can be established as typical of all other communities is supported by studies of other groups and conditions—studies that challenge the Chicago school on different grounds and note forces and circumstances occurring neither in New York nor in Chicago. See Howard Chudacoff, *Mobile Americans: Residential and Social Mobility in Omaha* (New York: Oxford University Press, 1972), pp. 77–79 and Humbert Nelli, *Italians of Chicago 1880–1930: A Study in Ethnic Mobility* (New York and London: Oxford University Press 1970), pp. 44–46.

Unfortunately, these revisions and new conclusions cannot be tested for other Jewish communal experiences. Most American Jewish communal historians fail to even note the older theoretical assumptions, let alone test them against local conditions. Even in the otherwise sophisticated communal studies of such larger Jewish urban areas as Baltimore, Milwaukee and Buffalo, limited attention is granted to immigrant movement within the city. Historians have contented themselves with identifying their local ghetto areas—sometimes remarking that a particular neighborhood was that community's equivalent of the Lower East Side—and with noting in a few terse sentences the chronology of out-migration. The issues and questions raised in this present work have, in truth, rarely interested Jewish historians. See, for examples, Fein, *History of Baltimore Jewry*, pp. 159–164; Louis J. Swickow and Lloyd P. Gartner, *The History of the Jews of Milwaukee* (Philadelphia: Jewish Publication Society of America 1963), pp. 166–168; Selig Adler and Thomas E. Connolly, *From Ararat to Suburbia: The History of the Jews of Buffalo* (Philadelphia: Jewish Publication Society of America, 1960), pp. 256–57.

Most regrettable, however, is the total absence of modern critical studies of the three largest Jewish immigrant cities other than New York: Chicago, Philadelphia and Boston. We know something about the Boston community at the turn of the century derivatively from Warner's work *Streetcar Suburbs*. Discussions of Chicago comprehend only the early annalistic writings and Wirth's sociological study, *The Ghetto*. And Philadelphia, with the exception of Morais's earliest American Jewish communal history (*The Jews of Philadelphia*, 1894) has not been studied at all intensively beyond the Jacksonian Era in American history. If useful volumes on these communities were available then historians could begin to rate the relative importance of the Chicago against the New York experience as models for understanding the general history of Jewish immigrant life.

7. See Moore, "The Emergence of Ethnicity: New York's Jews 1910–1940 (Columbia University, 1975) pp. 1–27 for a full discussion of the theoretical assumptions about what acculturation was supposed to mean to second-generation American Jews.

8. Rischin's *The Promised City*, an otherwise brilliant history of New York Jewish life between 1870–1914 is, once again, representative of these two important lacunae in most American Jewish historiography. Rischin fails to note the contribution of the German to the perpetuation of Judaism while acculturating the immigrants and does not discuss the deep commitment of the new elite East European Jews to Americanizing their own group. See Rischin, pp. 95–111.

9. See Aaron Rothkoff, *Bernard Revel: Builder of Modern Orthodoxy* (Philadelphia: Jewish Publ. Society of America, 1972), pp. 3–115. See also Gilbert Klaperman, *The Story of Yeshiva University: The First Jewish University in America* (New York: Macmillan, 1969), pp. 38–43, 59, 90 and *passim*. There is, unfortunately, no extant history of the Jewish Theological Seminary of this period to be consulted on this issue. And Abraham J. Karp's documentary *History of the United Synagogue of America 1913–1963* (New York: United Synagogue, 1963) does not deal in any significant detail with the question of the Seminary versus Orthodoxy.

Bibliographical Essay

This bibliographical essay is designed to identify and describe the several major areas of primary source material and the more interesting and useful secondary works examined in uncovering the history of Harlem Jewry. It is also intended as a guide to facilitate future researchers in investigating this and other inner-city centers of Jewish life which existed in the decades surrounding World War I. These sources and all other secondary materials are cited in the footnotes to this book. For a complete bibliographical listing of all materials consulted in writing this book see my "The History of the Jewish Community of Harlem, 1870–1930," (Ph.D. dissertation, Columbia University, 1977).

SYNAGOGUE AND LOCAL INSTITUTIONAL RECORDS

Harlem Jews were very poor record-keepers. Few if any of the small landsmanshaft synagogues kept minutes of organizational meetings, if indeed such official functions were ever held. Few of these institutions ever bothered to legally incorporate (or they did so after many years of existence), thereby depriving researchers of the names and addresses of their founders. Even the names of these synagogues probably would be unknown to contemporary historians if not for the *Jewish Communal Register of New York City, 1917–1918* published by the New York Kehillah, which canvassed each of New York's Jewish neighborhoods and recorded—albeit with many inaccuracies—the names and addresses of several thousand Jewish religious, social, cultural and fraternal organizations.

Most of the Harlem organizations which did keep records left them behind when their store-front synagogues were closed down and their larger institutions were converted into churches in the 1920s and 1930s. A few historically minded communal leaders preserved Harlem records when their institutions successfully shifted from uptown to the Bronx. But thirty years of subsequent intracity migrations have destroyed these synagogues, and with them their records, for the 1970s student of Harlem history. Interestingly, we do know what types of records were salvaged from Harlem in the 1930s due to the work of the Works Progress Administration Writers Project, which during the Depression surveyed the historical record collections of several hundred New York churches and synagogues—including those of the several formerly Harlem-based institutions. Their manuscript survey is maintained at the New York City Municipal Archives. My attempt to contact the recording secretaries and the other officially designated record-keepers through their 1938–1939 addresses, thirty-five years later was totally unproductive. The paucity of local Jewish documentation extant from Harlem is ironically a function of the same processes of rapid group intracity migration and resettlement that this study seeks to examine.

Several incomplete sets of uncatalogued synagogue and other Jewish institutional records have survived and were consulted. Congregations Ohab Zedek, Shaarei Zedek, and Anshe Chesed, each formerly of Central Harlem and now of Manhattan's West Side, maintained their records in varying degrees of disorder within their respective synagogue archives. Institutional Synagogue of Harlem (1917–1943) records are now part of the Yeshiva University archives in New York. The minutes of the Hebrew Tabernacle (1908–1922) as well as those of the Temple Israel Sisterhood (1891–93) have found their way to the American Jewish Archives in Cincinnati, Ohio. The Library of the American Jewish Historical Society in Waltham, Massachusetts, houses the *Constitution and School Regulations* of the Shangarai Limud Talmud Torah Society of Harlem (1876), uptown's first Jewish educational institution. The Yiddish Scientific Institute (YIVO) in New York is the repository of the records of the 92d Street YMHA, a Yorkville institution whose history bears indirectly upon Harlem Jewish history.

Regrettably, Temple Israel of New York would not open its records for my examination. Fortunately, Louis Marshall, Jacob Schiff, and

Felix Warburg, who were excellent record-keepers, were members of the boards of directors of several important Harlem Jewish social and educational organizations, most notably the Uptown Talmud Torah and the Harlem Federation. These important Jewish communal leaders very often received and retained copies of the minutes of these now-defunct institutions. It is through their involvement—often as outsiders—with local organizations that we know as much as we do about the insides of Harlem Jewish communal politics. The Marshall, Schiff, and Warburg Papers may be examined by scholars at the American Jewish Archives.

Finally, conflict within local communal circles sometimes led to legal litigation within New York municipal and state courts. The New York City Hall of Records has maintained the manuuscript copies of justices' decisions in cases involving Jewish litigants, including outlines of the objective facts of cases which often received less-than-objective treatment in the highly partisan Yiddish press.

PERIODICALS

The Yiddish press is of fundamental and invaluable importance to the researcher of the history of East European Jews in America. It is the source closest to the inarticulate immigrant masses and deals with every aspect of the Jewish communal experience. The scholar using the decidedly parochial and highly partisan Yiddish press must be sure, however, to examine and compare the accounts of each of the extant journals on every significant event or issue, to clearly determine the actual course of events. Indeed, some occurrences and activities given extensive and dramatic coverage in one newspaper are simply not chronicled at all in another.

The *Yiddishes Tageblatt, Jewish Daily Forward,* and *Morgen Journal,* the three oldest Yiddish dailies, were particularly useful in studying Jewish Harlem. The politically conservative and religiously traditional *Tageblatt,* extant from 1888, gave extensive coverage to the uptown migration, particularly on its daily English page. This section of the newspaper, explicitly dedicated to the new American-born generation of readers, was a forum for discussions ranging from the value of differing Americanization plans to the problems of maintaining older and newer forms of Judaism inside and outside of the ghetto.

The Socialist *Jewish Daily Forward*, extant from 1897, followed Jewish workers and their institutions out of the ghetto to Harlem and elsewhere. It is through the *Forward* that groups like the Arbeiter Ring and the Socialist Party maintained communication links throughout the city. The *Forward* reported sympathetically on meat and rent strikes and helped spearhead the Hillquit candidacy in 1916. This Socialist organ rarely reported on synagogue or religious educational activities, except on those occasions when it editorialized vitriolically against those uptown-bound Jewish "capitalists" who sometimes foreclosed on their downtown brethren's synagogues and then used the proceeds to build new edifices in Harlem.

The *Morgen Journal*, extant from 1905, was the voice of the old-line Orthodox in the ghetto and beyond. It consistently criticized the activities of the New York Kehillah as well as those of "do-gooder" communal activists in uptown society. It often found itself on opposite sides of labor issues with the *Forward,* and of religious issues with the *Tageblatt*. Scholars may examine the extant runs of each of these major city-wide newspapers, which are available on microfilm from the American Jewish Periodical Center in Cincinnati, Ohio.

Harlem also had its own local periodical press. The *Harlem Local Reporter* (extant 1890–1899) and the *Harlem Magazine* (extant 1914) are available at the New York Historical Society and the New York Public Library respectively. These journals give the researcher a feel for local white, native-American life in Harlem prior to and during the migration of Jews, blacks and other ethnic groups uptown. They are, however, disappointing as sources for determining their group's reaction to these massive incursions. The *Harlem Home News* (extant 1916–1917), a forerunner of the Bronx Home News, is also available at the New York Public Library. Published at the height of the Jewish heyday in Harlem, it concerns itself primarily—and disappointingly so—with the lives of former white Harlemites living elsewhere in the city. Harlem's own local Yiddish newspaper, the *Bronx-Harlem Presse*, lasted, as far as I was able to determine, only one year (1914). Its incomplete run for that year is kept at the Jewish Division, New York Public Library. Harlem's relatively close proximity to the Lower East Side and the presence of *Forward, Tageblatt,* and *Morgen Journal* offices uptown may well have obviated the Harlemite's need for his own local Jewish daily.

The major supplements to the Yiddish press for studying New York Jewry are the Anglo-Jewish weeklies. The *American Hebrew*, extant from 1879, covered the communal activities of the German-Jewish community as well as granting extensive coverage to their Americanization efforts on behalf of their East European brethren. Interestingly enough, as the first decade of the twentieth century proceeded and East European-run or -influenced institutions for Americanization began making their appearances on the New York scene, news of that new immigrant elite group's activities was also granted space. The *Jewish Messenger*, extant from even before 1870 until its merger with the *American Hebrew* in 1902, kept close tabs on the social, cultural and religious life of New York's major German-Jewish families and organizations.

The *Hebrew Standard*, extant from 1893–1894 and from 1900–1922, may well be described as the voice of the acculturating East European Jew and/or of the religiously progressive Modern Orthodox. This weekly focused on many of the same problems of concern to the *Yiddishes Tageblatt* English page readers. In fact, many times editorials from one organ were repeated in the other. The *Hebrew Standard* is a basic and critically important source for studying such nascent American Jewish religious movements as the Young Israel synagogue and the Institutional Synagogue-Jewish Center concept. All these periodicals are available at the American Jewish Periodical Center and the New York Public Library.

The growth and decline of the physical neighborhood in Harlem, fundamental to the story of its Jewish communal life and death, can be studied for over fifty years through the *Real Estate Record and Builders Guide*. This trade journal affords us the builder's and realtor's points of view in studying such issues as the effect of legislation and progressive agitation upon tenement conditions and intracity population mobility as well as the process of neighborhood succession. It can also be used in a quantitative study of property valuation and devaluation over time. Finally, it gives the researcher an interesting glimpse into what builders and architects had in mind when they designed and built the then avant-garde, now long-outdated architectural forms that made up the ghetto landscape.

MEMOIR LITERATURE

Memoirs, first person histories, filiopietistics, and other roman-
ticized accounts of immigrant life are important supplements or coun-
terpoints to the usually more laconic contemporary journalists' reports. The Lower East Side was one community abundantly blessed
with a plethora of reminiscences written by those who lived downtown and who remembered the ghetto experience. Harlem has not
been favored nearly as much with heroic prose. Abraham Cahan's
famous *Rise of David Levinsky* (1917, repr. New York: Harper, 1960)
is, for example, the single major immigrant novel which deals in any
great detail with the saga of the up-to-Harlem movement. Muckraker
Hutchins Hapgood's sympathetic *The Spirit of the Ghetto* (1902, repr.
New York: Schocken Books, 1966) notes in passing the story of one
forlorn uptown rabbi. And Michael Gold's *Jews Without Money* (New
York: Horace Liveright, 1930) comments on the mass exodus of Jews
to the Bronx and Brooklyn in the 1920s. This literary poverty may well
be the fate of a residentially mobile community in a transitional area
situated all-too-close to the hub of immigrant life.

To this meager list of lively accounts of New York–Harlem Jewish
life may be added the several pedantic, often colorless autobiog-
raphies written by uptown leaders and residents. Books in this latter
genre include Philip Cowen's *Memoirs of an American Jews* (New
York: International Press, 1932), Bernard Drachman's *The Unfailing
Light* (New York: Rabbinical Council of America, 1948), and Maurice
Harris' *A Forty Years Ministry* (New York: N.P., 1925). Samuel Rosenblatt wrote an understandably sympathetic biography of his father,
Yossele Rosenblatt: The Story of His Life as Told to His Son (New
York: Farrar, Strauss & Young, 1954). And Herbert S. Goldstein com-
piled an equally sympathetic annotated compilation of articles and
stories about his father-in-law, *Forty Years of Struggle for a Principle:
The Biography of Harry Fischel* (New York: Bloch, 1928).

GOVERNMENT CENSUS AND VOTING MATERIALS

The basic statistical information on the occupational distribution
and residential mobility of Harlem's residents between 1890 and 1930

was derived from a variety of census reports and manuscript materials. John S. Billings, *Vital Statistics of New York City and Brooklyn Covering a Period of Six Years Ending May 31, 1890* was particularly useful in studying the intracity migratory patterns of the Irish and Germans out of the Lower East Side and up to Harlem during the first decade of massive East European and Italian movement to the United States. The absence of 1890 federal or 1892 state census schedules for Manhattan precluded a study of the basic economic life of that early uptown group.

For 1900, microfilm copies of federal census schedules recently have been made available to scholars. The National Archives in Washington, D.C., houses the complete run of the nation's enumerations. However, those interested specifically in New York City census returns may examine—as I did—identical microfilm copies of federal schedules maintained, interestingly enough, by the Government at the Military-Oceanic Terminal in Bayonne, New Jersey. It may be symbolic of New York's contemporary condition that basic documents relating to its history are housed out of state.

Bound volumes of the 1905 New York State census schedules for the Manhattan area are also extant and can be examined at the Office of the New York County Clerk. Scholars working there are greatly facilitated in their labors by the existence of an extensive file system which neatly codifies by Assembly District, Ward, and Election District the location of all Manhattan addresses. The reader is directed to Appendixes I and II for a complete discussion of the methodology used in studying manuscript census data.

Statistical data on the residential changes which had taken place in Harlem's several districts by 1910 were provided by Walter Laidlaw, ed., *Statistical Sources for Demographic Studies of New York*, vol. 1 (New York: World Council of Churches, 1913), available in manuscript form at the New York Public Library. For information on subsequent demographic changes uptown, I consulted Laidlaw's published *Statistical Sources for Demographic Studies of Greater New York* (New York: The New York City Census Committee, Inc., 1923) and his *Population of the City of New York, 1890–1930* (New York: City Census Committee, 1932).

The basic governmental sources used in studying Harlem voting patterns were the maps of Manhattan's Assembly and Election Districts (1900–1924) available on microfiche at the New York City Municipal Reference Center and *The City Record: Official Canvass of the*

County of New York (1900–1924), published by the City Record Inc. The maps indicate the changing boundaries of Harlem election districts. The *City Record* gives the official returns of every election held within Manhattan.

GOVERNMENT REPORTS

As immigrants, as workers, and as tenement dwellers, Harlem Jews and their uptown neighbors were often included as subjects of government investigation and research. Among the more useful published reports on housing conditions were the Progressive-inspired *The Tenement House Problem: Including Report of the New York State Tenement House Committee* of 1900 (New York: Macmillan, 1903) by reformers Robert W. De Forest and Lawrence Veiler, and the subsequent *Reports* of the New York City Tenement House Department (1902–1929). The United States Industrial Commission *Reports,* volume xv (Immigrants and Education) (1901) was useful in tracing the migratory patterns and in determining the living conditions of Jews and other immigrants in the ghettos of New York. *Housing Conditions : Report of the Housing Committee of the Reconstruction Committee of the State of New York* (Albany: J. B. Lyon, 1920) was particularly helpful in exploring the saga of the physical decline of New York neighborhoods during the First World War. Also noteworthy is the *New York Market Analysis,* published cooperatively by the New York *Times, The News* and the New York *Herald Tribune* (1933), which examined the cost of housing and, more generally, the cost of living in more than fifty different neighborhoods in New York City.

The Reports of the Regional Plan of New York and its Environs on the *Tobacco Industry in New York and its Environs* (New York: Regional Plan of New York and its Environs, 1924) and the *Clothing and Textile Industries in New York and its Environs* (New York: Regional Plan of New York and its Environs 1925) were useful in tracing the movement of industry within Manhattan. The 16th *Annual Report* of the New York State Bureau of Labor Statistics was consulted for its discussion of construction unionist opposition to Jewish scabs in their profession.

One additional source of government materials which proved useful was the typescript and manuscript reports and studies undertaken by the Works Progress Administration, Federal Writers Project, in late 1938. Commissioned to write a multivolume history of ethnic group life in New York City, Jewish writers and their counterparts from other ethnic groups attempted to study almost every aspect of immigrant and minority group life. Several of these reports—particularly those which dealt with the history of specific Jewish labor unions—filled in important lacunae left from accounts in the Yiddish press. The Jewish Writers Group succeeded in publishing one book based on their research, *Die Yiddishe Landsmanshaften fun New York* (New York: I. L. Peretz Yiddish Writers Union, 1938). The manuscript of that work, along with all the papers and reports of this interesting government-funded, depression-time project, are available at the New York City Municipal Archives.

LAND-USE MAPS

It is important for the communal historian to understand the ecological dimensions of the city or neighborhood under study. Ideally, this can be accomplished by his literally walking the streets of his "Jewish quarter" and examining the types of buildings in which Jews once lived and worked. This was, unfortunately, not possible in my studying of Jewish Harlem. Two generations of neighborhood deterioration, coupled with intermittent urban renewal efforts, have had the effect of altering almost completely the face of the once-immigrant neighborhood. However, I was able to make effective use of the existing published sets of land-use maps, in reconstructing the actual physical character of Jewish Harlem. These maps tell the researcher what types of buildings once existed; their sizes and shapes; whether tenements or brownstones predominated; whether elevators and, later, fire-escapes were present in a building; and whether a given block either contained open spaces or was badly overcrowded. William Perris and Henry Browne's *Insurance Maps of the City of New York*, vol. 8 (1876), was consulted to gain a sense of how Harlem's early German settlers lived. George Washington Bromley's *Atlas of the City of New York* was examined for the years 1894, 1898–99 and 1905 as an aid in following the frequent changes in Harlem's physical appearance around the turn of the century. For a complete discussion of how information derived from these maps was used in this study, see Appendixes ı and ıı.

PRIVATE JEWISH ORGANIZATIONAL REPORTS

The Jewish communal self-survey first came into vogue during the era of the New York Kehillah, reflecting that group's Progressive-inspired belief in the efficacy of research as an important first step in meeting group needs. Kehillah-sponsored population studies and the educational reports by its leading pedagogues were gleaned of information on Jewish Harlem. The *Jewish Communal Register*'s neighborhood and district studies for 1917–1918 were found useful, especially when compared with earlier and later government population surveys. Alexander Dushkin's *Jewish Education in New York City* (New York: Bureau of Jewish Education, 1918) was valuable in comparing the problems of Harlem institutions such as the Uptown Talmud Torah and the Rabbi Israel Salanter Talmud Torah with those of other likeminded institutions in the city. Isaac Berkson's *Theories of Americanization* (NY-Teachers College, Columbia University, 1920) provided important background information on the Yorkville roots of the Institutional Synagogue-Jewish Centers movement.

Although the Kehillah itself died in the early 1920s, a variety of its services and agency activities lived on. The Bureau of Jewish Social Research continued the Kehillah's survey tradition, publishing in 1928 its *First Section: Studies in the New York Jewish Population. Jewish Communal Survey of Greater New York*. This study clearly points out the rapid demographic changes which had taken place in each of New York's Jewish neighborhoods over the course of the preceding decade.

The Jewish Welfare Board also undertook several smaller scale local population studies during this era. Its unpublished *Study of the Institutional Synagogue in Relation to Harlem, N.Y.C.*, conducted in 1938, also charts the out-migration of Harlem Jews from the early 1920s to that date. Finally, C. Morris Horowitz and Lawrence J. Kaplan's retrospective and prospective study of Jewish intracity migrations, *The Estimated Jewish Population of the New York Area, 1900–1975*, published in 1959 by the Federation of Jewish Philanthropies of New York, also proved useful.

WORKS ON NEW YORK JEWS

This present work joins an ever-growing body of significant studies of the history of the world's largest Jewish community. Among the more important historiographical contributions consulted in preparation of my Harlem Jewish history were: Hyman B. Grinstein, *The Rise of the Jewish Community of New York, 1654–1860* (Philadelphia: Jewish Publication Society of America, 1945), Rudolf Glanz, "German Jews in New York City in the Nineteenth Century," in *Studies in Judaica Americana* (New York: KTAV, 1970): Moses Rischin, *The Promised City: New York's Jews, 1870–1914* (Cambridge, Mass.: Harvard University Press, 1962), Arthur Goren, *New York Jews and the Quest for Community: The Kehillah Experiment, 1908–1922* (New York and London: Columbia University Press, 1970), Irving Howe, *World of Our Fathers* (New York-Random House, 1975). Alter Landesman, *Brownsville: The Birth, Development and Passing of a Jewish Community in New York* (New York: Bloch, 1971), Thomas Kessner, *The Golden Door* (New York: Oxford University Press, 1976) and Deborah D. Moore, *"The Emergence of Ethnicity: New York's Jews, 1920–40"* (Ph.D. dissertation, Columbia University, 1975).

WORKS ON HARLEM'S HISTORY

Much has been written over the last two decades on the history of the emergence of a black ghetto in Harlem. The reader is directed to the bibliographical essay appended to Gilbert Osofsky's *Harlem: The Making of a Ghetto* (New York: Scribner, 1963) for a complete listing of books both about native-white and black Harlem. Among the more important of those works used in this study were Osofsky, Seth M. Scheiner, *Negro Mecca: A History of the Negro in New York City 1865–1920* (New York: New York University Press, 1965), Howard Brotz, *The Black Jews of Harlem: Negro Nationalism and the Dilemmas of Negro Leadership* (New York: Schocken Books, 1970), the National League on Urban Conditions Among Negroes, *Housing Conditions among Negroes in Harlem, N.Y.C.* (New York: Poole Press Association, 1915) and Alonzo Caldwell, *A Lecture: The History of Harlem* (New York, 1882). Lawrence Royce Chenault, *The Puerto Rican Migrant in New York* (New York: Columbia University Press, 1938) is an early study of that group's settlement in the metropolis. Harlem's Irish and Italian communities still await their historians.

Index

Dewey, John, 125
Distillator, Rev. Samuel, 23
Dolgenas, Rabbi Jacob, 115-16, 118, 122
Drachman, Rabbi Bernard, 92, 111, 117, 119, 122, 131
Duncan, Dudley and Beverly, 137-38

Eastern Europe, Jewish education in, 90-91
East European Jews: immigration of, 145; migration to Harlem, 26-28, 32-34, 49-50, 161-62; occupations of, 29, 36-40, 54-55, 173-78; relationship with German Jews, 164-65; settlement in Harlem, 36, 40; see also Central Harlem, economic distribution of; East Harlem, economic distribution of
East Harlem, economic distribution of, 36-38, 52-53, 55, 182-84
East Harlem, economic distribution of Jews in, 52-53, 55, 182-84
Educational Alliance, 97-98, 189

Fischel, Harry, 105-9, 113
Frank, Henry, 81
Fromberg, Harry G., 123
Furriers' Union, 76

Galewski, Bernard, 25
General Jewish Labor Alliance of Russia, Poland, and Lithuania, 62-63
German Jews, 158-59; in Harlem, 17-18; relationship with East European Jews, 164-65; in synagogue life, 22-25
Glass, Henry, 109
Goldstein, Herbert S., 116-17, 122-23, 127-30, 131-36, 153, 166
Grossman, Rabbi Rudolf, 90
Group Charmigal, 72

Hapgood, Hutchins, 99
Harlem: blacks in, 50, 145-50, 166-68; decline of Jewish population, 143-46; economic distribution of Jews in, 50-55, 182, 184; German Jews in, 17-18; housing in East Harlem, 141, 182; housing shortage, 140-41, 182; Irish in, 17; Italians in, 18, 49-50; meat strikes in, 48-49, physical deterioration of, 139-40, 167-68; politics in, 73-85; Puerto Ricans in, 150; Rapid Transit, 14-15, 30-31; rent strikes in (1904), 48-49, (1908), 72-73; residential

construction in, 14-15, 30, 31-33, 44-45, 142-43, 183, 184; Socialist Party in, 73-80; synagogues in, see specific names, e.g., Congregation Anshe Emeth
Harlem Bakers' Union, 67-68, 72-76
Harlem Educational Institute, 101; see also Uptown Talmud Torah
Harlem Federation, 87, 94, 95-96
Harlem Hebrew League, 116, 122
Harlem Relief Society, 14
Harlem Socialist Press Association, 61
Harlem Socialist Sunday School, 63-64
Harlem Workmen's Circle, see Workmen's Circle Branch #2
Harlem Yeshiva, 110-12
Harlem Young Judea, 102
Harlem YMHA: nineteenth century, 11-13, 21-22; twentieth century, 116, 123-24
Harlem Young Men's Orthodox League, 77, 116, 121-22, 129-30
Harris, Dr. Maurice, 19-20, 94, 96, 98, 159, 180
Harrison, Francis Burton, 74
Hays, Daniel P., 14, 20, 95
Hebrew Educational Society of Brooklyn, 98
Hebrew Educational Union of Harlem, 94-96
Hebrew Orphan Asylum, 106
Hebrew Sheltering and Guardian Society, 106
Hebrew Tabernacle, 151-52
Hewitt, Mayor Abram, 35
Hillquit, Morris, 76-83
Housing construction, see Residential construction
Housing shortage in Harlem, 30, 140-41
Hurwitz, Rabbi Schmarya Leib, 109-10

Industrial Removal Office, 43
Institutional Church, 191
Institutional Synagogue, 116, 129-34, 153
Intercity migration: Harlem's deviation from the theory of, 56-59, 161-62, 185-86; theory of, 55-56, 160-61, 162-63, 185-86
International Ladies' Garment Workers' Union (ILGWU), 76
International Painters' and Paperhangers' Union, 66
Invasion-succession theory (Burgess), 137, 163

Index by Beth Anshen Braunstein